LOUISE S. SPINDLER
Stanford University

D0768439

Culture Change and Modernization

*Mini-Models and
Case Studies*

Waveland Press, Inc.
Prospect Heights, Illinois

For information about this book, write or call:

Waveland Press, Inc.
P.O. Box 400
Prospect Heights, Illinois 60070
(312) 634-0081

Foreword

THE AUTHOR

Louise Spindler is Research Associate and Lecturer in Anthropology at Stanford University. She received the first Ph.D. in this field at Stanford in 1956. During Felix Keesing's chairmanship of the Department of Anthropology she was assistant, then associate in the long-term culture change project initiated by him.

She has done fieldwork with the Menominee Indians of Wisconsin, the Blood Indians of Alberta, Canada, among the Mistassini Cree, and in Germany. She has been particularly influential in the collaborative fieldwork with her husband in calling for equal samples of males and females, thus exhibiting her conviction that the two sexes do adapt differently and that the world view of women in different cultural contexts is badly understood. She has also brought a needed emphasis on the experience of individuals in culture change situations through her use of an "expressive autobiographic interview" technique and her focus on social interaction, social role, and self-concept.

She has published a memoir of the American Anthropological Association on changing Menominee women (Memoir No. 91, 1962), articles on male and female roles, a collaborative text in cultural anthropology with Alan Beals and George Spindler, on methodology in the study of culture change, on witchcraft, and most recently an ethnographic chapter on the traditional Menominee culture for the *Handbook of North American Indians* (1978), Vol. XV, Northeast, a chapter on the psychology of culture change for the Ninth International Congress of Anthropological and Ethnological Sciences, and a review of the Spindler's work for *The Making of Psychological Anthropology* (1980).

THIS UNIT

No sector of contemporary cultural anthropology is more challenging than the one with which this unit is concerned. Terms such as culture change, acculturation, psychocultural adaptation, innovation, identity maintenance, modernization call up a variety of images and constructs in anthropological minds. Few of us study cultures and social systems in anything resembling a steady state. The world is changing faster than we can study it. Sociocultural anthropology has become the study of culture change. But the words we use to describe what we study are grossly inadequate. What is studied, for instance, is not "culture change" in a restricted sense—it is the complex of processes involved in the continuing adaptation of the human population to its manifold environments, in the total sense of the word "adaptation."

It is not strange, then, that this field has suffered from a lack of ordering. Though it is a subject of great importance, it is very difficult to teach a coherent course in it. To attempt a comprehensive ordering of all the relevant theory at this point in the evolution of the field is beyond the intention and scope of this unit. This unit does, however, have an integrative plan. Louise Spindler starts with a master model of dimensions and relationships that includes the individual, social interactional and cultural system levels interrelated with each other and interacting with the environment consisting of physical and natural events and cataclysms, and other cultures and human populations. She has coined the term "mini-models" to carry the ordering further. Each mini-model is a partial theory at the middle level of complexity and inclusiveness. Each mini-model focuses on certain change processes and certain approaches for securing and analyzing data. Each one is related, in her continuing analysis, to the appropriate level of the master model.

Particularly noteworthy, besides the systematic attention to the ordering of relevant processes at the middle level of theory, is the illustration of each mini model with appropriate case materials, drawn from a wide variety of sources. The models are not left in a no-man's land between theory and observation. This relatively slim volume covers a very wide range of phenomena and locales. The traditional field sites of anthropologists are included, but attention is also turned to our own contemporary and very dynamic American society.

Special attention to the needs of students is reflected in overview, review, and question sections at the end of this unit, and in a selected reading list of recent works on culture change and urbanization/modernization (1979-84).

A basic anthropology unit* such as this makes it possible to avoid the constraints of a big textbook. It can be creatively combined with other materials, including case studies. And yet this volume is substantial enough to stand on its own. Knowledgeable readers will be impressed with how much has been packed into this relatively short book.

GEORGE SPINDLER
Stanford University

---

*See also basic units by Merwyn Garbarino (*Sociocultural Theory in Anthropology: A Short History*), and Ernestine Friedl *(Women and Men: An Anthropologist's View)*, published by Waveland Press.

Preface

THE PLAN FOR THIS UNIT

This Basic Unit is intended for use as a major or ancillary text in intermediate and upper division courses in sociocultural change, acculturation, cultural dynamics, modernization, and urbanization and as recommended reading in introductory anthropology and sociology courses where such topical areas are included. Since the concerns covered in this unit overlap with various sectors of applied anthropology and with the anthropology of development, it should prove useful in those contexts as well. The unit offers an orderly conceptual structure that is illustrated and made meaningful through the presentation of specific cases of sociocultural change occurring in the twentieth century. The focus is on contemporary models and theories with occasional reference to their historical antecedent.

The cases described in this unit are all concerned with what anthropologists term microtemporal changes. They occurred in single sociocultural systems within a limited time period. These changes are consequent to new ideas or things introduced to a group through innovation or diffusion, or occur as adaptations to alterations in the conditions of existence brought about by nature or by human agencies. By focusing on cases it is possible to illustrate how changes and adaptations actually occur. The reader is given information on the behavior of peoples under conditions of change that makes it possible to understand abstract concepts and theories about this behavior.

Most of the anthropologists whose works are described in this unit are eclectic in their use of concepts and strategies in the analysis of change. They have, however, constructed a variety of specific models, termed mini-models in this book, to be used as they fit the problem. This unit puts the cases of culture change and the mini-models together. References that will carry the interested student beyond the treatment possible in this unit are provided.

Practically all aspects of anthropology deal in one way or another, implicitly or explicitly, with change. Many books have been written on long-term evolutionary change and the field of prehistory is entirely about culture change. Therefore it is necessary in this brief unit to be highly selective. Although there is in this unit a strong convergence in focus with the work of specific evolutionists, case materials on evolutionary processes are not included. The general evolutionists, by inference and reconstruction of the past, deal with macro time periods including all of human development over time on the earth, beginning perhaps 3 million years ago. The specific evolutionists analyze the development of local cultures through relatively shorter time periods, focusing on environmental factors as they relate, in the main, to the technological system. Since their aim is to seek cross-cultural regularities, they rarely do complete case studies of single systems. Many important ideas, concepts, and trends formulated by contemporary evolutionists have been adopted by other anthropologists and are represented in this unit.

Although this unit focuses on microtemporal changes, it is acknowledged that all anthropologists writing about change do at least some limited reconstruction of history in order to decide on a base line from which change occurs. In the cases included here reconstruction is minimal; authors rely at times upon historical materials but usually derive their data for reconstructing from older living members of the culture and are concerned with a limited time span.

The guiding presumption made in writing this unit is that a student understands sociocultural changes better when they are contextualized in the varied matrices in which they occur—a specific sociocultural system activated by individuals continuously making choices in a given environment.

In Part I of the book, *Models for Culture Change,* a grand model is described for the study of sociocultural change, identifying and defining the various processes at three levels of analysis (cultural, social, and individual), with emphasis on the stimuli for change, both internal and external to the system. The use of mini-models is rationalized and the term defined in this first section, contrasting them to the grand model.

Part II, *Mini-Models and Cases,* includes all of the mini-models, the strategies used by anthropologists studying culture change. The models are given meaning through case materials from changing cultures around the world. The mini-models include Innovation, Diffusion, Ecological, Acculturation, and Modernization-Urbanization. Several Psychocultural Mini-Models are included: Innovation, Mazeway Reformulation, Revitalization Movements, Sociocultural Change and Psychological Adaptations, Behavioral Analysis, Raising the Level of Cultural Awareness, and Decision-Making.

Part III, *Change and Persistence in Special Areas,* includes: "Women's Adaptations" and "Coping in Contemporary U.S.A." In the first section case materials are presented that deal with women adapting to changes in their sociocultural environment. Since most cultures are male oriented, women tend to live in separate cognitive universes. There is, however, great variation cross-culturally as to the amounts and kinds of prestige women are accorded. This fact plays an important role in determining what happens to women as they adapt to sociocultural change.

"Coping in Contemporary U.S.A." is divided into three sub-headings: 1. American Values: Change and Persistence, including results of research on what is happening to traditional, core American values; 2. American Youth Cults, including studies of Hippie groups and religious groups such as the Hare Krsna group. These groups have embraced alternative ways for solving the problems of life and, in turn, have provided a potential for change in the preexisting solutions for these problems; 3. U.S. Minority Groups, including descriptive materials on strategies used by minorities for survival. Studies of Blacks, Mexican-Americans (Chicanos), and Indians (Native Americans) will be drawn from.

Part IV, *Overviews,* consists of overviews of the book. The first, "Comments on

Methods" is an overall analysis of the strategy of the book and explores further the reasons for its use. The Grand Scale Model for change is compared to the mini-models, and the interrelationships between all of the models are discussed. The second overview, "Looking into the Future," discusses some of the implications of the kinds of logic, methods, and case materials used in the book for estimating developments and problems of the future.

Part V, *Study Aids,* includes "Questions To Help Guide Review" for Parts I, II, and III, and a section, "Highlights for Review," consisting of a summary of the important ideas, processes, and foci of the book.

Louise S. Spindler

Contents

Foreword   iii

Preface   v

Part I   MODELS FOR CULTURE CHANGE:
         GRAND AND MINI   1

Introduction, 3
A Grand Model for the Study of Sociocultural Change, 4
Mini-Models, 9

Part II   MINI-MODELS AND CASES   11

1.   Innovation Mini-Model   13
     Some Innovations, 4
     Spread of Innovation, 16

2.   Diffusion Mini-Model   17
     Modern Man—An Example of Diffusion, 18
     Syncretism and Reinterpretation, 19
     Reciprocal Borrowing, 22

3.   Ecological Mini-Model   25
     Coping with Change (Tibetan Nomads, Maori, Tanala,
         Yungay, Skolt Lapps), 25

4.   Acculturation Mini-Model   31
     Background, 31
     Acceptance of Change, 33
         Emulation (Palau, Manus, Kaktovik Eskimo), 33
     Resistance to Change, 37
         Boundary-Maintaining Devices (Nilgiri Tribes, Gypsies and
            Hutterites, Ixtepejans, Navajo and Zuni, Jigalong Mob, 37
     Introducing Change, 48
     Forced Acculturation (Indians of Brazil, Tiwi), 48
     Attempts To Secure Support from the People (Swazi, Lugbara), 50

5.   Modernization-Urbanization Mini-Model   53
     Introduction, 53
     The City, 54
     Peasantry, 56
     Developing Societies, 58
     Models for Modernizing, 59
     Postpeasant Stabilization, 60
     Network Analysis, 60
     Variations in Coping (Gopalpur, Vasilika, Kippel, Orašac,
       Benabarre and Almonaster), 61
     Resistance and Persistence (Toba Batak, Qemant, Zinacantecos,
       Burgbach), 73
     Nonrevolutionary Modernizing (Japan, Taiwan, Malta), 78
     Concluding Remarks, 83

6.   Psychocultural Mini-Models   85
     Innovation, 86
     Mazeway Reformulation, 86
     Revitalization Movements (Xhosa, Melanesia, Menominee
       Peyote Cult), 87
     Sociocultural Change and Psychological Adaptation (Northern
       Ojibwa, Menominee, Blood Indians), 89
     Behavioral Analyses (The Vicos Project, Tri-Ethnic Project,
       Cook Islands), 92
     Raising the Level of Cultural Awareness, 96
     Decision-Making (Manus, Fur of Darfur, Schönhausen), 97
     Concluding Remarks, 102

Part III   CHANGE AND PERSISTENCE IN SPECIAL AREAS 103

7.   Women's Adaptations   105
     Introduction, 105
     Blood Indian Women of Alberta, Canada, 107
     Menominee Indian Women of Wisconsin, 107
     Adapting German Peasant Women, 110
     Kaktovik Eskimos of North Alaska, 110
     Concluding Remarks, 111

8.   Coping in Contemporary U.S.A.   113

     American Values: Change and Persistence   113
     Background, 113
     Traditional to Emergent Values, 114
     Values Projective Technique, 114

Minority Group Values, 117
Concluding Remarks, 118

American Youth Cults   119

Background, 119
The Proliferation of Cults, 120
The Hippie Ghetto, 122
The International Society for Krsna Consciousness (ISKON), 123

U.S. Minority Groups   126

Introduction, 126
Urban Black Families, 127
An Urban Black Delinquent Group (The Vice Lords), 129
Mexican Americans (Chicanos), 131
Chicano Prisoners, 134
American Indians (Native Americans)

Part IV   OVERVIEWS   141

Comments on Models   143

Looking into the Future   146

Part V   STUDY AIDS   151

Questions To Help Guide Review   153

Highlights for Review   156

Selected Recent References   164

Bibliography   167

Index   175

PART I

Models for Culture Change: Grand and Mini

INTRODUCTION

Until recently nearly all scientists writing about sociocultural change have been products of Western culture and have been socialized to its standards and assumptions. This fact must be constantly acknowledged and taken into account. For example, in Western culture we automatically view change, major or minor, as something both inevitable and good. This assumption is so much a part of both our overt and covert culture that it can be termed a cultural "compulsive" (Calverton 1931). Without retraining we cannot think otherwise. Along with this compulsion are others such as the belief that humans are the most important living beings on earth and that they *must progress* by continuously exploiting their environment, both social and physical, in the name of that progress. These beliefs and values could remain unchallenged were we never to see and understand how people live with contrasting cultural compulsives. As Ben Calfrobe, a Blood Indian, once told me:

> God put Indians on this side of the world to live, and you white people on the other part. The Indian lived just with what was here—the meat, the berries, the hides of animals. . . . You white people have a different kind of brain. Your mind is open to everything. You learn new things all the time. You're always inventing something. We Indians just lived. We took what God put on this earth in its regular form and used it. We didn't change nothing. . . .
>
> You have factories to make cars, everything you need. You have scientists, and they take what's in the ground and make atom bombs. Someday there is going to be a terrible war and you'll blow yourselves all up. (Pause) Then maybe we'll be the only ones left around.

He was aware of the difference between his culture and ours and of the implications of this difference for change.

Whether we like it or not, changes are constantly taking place. Sometimes they transform whole ways of life and basic relationships between humans and between society and nature, as did those changes resulting from the Industrial Revolution. Or they may be a less obvious kind, such as modifications in the culture that a new generation always introduces. Archeologists and historians document changes after they occur. Anthropologists are devising

3

methods for studying change as it is taking place, now. The focus of this book is on results of studies of change taking place in our world today.

Though all cultures are changing, the persistence of cultural forms is also universal. Any culture will be made up partly of ways of doing things and thinking that are in the process of change, and partly made up of ways of doing and thinking that have persisted, sometimes past the point where they are useful. The anthropologist tries to find out why some cultural forms change and others persist. When viewed from a long-term perspective of hundreds or thousands of years, persistence looks more like change occurring at a slow rate rather than the survival of an unchanged form. No cultural forms are static. Other perspectives, as in the study of social and religious movements, call attention to some forms of cultural persistence as the result of self-conscious rejection of change. In any event, viewed as one of the tendencies always present in varying degrees among human groups, cultural persistence as well as change must be understood if we are to understand the dynamic characteristics of human culture.

In the following section an attempt is made to define and outline as simply as possible the major concepts and processes involved in sociocultural change. The emphasis in the remainder of the book is on cases that illustrate these processes.

A GRAND MODEL FOR THE STUDY OF SOCIOCULTURAL CHANGE

When the term "culture" is used in a study, it is important to know what is meant. Different authors in different times vary in their interpretations of the term. Culture, as used here, refers to shared designs for living. It is not the people or things or behaviors themselves. Culture can be equated with the shared models people carry in their minds for perceiving, relating to, and interpreting the world about them (see Goodenough 1961). These models are not replicas of each other. Every individual has his or her version. There is more variation among individuals than was formerly thought to be the case (further discussion will be included in the section on psychocultural models). When we add "social" and refer to sociocultural change, behavioral changes which occur in the *interactions* between individuals are included as well as changes in the shared *patterns* for behavior. For example, if people adopt Christianity, they have a new model for thinking about the supernatural in their minds and cultural change has occurred. When they actually go to a Christian church service for the first time, social change has occurred. New groupings, statuses, roles, and interactions have been generated. We use the term "social" here also to include economic and political aspects of behavior involving social interaction. Since the two concepts are interdependent, the term "sociocultural' seems best suited to the change phenomena that will be discussed in this basic unit.

There are many factors involved in the analysis of sociocultural change.

The diagram (page 6) will serve as a simplified device for summarizing the basic elements involved in the dynamics of sociocultural change. It is a skeletal form to be fleshed out with examples to be presented later.

"Sociocultural system" is a term that covers both the social and the cultural aspects of human life. The diagram based upon this concept presents a "grand model" for the analysis of "culture change," as contrasted to a "mini-model." Culture consists of customary, shared patterns for behavior (including patterns for regulating behavior when there is minimal sharing), as represented in institutions such as kinship and marriage, political and economic organizations, and religion. The social aspects include the interactions among people as they react to the demands placed upon them, many of which stem from their culture. People are not robots so their interactions are rarely exactly what the culture would predict. They sometimes react against culturally patterned conventions, role expectations, and demands. And they are always exercising individual choice within the framework of possibilities provided by their culture, even when they accept their culture in the main. Sociocultural systems therefore include customary, agreed upon, institutionalized solutions which influence most individuals to behave in a predictable manner most of the time, but never all of the time. The system also includes a variety of rules and statuses whose patterns for behavior are complementary. That is, even when operating within the system, individuals do not replicate each other. They are not endless duplicates of a basic prototype. And these individuals interact with each other. For these reasons the concept of "social" or of society alone, or a concept of culture alone, is inadequate. Sociocultural system is therefore the basic concept we work with in this book, and it includes cultural patterns for behavior, social interaction, and individual adaptation. Since saying sociocultural system constantly gets cumbersome, the terms culture or system are frequently used as shortcuts for it. You will be able to tell when this is the case from the context in which the term is used.

For analytic purposes, however, it is very important to keep reminding ourselves that the cultural, social, and individual aspects, or "levels" of human life, are not the same thing. The cultural level includes patterned ideas about the universe and human relations to it, to other humans, and to the supernatural. A culture can be viewed as a sifter of ideas. Certain ideas, patterned in certain ways, and including basic assumptions about how the world works, distinguish one culture from another. These ideas and assumptions are expressed in social interaction and other behaviors, but they are not the interactions or the behaviors themselves.

The social interaction level indicated on the diagram (Figure 1) includes behavior that is culturally directed, and behavior that is not. When two or more people meet and interact they are usually treating each other in special ways, according to the status of each. Their individual personalities will influence this interaction, but within a frame determined by custom. Usually, an individual interacts differently with a priest than with a prison convict, but the saintly character of a given convict might evoke behavior more like

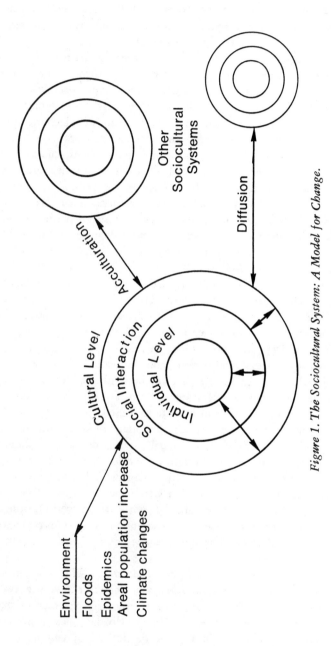

Figure 1. The Sociocultural System: A Model for Change.

that one would expect in the presence of the priest. Also, basic characteristics such as age and sex set a culturally specified framework for interaction, but two people of opposite sex and appropriate age will act very differently if they are "in love," a culturally specific notion, than if they are really platonic (sexually disinterested in each other), or if they have homosexual tendencies. Culture is always lurking about, one might say, ready to set the rules for behavior, but these rules rarely work out exactly as they may be coded.

Sometimes social interaction and spontaneous behavior determine culture, and this is indicated by arrows in the diagram going in both directions between the cultural level and the social interaction level. That is, a certain behavior, such as slapping hands instead of shaking hands as a greeting, may start spontaneously in a small group. If this pattern for behavior is accepted by the group it may spread to others. When that happens, cultural change is occurring.

It is also important at times to focus upon the individual. Many anthropologists have concluded that most culture change begins with individuals—with individual perceptions of a new situation or invention, the assessment of it, and then the decision to accept or reject it. The "cultural compulsives" play a strong role in how the individual perceives, but often the individual goes beyond the specific cultural determinants. If this were not so it is difficult to see how any changes could occur. Once a change of any kind has been adopted, it becomes a part of the culture and simultaneously a part of the normal social interaction process. When studying the individual as a focal point for change, the anthropologist may focus on the mentalistic processes of individuals. Each person carries in his or her mind a special, unique way of interpreting the world. These ways are influenced by culture patterns, but not identical with them. The deviations, from cultural norms represented in individual minds are the source of change and therefore have to be studied. That is, the anthropologist interested in culture change cannot always stop at the cultural or social interactional level. He or she must often, not always for certain problems at the systems level, go on to very specific studies of individuals and their thinking and perceiving processes. The study of individuals is an important part of this book. The reciprocal interactions between the individual, social, and cultural levels are indicated in the diagram of sociocultural system by double-ended arrows.

Sociocultural systems also act upon each other as stimuli for change, as indicated in the diagram. This process is usually referred to as "acculturation." The relative size and prestige of each system in contact is important. A large section of this book deals with this process and with case materials that illustrate it.

The process of cultural diffusion, also indicated as a source of change in the diagram of the sociocultural system and its environment, is closely related to acculturation. It is different in that the process of diffusion can occur whether or not two cultures are in proximity to one another. It is the process by means of which one sociocultural system acquires parts of another. A new idea, a new object, a new food can come from another culture, over great distances, without any direct contact between members of the two sociocultural systems. Acculturation is more total. It is an adaptation to changes in the conditions of life brought about by the impact of one sociocultural system upon another. The process is actually always a two-way one. Both cultures are affected, but when one sociocultural system is technologically and materially dominant it may seem that the process of adaptation is entirely one way.

Figure 1 also shows the environment as a source for change. All human communities are, to a greater or lesser degree, subject to the vagaries of their environments. Humans as yet can do little to prevent or affect natural phenomena such as earthquakes, climatic changes, and floods; and not even epidemics or population explosions are under control. People in all cultures must therefore try to understand and adapt to the limits imposed upon them by their natural environment. Modern Westerners, with their impressive array of technological paraphernalia and their science, can and do alter the environment decisively, even changing its chemical and physical constituency by pollution or by extraction of elements. These changes themselves constitute, however, a new and possibly uncontrollable environmental force that humans are just beginning to understand and learn to cope with.

The grand model of sociocultural system that has been described above and that is represented in Figure 1 implies that the parts of such a system are functionally interrelated. This is called "functionalism." When systems of this kind and concepts of functionalism were first developed, particularly in British anthropology, the notions of equilibrium and functional interrelatedness were carried to extremes. If all of the parts worked together so well, how could change occur? There is no point in altering or repairing a perfectly working machine. The English "fathers" of functionalism posited a stable kind of equilibrium which left little room for change. The sociocultural system, adjusting to changes in the environment or to new stimuli, operated to keep its status quo (Radcliffe-Brown 1952; Malinowski 1945). Modern English functionalists, however, view a sociocultural system as being in only *relative* equilibrium, with room for dysfunction and change. Most contemporary American anthropologists use functional concepts in quite modified form. Sociocultural systems are seen as adaptive, and when the introduction of new ideas or things disrupts parts of the system, adaptive changes are conceived as occurring in other parts. However, unlike many early functionalists, it is assumed by contemporary American anthropologists that while the system is adapting to the disruption, it is often making new and further changes. At the same time, contemporary analysts of culture change agree that a tendency toward stabilization of some sort is exhibited. When the parts of a sociocultural system are no longer interrelated, when the system exhibits no tendency toward stabilization, it ceases to function.

The position taken in this book, as Figure 1 indicates, is that a sociocultural system adapts to stimuli from within and without. Ideas or things are accepted, rejected, or reinterpreted. They are made to fit by synthesizing and integrating the new with the old. And even in isolated societies there is always some degree of conflict and contradiction between individuals regarding certain segments of the system. Some members are always frustrated enough by society's goals and constraints to challenge them and threaten the very values supporting the system. The adaptive strategies used by individuals have repercussions at all three levels of the sociocultural system as represented in Figure 1.

MINI-MODELS

Anthropologists studying change have developed a variety of research strategies and methods. Some adopted a kind of master model of sociocultural system, with its functional implications, but most use several models from several fields.

We can think of a model as a statement or description of working relationships between processes within a problem area. The model offered in Figure 1, describing relationships between parts of the sociocultural system, relationships between sociocultural systems, and relationships between the systems and their environment, must be considered a grand-scale model composed of many interrelated parts. The term "mini-model" used in this book refers to the more circumscribed subprocesses contained within the grand-scale model and to the various specific working relationships attributed to them. The two kinds of models might also be thought of as macro (grand) and micro (mini) models.

The mini-models represent special focuses and emphases. Some have been in use for a long time; others represent new approaches for defining what is to be studied. The mini-models deal with relatively limited relationships between selected processes within the field of action that has been broadly delimited by the grand model of sociocultural system furnished in Figure 1. For the purposes of this book, mini-models serve as a way of organizing the bewildering array of case data now available in the field of culture change. They should help the reader understand what kinds of data and understandings are related to different types of analytic strategies employed by anthropologists in the study of culture change, urbanization, modernization, and related phenomena.

The mini-models that will be described and illustrated in this Basic Unit include the following: innovation, diffusion, ecological, acculturation, modernization-urbanization, and psychocultural.

PART II

Mini-Models and Cases

1

Innovation Mini-Model

Innovation is dealt with first, as it is considered by many anthropologists to be the basic source of culture change. Innovation is closely linked with diffusion and acculturation. An innovation is usually a recombination of existing ideas into a new idea. As it is accepted by a large number of people, it is diffused both within the sociocultural system and to other systems. Innovations that become a part of the culture may either be produced within the cultural system or are the result of diffusion. They more often occur as a result of the latter. When diffused cultural patterns or traits are reworked to fit the receiver's system and accepted by others in the group, an innovative process is occurring. Processes of cultural reinterpretation and syncretization, to be discussed under the Diffusion Mini-Model, are also a part of the innovative model. The focus is on the newness of the idea or trait and on the creative process involved in producing it. Every cultural pattern has its origin in an innovative act performed by someone. As stated, that someone is more often than not someone in another culture. Most of our basic innovations such as the wheel, domestication of animals, writing, a system of mathematics, and most domesticated foods came from outside western European culture.

The process of innovating is universal. It is occurring all the time in all cultures. Most innovative recombinations, such as a unique hairdo or an unusual food combination, are so transitory or are considered so impractical that they are discarded. They never become cultural patterns. Innovative configurations of ideas, when accepted by the majority of persons in a culture or subculture, constitute culture change and may be expressed either in physical artifacts (axes, arrows, art work) or social inventions (the League of the Iroquois, the United Nations, etc.) or in concepts such as the Freudian "unconscious." Some innovations occur even in patterns of behavior as people respond and interact with each other. Individuals' modes of interaction may be both deviant and innovative, as those found among Hippies who have created a new subculture.

Anthropologist M. Herskovits (1950) used the concept of *cultural focus* to express what he described as a tendency in every society to concentrate interests and innovative ideas upon a special area where production of and receptivity to innovation are high. Among many traditional African cultures it was in the area of cattle raising. The cultural focus for the mainstream society in the United States could be said to be on technological innovation.

SOME INNOVATIONS

Since every cultural pattern for behavior was once someone's innovative idea, the range of types of innovations and their importance is great and some examples are given below.

The Cheyenne Indians explained how their first lodge was supposedly created:

> The first lodge of modern shape is said to have been suggested by a man who was handling a large poplar leaf, and quite by accident bent it into the shape of a cone—that is to say, of a lodge, such as are used today. As he looked at the leaf it flashed into his mind that a shelter like it would be better than those they then had. He showed it to the people and they made lodges in the shape of this leaf, and have used them ever since. (Grinnell 1923:50, quoted in Hoebel 1949:471)

If and when a Cheyenne man actually went through a process of combining the idea of the cone formed by the leaf and the idea of a lodge, he was innovating. And, since the group *accepted* the idea, culture change occurred.

An example of a special innovation in the technological sphere occurred in about 1900 when a Gilbert Islander settled on the island of Hiva Oa in the Marquesan Islands. He took a native wife and earned his living as a fisherman. If he had come twenty years earlier, he would have been considered a poacher since the old Marquesan patterns for fishing were carried on as a semicommunal activity, with canoes kept in a sacred place, and a resident priest directed all fishing activities and watched the canoes. By the time the Gilbert Islander arrived, however, the old customs had broken down and fishing had become an individual matter. In the new situation, canoe stealing became very commonplace and was a great annoyance for the man who might find his stolen canoe days later in a neighboring cove. The priest was no longer there to watch the canoes, and, with the breakdown of the old religion, the magically supported taboos were ineffective. Ralph Linton, who worked in this area, described what occurred when the Gilbert Islander became annoyed with the situation:

> We may imagine that the Gilbert Islander, being a stranger, was subjected to more annoyance in this respect than the local fishermen. The Marquesans combine with their light-fingered tendencies an almost sophomoric delight in practical jokes and hazing.
>
> Whatever the reason, the visiting fisherman invented a new type of detachable outrigger. This contrivance was quite different from the outrigger of the home islands and, as far as I know, from that used in any other part of the Pacific. The float was indirectly attached to the crosspieces which held it to the canoe. The uprights which connected the float with the crosspieces were made from staves of European casks and were fitted solidly into the float at the bottom. They were pierced with holes a few inches below the top and lashed to the crosspieces, and the crosspieces in turn lashed to the canoe, with a single continuous piece of rope. When the owner beached his canoe, he undid the lashings, laid the float and crosspieces side by side, wound up the rope around them and carried the whole up to his house on his shoulder.

Since the canoe could not be used without an outrigger, it was quite safe from theft, while when he wanted to use it himself he could put on the outrigger in five minutes. (Linton 1936:313–314)

It is not difficult to understand why this simple, yet ingenious, device was quickly accepted by the community. Because it was accepted it became a cultural change. A real need had existed for this innovative act. It is probably not coincidental that the innovator was a foreigner, who saw the situation in a fresh manner, unencumbered by the weight of past customs. Innovators are often "marginal men," who are, for a variety of reasons, somewhat divorced from the core of their culture and thus more free to create.

Not all innovations, however useful to an individual at a given time, become sources of cultural change. The author and her husband were once forced to make a small-scale, substitutive technological innovation. While they were en route to a Cree Indian trading post near Hudson Bay, the outboard motor on their boat suddenly stopped. The water was turbulent and dangerous in an unbroken stretch miles long. After paddling to a small island and devoting much thought to the situation, an innovation was made. The needlepoint brass screw that controlled the carburetor input had fallen out. There was no way it could be replaced. By whittling down twigs of spruce to a fine point to replace the screw, and trying them, one after another until one worked, the motor was eventually made to run. The new "screw" lasted all summer and served as well as the original brass one. The innovation in this instance was in the nature of the materials used. At first glance, spruce twigs and finely machined brass screws seem to have nothing in common. However, the substitution of twigs did not become a cultural change, as it was not accepted by a large number of people. There was no general need to substitute spruce twigs for brass screws.

Innovative ideas on the part of a Paiute Indian started a new religious movement, which then spread to other tribes over a vast area. Wovoka, or Jack Wilson, was a Paiute Indian living in Nevada in the 1890s. The Nevada Indians, with their hunting and gathering routes broken up by White infiltration, were in bad shape. They were forced to modify their old patterns, hunting and gathering only part time and working for whites part time. Their culture was being extinguished, and no one cared (Underhill 1953:Chap. 11). When things became unbearable Wovoka, as his father had done in 1870, had a trance and "saw God." As a result of this, he encouraged his people to return to the old ways and to love each other. He told his people to dance in a circle five nights in succession, and he reintroduced the old Basin dance with the old songs about wind, cloud, and animals sung in the traditional manner typical of the Basin groups. Wovoka claimed that if his advice were followed, the whites would disappear and the dead Indians return. This became the famous Ghost Dance and swept Indian country. It spread eastward through the Plains Indian tribes, with tragic results among the Sioux in the massacre at Wounded Knee. The message of the Ghost Dance was enthusiastically welcomed by oppressed Indians. It even spread to some eastern Woodlands tribes, becoming modified to fit local cultural circumstances. This kind of "revitalization" movement is explained in psychological terms in the Psychocultural section.

Wovoka, the Gilbert Islander, and the Cheyenne Indian comprise only a very small sample of the many kinds of innovators cultures throughout the world produce. They represent some of the creative potential which is a part of being human.

SPREAD OF INNOVATION

Novel, deviant, or innovative behavior is the beginning of some kind of social or cultural change. As has been stated, however, an innovation does not become a cultural change until it is integrated into the patterned way of life of the group.

Sociologists and anthropologists agree on the kinds of preconditions necessary for new ideas and traits to be accepted. These preconditions include the following:

1. Individuals must be able to assign some sort of meaning to an item. It might, however, result in the item being used in an unintended fashion, such as using light bulbs or tin cans as ornaments, and so on.
2. The new items or ideas should make it possible for individuals to feel that the values gained from the innovation are greater than the value lost.
3. The innovation must be compatible with existing values and experiences.
4. The idea behind the innovation must be communicable. The concept of a steel axe is far easier to communicate than a concept such as "honor" or "shame."

In researching the communicability of innovations to newly developing countries, sociologists have discerned that mass media alone do not effect change. Along with the mass media (such as television and radio) must be neighbors, peer groups, salesmen, and local specialists to mediate, influence, and inform. Since 1940 social scientists have termed this the "two-step" process. First the mass media inform, and second the personalistic relations with others do the convincing. Everett Rogers, a sociologist, feels that this widely used model is too simplistic (1969:222). He contests that it implies a dichotomized relationship between opinion leaders and followers. Further, he claims, the two-step flow model ignores stages in the decision-making process about a new idea. Rogers describes how the mass media are most important in creating knowledge or awareness of a new idea, whereas the interpersonal communication channels (referred to in the two-step flow model) are most important at the attitude-change stage.

In discussing why or how innovations spread, we must revert again to the concepts of "cultural compulsions" and "world view"—those deep, underlying, unrecognized assumptions and values that individuals in a culture carry around in their heads and which channel their behaviors. The world view of a culture— its unique thought patterns for viewing the relationships of man to nature or of man to the supernatural or of man to man—plays a crucial role in decisions to accept or reject an innovation.

2

Diffusion Mini-Model

Next in importance to the innovative process is the diffusion (cultural borrowing) process. Although innovations must diffuse if they are to become cultural changes, the innovative process is separate from the diffusion process. Cultures grow and evolve through innovations made from within the system, but the great bulk of cultural growth is due to borrowing ideas and things that have been invented elsewhere.

The relationships posited for the Diffusion Mini-Model by contemporary anthropologists and sociologists deal with the acceptance or rejection of diffused items by individuals or groups in different cultural systems and what happens to them after they are accepted. Processes such as syncretization (the blending of traits from separate traditions into something new) and the reinterpretation of new traits to fit the adopting system are part of the mini-model. Another posited relationship in the mini-model is the reciprocality aspect of borrowing. The borrowing is a two-way flow, even though the flow is greater from a prestigeful or technologically superior culture to an underdeveloped culture. One important difference between diffusion and acculturation is that ideas and items can be diffused without two or more systems being in physical contact. This mini-model would be related to the social and cultural levels of the grand model, as the paramount question is always: Will the diffused ideas or items ultimately be accepted or rejected by the group?

The older diffusion models played an important role in anthropology in Europe and the United States in the early part of the twentieth century. Unlike the evolutionists, the proponents of the various models viewed man as a borrower rather than as a part of a predetermined scheme. The English "Pan-Egyptian" Diffusion Model was on a grand scale. Relationships were assumed between an original culture that developed in Egypt and then spread to the remainder of the world (see Perry 1923). During this same period in Germany proponents of a "Culture Circle" model claimed that culture was invented independently in several different areas of the world and then spread, over time, from the so-called "center" of an assumed circle to the peripheral areas (Schmidt 1939).

Under the direction of Franz Boas, the "father" of American anthropology, great emphasis was placed on tracing the distribution of traits through diffusion between groups both in small circumscribed areas and on a global scale. Elaborate criteria were devised for determining whether a trait was diffused or independently invented (see Bee 1974:76–82 for a good discussion). Those involved in trait tracing were not very interested in what happened to the traits after they had diffused (Rohner 1969). By 1940 the strong interest in these attempts had almost ceased (Driver 1961).

The model for the American historical school (a diffusion model) related groups or complexes of similar culture traits to a common "Culture Area." The model became elaborated with the relating of the most dense clustering of traits and complexes to the center of the area where the ecology was presumably most favorable for their development (see Kroeber 1944).

Although the American model did not allow for the role of the individual as a selector and posited the physical environment as a major causal factor for diffusion and change, many valuable limited studies of historical reconstruction were products of this model.

In the past anthropologists were more concerned with the diffusion of ideas between societies than with the spread of an idea within a society. Today anthropologists and sociologists are focussing on reasons why individuals accept or reject diffused items.

Some anthropologists dismiss all diffusion models as outmoded. The sociologist Everett Rogers, however, wrote a book dealing with the diffusion of innovations (1962) in which he cited 503 diffusion studies made by contemporary social scientists. Today sociologists use the diffusion model to analyze what happens within a given culture when new traits are diffused to it. This includes a study of diffusion through mass media such as books, journals, and radios—as mediators. Sociologists and anthropologists focus today on a particular culture or culture area and on how and why diffusion occurred.

Following are some case materials dealing with the diffusion process.

MODERN MAN—AN EXAMPLE OF DIFFUSION

Our solid American citizen awakens in a bed built on a pattern which originated in the Near East but which was modified in northern Europe before it was transmitted to America. He throws back covers made from cotton, domesticated in India, or linen, domesticated in the Near East, or wool from sheep, also domesticated in the Near East, or silk, the use of which was discovered in China. All of these materials have been spun and woven by processes invented in the Near East. He slips into his moccasins, invented by the Indians of the Eastern Woodlands, and goes to the bathroom, whose fixtures are a mixture of European and American inventions, both of recent date. He takes off his pajamas, a garment invented in India, and washes with soap invented by the ancient Gauls. He then shaves, a masochistic rite which seems to have been derived from either Sumer or ancient Egypt. (Linton 1936: 326–327)

When returning to his bedroom, our American uses a chair of southern European type, puts on clothes patterned after the skin clothing introduced by Asiatic nomads and shoes made from skins, using a process invented in Egypt. His bedroom window is made of glass, also invented in Egypt. At breakfast his plate is made of pottery originating from China, he uses a fork invented in medieval Italy and a spoon derived from a Roman model. His breakfast consists of *borrowed* items: orange (eastern Mediterranean), cantaloupe (Persia), coffee (Abyssinia), sugar (India), wheat for his waffles (Asia Minor), syrup (invented by Indians of the eastern Woodlands), egg (Indo-China), and ham (eastern Asia).

When our friend has finished eating he settles back to smoke, an American Indian habit, consuming a plant domesticated in Brazil in either a pipe, derived from the Indians of Virginia, or a cigarette derived from Mexico. If he is hardy enough he may even attempt a cigar, transmitted to us from the Antilles by way of Spain. While smoking he reads the news of the day, imprinted in characters invented by the ancient Semites upon a material invented in China by a process invented in Germany. As he absorbs the accounts of foreign troubles he will, if he is a good conservative citizen, thank a Hebrew deity in an Indo-European language that he is 100 percent American. (Linton 1936:326–327)

Linton, the author quoted above, claims that over 90 percent of any culture's content, including our own North American culture, is borrowed. Most cultures continue to grow by borrowing traits that have been invented elsewhere. The complexity of our modern civilization is due in large part to the receptivity of our ancestors who saw advantages in the ideas and material artifacts of other peoples.

People exercise a high degree of selectivity. They never borrow all the items available. And after a trait is borrowed, it must be made to "fit" the sociocultural system. One method for achieving this is termed *reinterpretation* (Herskovits 1950:553). Individuals in a system give the trait their own interpretation. Sometimes this takes the form of *syncretization*, combining meanings of the new trait with those existing for comparable items in the recipient's group. These processes are illustrated in the following examples.

SYNCRETISM AND REINTERPRETATION

After the Brazilian Negroes had been brought to South America from Africa as slaves and converted by force to Christianity, they identified, through the process of syncretism, their African deities with the saints of the Catholic Church, a widespread practice among converts. Today the descendants of the African slaves can still worship African gods and be professed and practicing Catholics as well as members of African cult-groups. The syncretic process has been carried to great lengths here. For example:

A hollow-log drum that has not been "baptized" will not call the proper deities to the dance, since it does not have the disciplined spiritual control that goes with baptism. In Salvador, Bahia, a novitiate, after a long period of initiation into cult-practices in the cult-house of her group, will immediately on emerging from her training make one pilgrimage to the shrine of the principal saint of the city, and another to worship at the altar of the saint that is identified with the African god to whose worship she is vowed . . . even in a single city, one cannot flatly say that a given African deity is always identified with a given Catholic saint. In Recife, for example, though the African water-goddess named Yemanja was identified by the members of four cult-centers with Our Lady of the Immaculate Conception, Shango, the African thunder-god was held by one group to be the same as St. Jerome, by another as St. Anthony, and by a third as St. John the Baptist. (Herskovits 1950:570–571)

Missionaries and priests have long recognized the importance of syncretism. Over one hundred years ago an Episcopalian missionary, realizing the possibility of misinterpretation of the Christian rite of Communion by the Tsimshian Indians, with whom he was working, decided to omit the rite from his services. H. Barnett described the historical incident:

> Cannibalism among the Northwest Coast Indians, although quite different in meaning for the Indians, was too similar to communion in form and function. Not only in this but in other points as well did Duncan, the missionary in question, deliberately and as a matter of policy eliminate "many of the potential danger spots in Christian metaphysics for a native whose only basis for interpreting new belief was in terms of the old." (Barnett 1942:24)

While doing fieldwork among the Blood Indians of Alberta, Canada, the author had an interesting incident related to her. An elderly, traditional Blood Indian, also a nominal Catholic, was supposedly dying in the hospital. The priest stood on one side of his bed and the medicine man on the other. Each, in turn, waved his sacred items over the patient—one the cross; the other a sacred bundle—in order to transfer to him a special "power"—blessings and salvation in one case; medicine power in the other. The ill man, the medicine man, and the priest all understood this common denominator—power. The man recovered, but no one knew to whose power the miracle should be ascribed. The combination of the priest's power and the medicine man's power constituted a form of syncretization for the patient.

Another anthropologist, E. A. Hoebel, while attending a Northern Cheyenne Indian peyote meeting, in itself a syncretization of Christian and Indian beliefs and ritual, noticed a special decorative staff being used. There were carved scenes of toreadors and charging bulls. The Mexican eagle was sitting on his cactus but the usual snake in his claws had been scraped out:

> Black Wolf, the peyote leader, explained that the staff had come from Mexico, and he pointed out that the eagle is good medicine. The toreador confronting the bull suggested the vision-seeking Indian confronted by a bison. However, he said, "Those people down there worship snakes, but we don't. So we took the snakes out. We can't have any snakes in our ceremony." The Cheyennes, in point of fact, are not simply neutral with respect to snakes. In their mythology, the Horned Snake (or the Plumed Serpent) is a creature much to be feared and avoided. (Hoebel 1972:656)

By simply removing a part of the diffused item, it could easily be reinterpreted to fit the adapting culture's belief system.

Sometimes important individuals combine and syncretize elements from two cultures to fit their needs. And if enough followers imitate, the combination becomes a part of the system. An example of syncretism occurred when the sister of the Queen Mother of the Swazi (South Africa) combined Swazi and Christian elements in her own special way. The Swazi male aristocrats had resisted conversion to Christianity, as they wished to continue the practice of polygyny. Their wives and mothers, however, were more responsive. The late Queen Mother, Indlovukati Lomawa, supported a Christian church, though the Swazi National Council ruled that full conversion and the wearing of Western clothing were incompatible with the ritual duties of her position. She was particularly in sympathy with the Zionist Separatist Church, whose charismatic— and flexible—leader had recognized the claims of hereditary kingship exercised by her son. Hilda Kuper, the anthropologist working with the Swazi, reports:

> When she died, she was buried according to custom away from the capital in a former royal village, so that her son would not be weakened by contact with death or the dead. At her funeral—which her son was not permitted to attend —various church officials paid their respects. Despite the fact that leading councilors tried to follow traditional practices, the entire mortuary procedure was interrupted for a few hours when her sister, who later succeeded to the position of queen mother, found that the church membership cards of the deceased (described as her "tickets across the Jordan") had been left behind at the capital. These were fetched and placed beside the dead woman in a wooden coffin that had been specially shaped to hold her body which was bound in fetal position and wrapped in a shroud of black cowhide. (Kuper 1963:67)

The sister, later to become Queen Mother, viewed the journey across the Jordan as an important route at death. Because of her special status, this type of reinterpretation would be embraced by many.

Sometimes the reinterpreting might seem simple and logical to a few people and unacceptable to the majority. This occurred when a group of missionaries in Swaziland thought they were doing some simple "substituting." Most of the schools in Swaziland are mission controlled and opposed to traditionalist values. The Swazi king attempted to reconcile the gaps between the Christians and traditional Swazi by suggesting the introduction of a modified age-class system in the schools. In the traditional culture, all boys of the same age group belonged to special "clubs." The missionaries could not allow a polygynous king to influence the "system," so they offered what they thought was a logical substitute—a "Pathfinder Movement" similar to the Boy Scouts (Kuper 1963:56). It didn't work.

Another example where reinterpretation could not be done simply is the case of the Yir-Yiront, a "stone age" people of Australia and a classic example of culture change. They substituted steel axes obtained from missionaries for stone axes and, in doing so, undermined their entire system. The polished stone axe was the most important tool for the Yir-Yiront. It was essential for obtaining firewood (woman's job) and for making domed huts and platforms. It was also essential as a tool in hunting and fishing and in gathering vegetables or animal food. The axe was a symbol of masculinity; only senior men could own them and women and children had to borrow them from close male relatives. The stone was obtained from trade partners in exchange for stingray spears. And the trading took place at important annual ceremonial gatherings. Of great importance was the role played by the stone axe in the Yir-Yiront totemic cosmology. It had a special origin myth and was considered sacred to one clan.

With an understanding of the functions which the stone axe played in Yir-Yiront culture, the result of the availability of steel axes to young men and women who won the favor of the mission staff could be predicted. The undermining of the dependency upon older males had important repercussions for the authority structure of the community, for male-female role definitions, for the structure of interpersonal behavior, and for the patterns of kinship behavior. A man who wanted a stone axe could depend upon established relationships with other men and with nature to get one. A man wanting a steel axe could not be self-reliant; he had to assume a dependent relationship with a missionary who gave them out erratically (from the native point of view) to "better" aboriginals or to those who did odd jobs for the mission. Dependency was substituted for self-reliance. Even women and young boys would get steel axes from the missionaries occasionally, which they considered their "own" in a new concept of possession, while some older men would be left with only stone axes. These older men would then borrow steel axes from their women and sons in a drastic reversal of roles and consequent loss of dominance and respect.

The most disturbing aspect in the situation was that the steel axe could not be incorporated into the cosmological scheme, so importantly linked with the ancestral past. As Lauriston Sharp, who worked with the group, wrote:

> The steel axe . . . has no distinctive origin myth, nor are mythical ancestors associated with it. Can anyone, sitting in the shade of a ti tree one afternoon, create a myth to resolve this confusion? No one has, and the horrid suspicion arises as to the authenticity of the origin myths, which failed to take into account this vast new universe of the white man. The steel axe . . . is not only replacing the stone axe physically, but is hacking at the supports of the entire cultural system. (Sharp 1952)

This example of borrowing an item that could not be reinterpreted to "fit" illustrates well the concept of functional interrelatedness of the parts of a cultural system.

RECIPROCAL BORROWING

It is usually assumed that most borrowing is from the culture with most prestige—often Western culture—by the less technologically developed culture.

Often this assumption is justified, but borrowing between cultures is also a two-way process, as can be seen by what we have borrowed from the American Indian.

We in the United States, viewing the small minority of Indians whose traditional cultures have for the most part been broken for several decades, naturally assume that borrowing has been a relatively one-way process: from us by them. But this is not so. Our borrowings from the American Indian have been numerous and can be found in many different areas and segments of our culture, and, perhaps, even in our personalities. A glance at the various types of things and ideas that have been borrowed is rather startling. For instance, plants domesticated by American Indians furnish almost half of the world's food supply today (Driver 1961:584). A few of the better known plants include "Irish" potatoes, corn, beans, squash, and sweet potatoes. Among drugs and stimulants, tobacco is the most widely diffused of the plants borrowed from the American Indian. Of the many native American drugs which are found in modern pharmacology, the best known are coca in cocaine and novocaine, curare in anesthetics, cinchona bark as the source of quinine, ephedra in ephedrine for clearing sinuses and nasal passages, datura in pain-relievers, and cascara in laxatives (Driver 1961:587).

We acquired the woolen poncho, the parka, and moccasins from Indian cultures. The commercial cottons used today are derived principally from the species cultivated by American Indians, and thus native American varieties of cotton supply much, if not most, of the world's clothing needs at the present time (Driver 1961:589).

American Indian music had a decisive influence on some American composers. One composer commented, "Many devices of the ultramodern composers of the present day have long been employed by Indians—unusual intervals, arbitrary scales, changing tune, conflicting rhythm, polychoral effects, hypnotic monotony" (Skilton 1939). The composers turned to the Indians. Edward McDowell composed the famous *Indian Suite* in 1891–1892. And in the early 1900s a number of composers visited Western reservations, gathering and arranging melodies and borrowing themes (Hallowell 1957:207).

Literature in the United States also reflects the influence of the Indian. Most readers are familiar with Longfellow's *Hiawatha* and James Fenimore Cooper's *Leather-Stocking Tales*. The hero of Cooper's novels, Natty Bumppo, became the epitome of pioneer character, combining the best personality traits of both Indians and Whites (Driver 1961:610). Cooper was the first novelist to dramatize the psychological consequences of the acculturation process (Jones 1952).

It is obvious today that the present-day Indian has taken over large areas of the Euro-American culture. But we can see from this brief sketch of the contributions of Indians to modern life that parts of their culture are alive today in the American way of life. The borrowing has been a reciprocal, two-way, process.

3

Ecological Mini-Model

The relationships posited for the Ecological Mini-Model are the interactions between an environment and the sociocultural system. This places the mini-model at either or both the social and cultural levels of analysis (see Figure 1). Anthropologists focusing on the ecology of a system are interested in the unique kinds of strategies devised by different systems for coping. This is an important area since a large proportion of an individual's behavior is consciously or unconsciously involved with solving problems posed by the environment. The natural environment does set limits, especially for people without advanced technology in severe environments. However, the environment alone cannot determine the nature of a particular system. The interpretation of the environment, in terms of a group's particular belief system and values, makes the environment something different for each group. There is no one "best" solution to the problems posed by the natural environment.

This mini-model is only indirectly related to other mini-models. It is only after a group of individuals have reacted to the environment that they innovate, make decisions, or devise personal coping strategies.

Although it is not directly related to a situation of change, the research done by Edgerton (1974) as part of a culture and ecology project under the direction of W. Goldschmidt should be mentioned, as it is an excellent example of the dynamic relationships existing between sociocultural systems and their environments. The research reveals interesting relationships between subsistence techniques practiced by pastoralists and farmers, attitudes toward their environment, and special psychological values.

COPING WITH CHANGE

Tibetan Nomads

The adaptation of Tibetan nomads to their natural environment served as a real protection for them against threat from radical changes taking place in their sociopolitical environment. They used their tight ecological fit they enjoyed as an effective weapon against the invader.

The Communist Chinese takeover of Tibet (from 1950) posed threats to the culture of the independent Tibetan pastoralists who pastured their herds in high, rough country. It takes a long period of adjusting and acclimatizing, more than one life cycle, in order to operate well at 16,000 feet above sea level in rough terrain. Thus, when the Chinese decided to eliminate the nomad's way of life as nomad economy did not fit into their conception of the socialist state, they had real problems, for the nomads did not give up their culture easily. At first there was open conflict.

R. Ekvall, who worked with the nomads over a period of nine years, describes the first Chinese attempt, made by veteran fighters, to defeat the nomad horsemen:

> Veterans who—fighting by day and marching by night—had made their way across half of China could not even come to grips with the horsemen who sniped at them and vanished. Those swift riders did not need to close in for the kill. They knew that cold, hunger, and heart strain, from the exertion of trying to match horsemen in mobility at high altitude, would take their toll as the Chinese died by the many thousands. (Ekvall 1968:95)

However, the Chinese people badly needed the beef and mutton of the high pasturage, and the wool, hides, salt, and borax produced by the nomads were needed by the industries of China. The Chinese, recognizing the dilemma, after the initial period of conflict, left the pastoralists alone, paying them good prices for their products. Later, they met with partial success by providing fixed homes, schools, and medical care for part of the year plus huts for the aged and supplementary feed for the herds during the starvation period. These attractive enticements were offered to tie the pastoralist to a fixed locale to which he must return, curtailing his mobility and making it easier to exert some controls. As Ekvall summarized the situation:

> Together with such enticements the nomadic pastoralists still receive preferential treatment—whenever they are not involved in outright confrontation. As late as 1963, when all of the Tibetan agriculture had been fully collectivized, the nomads were still being allowed private ownership of all their stock, and were being told that if they would just keep producing animal products in ever increasing quantities, they were under no pressure to accept immediate socialization of their economy. (Ekvall 1968:97)

Thus the Tibetan nomads succeeded in saving large portions of their culture from destruction because that culture was so well adapted to its special environment.

Maori

In spite of their adaptation to a new natural environment, the Maori of New Zealand were able to preserve the "core" of their old culture. In about 1350 A.D. the Maoris migrated, in a great flotilla, from central Polynesia to New Zealand. Here they found that the colder climate would require some radical changes. The Maori carpenters were forced to build insulated planked longhouses rather than their customary airy thatched houses. They could no longer wear tapa cloth garments both because the plant from which they were made would not grow and because warmer clothing was required. Thus they developed a process of weaving flax. Their former diet of bananas and coconuts was replaced by roots and buds.

In spite of these changes forced upon them by the natural environment, important aspects of their culture remained stable—the family organization, the government, religion, and mythology. And their language is still recognizable today as a central Polynesian dialect.

Tanala

Another group, the Tanala of Madagascar, were unable to keep their old culture intact, so quickly proceeded to create a new system that would fit the environment. When land was no longer available for the traditional dry-rice type of cultivation, the people either had to face starvation or adopt the new technique of wet-rice cultivation. Under the old system, the Tanala moved their villages from one site to another as land became exhausted. It was a system based on the cooperation of several families. The new irrigation system required only a single family to tend a field, and the new techniques called for permanent villages. The old practice of moving from one site to another made each joint family an integrated unit. The anthropologist Ralph Linton, who studied this group, describes further changes brought about as the group adapted to its new environment:

> The process brought further changes in the patterns of native warfare. The old village had to be defended; but not at so great a cost nor with the necessity for permanent upkeep. When the village became permanent the defenses had to be of a powerful kind, involving big investments and permanent upkeep.
> Slaves, who were of no economic significance in the old system, now acquired economic importance. This gave rise to new techniques of ransom. Thus the tribal organization grew in solidity; and with the change the old tribal democracy disappeared. The next step was a king at the head who exercised control over the settled elements but not over the mobile ones. The kingdom came to an end before any adequate machinery of government could be established. This king built himself an individual tomb, thus breaking an ancient custom. (Linton 1939:282–283)

The democratic and individualistic Tanala were transformed into a class-structured society with a change in family life from permissive to authoritarian types of control. The ecological system had to be transformed drastically, as the old social environment was reworked to fit the new demands of the natural environment.

It is apparent in viewing these examples of the adjustments made by a group to its natural environment that the social environment plays a crucial intermediary role. In the case of the Tanala, a new social order was forced into existence. In the case of the Tibetan nomads and, in perhaps most cases of real disaster, the members of the system will attempt to maintain or recreate their traditional patterns of behavior. The next case illustrates this point:

Yungay

The earthquake of May 31, 1970, in the mountain areas of north central Peru was the most destructive in the history of the western hemisphere. It would qualify as a disaster of the first order, as disasters have been defined as disruptions of the social system to the degree that some, if not all, of the essential functions of the society are not fulfilled. A section of an avalanche buried an entire town (Yungay) of 4000 inhabitants, leaving only 250 survivors. Approximately 70,000 people in Yungay and the surrounding area were killed.

The situation demanded immediate modifications of preexisting behaviors to fit the emergency situation. Survivors of the buried city, on the day of the disaster, joined by nearby peasants who had lost their homes, established a refugee camp near the site of the buried city and named it "Yungay," after their old city. Aid for the necessities for existence was quickly made available to members of the refugee camp. Anthony Oliver-Smith, an anthropologist, studying the aftermath of the disaster, writes that almost from the time of its conception the refugee camp began operating under the preexisting social guidelines:

> Although there was an initial period of brotherhood and sharing between all social classes, typical of most disaster communities, it was soon dispelled with the arrival of aid. People began to be differentiated on the basis of their predisaster social identity as well as the new referent of disaster identity. Thus, not only was the camp composed of "decent people" [upper and upper middle class] and *Cholos* [Indians], but these lines of class demarcation were cross-cut by the disaster identity of *sobreviviente* [survivors who had homes buried] and *damnificado* [survivors who suffered only the effects of the earthquake]. Thus, if it could be concretely proven to him, an upper class person might recognize the right of an Indian or *Cholo* to receive a limited amount of aid providing he waited in line after the "decent people" had received their aid.
>
> In the eyes of the "nobles" of Yungay, there were very few survivors of the urban area in the camp. Most who claimed urban origin were considered imposters. In addition, middle and upper class survivors who remained in the camp considered themselves to be surrounded by "Indians"—a term employed to demonstrate one's scorn for a lower class person. (Oliver-Smith 1973)

Upper class survivors were bitter about the rural lower class who migrated to the new Yungay settlement and about the Indians who stayed in their communities and received aid. One survivor commented:

> The disaster has put some people up and some people down. The Indians are way up now. When did they ever have beds, sofas, stuffed chairs, tables? (Oliver-Smith 1973:176)

When authorities decided that the site of the refugee camp could later become dangerous and announced that the capital of Yungay would be relocated in an area 15 kilometers to the south, urban survivors of Yungay immediately rejected the plan. Hand-painted signs appeared saying, "Yungay Stays Here." Leaders were far more than sentimentally involved with the old site. They understood too well what would happen to the very foundations of their old class structure if the city were to be moved to a new area. A tradition of peasant labor had existed for a long period for the benefit of Yungay (i.e., road maintenance, street cleaning, minor construction). These traditional demands were already weakening since the disaster. Immediately after the earthquake, peasants were paid by authorities for their labor. Leaders were resisting a project which would mean radical structural change in their society. Thus leaders were willing to place greater value on the maintenance of their former ecological adjustment than upon the possible physical dangers inherent in the situation. The consequences of this confrontation with aid officials was a stalemate and postponement of action and decision which seemed to heighten the insecurities of the traumatized population.

Skolt Lapps

P. Pelto's study (1973) of the snowmobile revolution among the Skolt Lapps of northeastern Finland furnishes another illustration of the use of the Ecological Mini-Model. The main focus of his study is on the mechanization of reindeer herding. Prior to the 1960s the economy of the Skolt society was based on reindeer herding. Reindeer were important for both subsistence and transportation in the harsh arctic climate, and males took great pride in their skills as herdsmen. Skolt society was very egalitarian. As most individuals had equal access to crucial economic resources, there was little opportunity for the development of social or economic differences among them.

Beginning in the early 1960s, snowmobiles were introduced into northeastern Finland, and the Skolts eagerly accepted them. As Pelto found, this technological innovation had repercussions on almost every facet of Skolt life. Their economic system, mode of transportation, and patterns of social interaction were radically altered within a decade, and the egalitarian character of the society appears to be in the process of a major transformation.

In explaining the importance of the ecological approach for the study, Pelto writes:

> To understand the many-sided influence of the snowmobiles we have to take a quite eclectic ecological approach to this instance of human social adaptation. The web of interactions among the Lapps, their new machines, and the reindeer takes particular shapes because of the physical landscape on which they operate. The social environment, made up of neighboring groups, structures of government and economic enterprise, as well as international boundaries, must be carefully considered in the picture. (Pelto 1973:iv)

As part of the ecological model, Pelto (1973:11) treats human cultural behavior as a "heterogeneous and flexible system of adaptive responses." The various responses made by individuals to the new technical and economic situation brought about by the machines were summarized under two concepts: "delocalization" and "technoeconomic differentiation." The first process—delocalization—is common to the modernization process wherever it occurs. It refers to the transfer of local energy sources to commercially distributed sources.

And the use of the snowmobile and other machinery made the Skolts dependent on outside sources of fossil-fuel energy. But the cost of transferring from sleds to snowmobiles had many ramifications. It took effective resources management and manipulation of the socioeconomic network to meet these costs. It also took new sets of knowledge and skills for those who were to succeed in owning the machinery. The second process—technoeconomic differentiation—refers to the sharp contrasts existing in the contemporary "material style of life" between those who have the items from advanced technology such as the snowmobile and those who do not.

The strong egalitarian character of the Skolt sociocultural system is undergoing change due to the differential accumulation of material possessions by individuals. The possession of telephones and automobiles, for example, confer adaptive advantages on the individuals who can afford to acquire and maintain them. Social differentiation is beginning to occur and even schoolchildren are aware of who the leading snowmobile owners are. Those who still herd with sleds have feelings of inferiority in dealing with the machine men. Those who have been forced out of reindeer herding activities suffer a loss of self-esteem, according to the author.

The study is a good example of the relationships between a sociocultural system and its total environment and the relationships between its parts, showing how a change in one important aspect of the system can affect the equilibrium of all other aspects.

In attempting to understand the relationships between human beings and their environment, the anthropologist using an ecological mini-model must always be aware of the fact that scientific realities and sociocultural realities are often different and in conflict with each other.

4

Acculturation Mini-Model

BACKGROUND

Acculturation refers to the reciprocal modifications that occur when individuals from two or more different sociocultural systems come into contact. This definition is in keeping with more modern usage. Emphasis is placed upon the Acculturation Mini-Model since a large number of studies of sociocultural change are made with this model in mind. Early studies of acculturation were dealing mainly with the results of colonialism in the British Empire and forced acculturation. America and England furnished the technologically superior models to which other cultures were expected to adapt. And these kinds of expectations and biases ruled out any focus on "reciprocal" influences which contemporary anthropologists are at present attempting to include in the model.

The Acculturation Mini-Model must take into account such factors as the relative size of the system, the status and power exerted by the systems, and the number of individuals making contacts with each other in the systems. When a group is being "forced" to acculturate, the dynamics of the situation differ from those where the process is one of choice. For the American Indian, for example, the chain of events were special when the acculturation occurred between the fur-traders and the Indians, and differed radically from those occurring later between the Indians and the United States government. The process differed even when contacts were made by Indians with the Jesuit missionaries and when they were made with Franciscan mission communities.

After the early 1930s anthropologists became dissatisfied with the popular diffusion studies, where traits (mostly material) were traced as they diffused from one culture to another. Anthropologists were beginning to study what happened to systems when new traits were introduced through contact with other systems. In 1936 a group of leading anthropologists drew up a model for the study of acculturation (see Redfield, Linton, and Herskovits 1936). The focus, however, was still on traits as the unit of analyses—how they were syncretized, reinterpreted, and the amount of convergence. The studies were not upon the processes of reinterpretation, but on the accomplished results in terms of changes in the systems. Some of the earlier acculturation studies made in Mexico were composed of long lists of traits—one listing Indian elements, another Catholic, and another "combined."

In 1954 another attempt in the form of a memorandum was made to systematize the "acculturation" approach (SSRC Seminar 1954). This memorandum was more inclusive than the earlier one. The main focus was still upon the "systems" in contact and the end results of the acculturation process. Role-playing between individuals in contact, however, was described as the important method by means of which ideas and traits could be introduced and the authors of this later memorandum did therefore include the social interaction level of analysis (see Figure 1) in dealing with acculturating systems. They were still mainly interested, however, in the end results of intercultural role-playing, and systems were classified in terms of the results of the role-playing (that is, fusion, stabilized pluralism, etc.). There was no place allowed for changes in basic attitudes or world views or the perceptions of individuals, even though they might be shared. The process of acculturation was conceived as one coherent, organized system responding—through representative individuals (who *share* patterns for behavior)—to the impact of another system (G. and L. Spindler 1963). It is difficult to understand where the nonrepresentative deviants (missionaries, leaders of nationalistic movements, fur traders, etc.) who were responsible for many sweeping changes, fit. As long as there is a coherent culture, shared by a community of people, the formulation described in the 1954 memorandum is useful. But when the system begins to disintegrate and individuation takes place, a new focus on the individual is necessary—on how he or she perceives new alternatives and finds new ways of coping with the demands of change.

The Acculturation Mini-Model used by most contemporary anthropologists who deal with the acculturation process would fit any one or all three of the levels (social, culture, or individual) represented in the grand model (Figure 1), depending on the focus of the problem. The modern mini-model emphasizes the reciprocal relationships between sociocultural systems in contact, unlike the earlier models, where the flow was only from the dominant to a subordinate sociocultural system. The individual plays an important role in many of the contemporary studies. The contemporary Acculturation Mini-Model includes the reactions of individuals to new ideas from the system in contact, often with elaborate analyses of *why* particular individuals accept or reject. Emphases are placed on "coping strategies" used by individuals and strategies for maintaining special "identities" during the acculturation process.

One of the main drawbacks of the earlier acculturation models was that they could not be used to study large heterogeneous sociocultural systems (such as the U.S.A.) in contact with others. The contemporary Acculturation Mini-Model offers a solution to this problem by dividing the sociocultural system into subcultures. The researcher can study relationships between these smaller manageable parts as they are affected by stimuli from another sociocultural system. A subculture would include organized groups such as Hutterites and some Hippie groups, or special geographically located groups such as "Hill-billies." The contemporary model does not posit "assimilation" of one group by another but allows for retention of "ethnic identities."

The acculturation model has been critized by contemporary anthropologists because some of the earlier work seemed to assume that the end-result of acculturation was always assimilation—by the powerful dominant culture of the smaller, less powerful. This tendency was at least in part a reflection of the pervasive colonial mentality that has afflicted the West for some centuries. Internal colonialism—the tendency of the Anglo middle class in America to try to make over others in their image—has both affected reality conditions and the interpretations of anthropologists and other social scientists as they viewed the interactions between Native American and other nonmainstream communities and the dominant Anglo-American segment. Acculturation is not understood so much now, however, as a process leading to assimilation. It is seen rather, in its various forms, as adaptive strategies used by people who have to cope with the economic, social, and political disadvantages of their position as minorities. For these reasons we are less prone to see continua of acculturation leading to some state resembling assimilation, and more prone to recognize a variety of coping strategies, including reaffirmation of seemingly traditional values and behavior patterns, biculturalism, cultural syntheses of conflicting cultural elements, and managed identities. In the latter instance ethnic identity is symbolized and used as a means of obtaining social and political goals as well as to provide reference points for personal identities. There are many books and articles that put forward these interpretations, among them the American Ethnological Society volume *The New Ethnicity* (Bennett 1973). The reinterpretation of the Menominee response to the impact of Anglo-European culture takes the point of view that what had once been understood as acculturative segments of a continuum are better understood as adaptive strategies (Spindler and Spindler 1971). All of our concepts and models are in a constant state of flux as new understandings emerge.

The following case materials used to illustrate the Acculturation Mini-Model are grouped in terms of various types of acculturative processes that occur. Sometimes "free" choice is allowed the recipient culture and other times the adoption of ideas and items is "forced." The categories to be used include: examples illustrating the emulation of a technologically superior culture; examples of sociocultural systems resisting new ideas and things by erecting psychological and social barriers to change (boundary-maintenance); examples of cases of forced acculturation, where the receivers did not have a free choice; examples of acculturation that occurred with the support of the people adopting the new items.

ACCEPTANCE OF CHANGE

Emulation

The products and habits of technologically superior sociocultural systems are frequently emulated by people whose technology and material culture are not so highly developed. Aspects of life in the nearest large city may be emulated by a rural peasantry. The behaviors of military and administrative personnel representing powerful and remote nations like the United States may be emulated by members of tribal communities. The way of life of the technologically advanced society, or urban sector, imperfectly understood as a rule by those who imitate it, becomes an "emulative model"—something to be admired and emulated. "Model" is used in this context with a different meaning than when referring to working interrelationships in a sociocultural system.

Palau

The United States, with a large contingent of Army and government personnel as representatives, became an emulative model for the Palauans. When Palauans came in contact with the Americans on their islands after World War II, they had no built-in antagonisms toward accepting change. Throughout their entire history they had welcomed economically efficient innovations introduced from the outside world, even though they feared making changes originating from within the culture. They seemed to lack confidence unless they had a good working model to copy. The Palauan views the foreigner as having great prestige and power and has been quick to adopt many customs of diverse origins. Palauan culture is a compound of Trukese, Yapese, English, Spanish, German, Japanese, and American and has been influenced by New Guinea and India (Barnett 1960:16).

The receptivity of the Palauans has been costly. One of the costs is a deep sense of inferiority. Most foreigners have contributed to this sense of inferiority, but the Japanese were the most systematic in reinforcing it during their administration, when they pursued a policy of forced acculturation.

> They taught school children that they were congenitally inferior to the Japanese and could never hope to match them in spirit or intelligence. True, Palauans are powerful and cunning, but so are animals. The children had no reason to question this doctrine and they were witnesses to its social consequences. Except for the few taken into Japanese homes as servants, they and their parents were treated with contempt. They were not allowed to enter Japanese homes unless, in the exceptional case, they were seated at the threshold on a mat to protect the floor. In mixed groups in public places the Japanese held their noses, objecting to the odor of coconut oil. On boats and buses they were segregated. (Barnett 1960:16)

District rivalry has been intense in Palau with a continuous threat of a flare-up over some political or prestige issue. When the Americans arrived, they had an idea that a central club house, built cooperatively by the Palauans, would inspire a feeling of unity and pride that would override the limits of district, village, and family loyalties. The idea had first to be sold to the Palauans in such a way that it would seem to have been their own. The Palauan system still functions at its best under the drive of pride and the excitement of competition (Barnett 1960:35). In engineering the acculturative process, the Americans stimulated, advised, and encouraged, with an understanding of the Palauan compulsion to succeed and excel. Thus the community center was completed in a little over two months, which astonished the Palauans and Americans alike. When Palauans saw the project as a contest, their enthusiasm was unbounded:

> Few Palauans grasped this lofty design, but many of them wanted a building of their own in the town of Koror, the hub of economic and political action; and the rest could not afford to let themselves be excluded. When several contenders for American patronage leaped at the chance to support the project, their adversaries did likewise. Planning committees were formed and their meetings well attended out of fear of losing influence or a chance to propose something. Craftsmen who carved and painted the thematic panels on the gables of the club house vied for public praise of their skill and at the same time selected episodes and heroic acts for portrayal that proclaimed the glory of their clans and districts. Even ordinary people, old and young, claimed the right to contribute some special material or service and receive credit for it. Some villages took pride in supplying a specialty, such as a kind of timber or a thatching material, for which their localities are famous. Old men, reviving their ability, braided the coconut fiber used throughout the building to hold its parts together and made thousands of fathoms of cordage and rope. They also made many of the hundreds of strips of thatch necessary to cover the immense roof of the building. Women and children were kept busy with the specialties reserved for them—feeding the men and cleaning up. (Barnett 1960:36)

The Palauans' sense of identity had been revived.

Manus

American army personnel also furnished a special emulative model, inspiring the people of Manus, who live in the Admiralty Islands of the South Pacific, to effect radical changes. After twenty-five years, the anthropologist Margaret Mead returned to restudy the group. On her first visit, twenty-five years earlier, she lived in and studied a community built on stilts out in the shallow salt lagoons and between the islands—a community made up of a people who had no comprehension of the world outside, knew no writing, handled the problem of social interaction and reciprocal obligation in terms of kinship, who wore G-string and grass skirts, and whose economic system Margaret Mead described as a "treadmill." When Dr. Mead returned, she was ". . . greeted by a man in carefully ironed white clothes, wearing a tie and shoes, who explained that he was the 'council,' one of the elected officials of the community" (Mead 1956:22). She was handed a letter, signed by the locally chosen school teacher, a man who had been a babe in arms when she was there before, that asked her if she would help him teach the children. A few days after her arrival she was asked by another elected official to help work out a list of rules for modern child care—feeding, discipline, sleeping, and so forth. When she explained that her comments would be based on the latest thinking of the International Seminar on Mental Health and Infant Development, held at Chichester, England, in 1952, under the auspices of the United Nations, this man, who was born into what was recently a technologically primitive "stone age" society, *understood what she was saying.*

The anthropologist had left an isolated, nonliterate people twenty-five years earlier. She returned to find them moving rapidly and purposefully into the stream of modern world culture. She found them searching for education that would permit them and their children to participate more fully in the modern world. And this occurred in one lifetime!

Why did this happen? Over a million Americans poured through the Admiralty Islands during World War II. They set up sawmills in the bush to make lumber to build barracks. They knocked down mountains, blasted channels, leveled airstrips. And they treated the Manus men who worked for and with them more like individuals than they had been treated by other contacts. The Americans furnished a special kind of emulative model for the Manus, and, for whatever the reasons, they were generous. The Americans also brought with them a special and powerful version of our highly technological material culture. The model was skewed and limited, as social interaction could only occur with a few highly selected persons.

In using Americans for a model to emulate, the Manus literally threw away their old culture and attempted to recreate a way of life modeled after the American way as they interpreted it. (An outstanding leader, Paliau, played an important role [see Decision-Making on page 97].) Anthropologists had long thought that rapid change was inevitably disruptive. Margaret Mead suggests the opposite. If change is desired by an entire group and if it affects all of the culture and its parts simultaneously, there may be less social disorganization and personal maladjustment than if changes occur, segmentally over a long period of time. (Mead 1956).

There is, however, one great danger in this rapid change for the Manus. They believe that by modeling themselves in the image of American society they can participate fully in a world dominated by the Western way of doing things and receive benefits from this participation. This may, of course, not be the case, as others have discovered.

Kaktovik Eskimos

Another sociocultural system, that of the Kaktovik Eskimos of North Alaska, represent a somewhat different process as they responded to the technologically superior United States model. The situation was unique and could be considered a success, as individuals were able to maintain their identity as Eskimos while realizing many of the "benefits" of U.S. material culture.

The village of Kaktovik was formed voluntarily when new employment opportunities were made available by the military and other governmental personnel connected with the DEW (radar) Line installation. The village was mostly made up of related families previously scattered along the coast. Many factors were responsible for the positive kind of adjustment made by the Kaktovik Eskimos to rapid change. Professor Norman Chance, an anthropologist living in the village, describes the situation well (Chance 1966). The smallness and compactness of the village offered maximum opportunity for intragroup communication. Chance writes: "At Kaktovik, the successful substitution of new norms was related directly to the high intensity of interaction and communication among the Eskimo" (1966:85). The new goals were formulated mainly in terms of desires for material goods. And these newly defined goals could be successfully realized since all men, regardless of age, had equal opportunity to receive salaried employment and participate in the new way of life. The sociocultural system itself did not deteriorate, since the basic ideologies and patterns for behavior were not radically changed. Traditional patterns of behavior associated with sharing and cooperation were unaffected. Norms regarding interpersonal behavior, religious behavior, and drinking were firmly held, according to Chance.

Another factor responsible for a positive kind of adjustment was the fact that kin ties bound together fifteen of the eighteen householders and the traditional kinship system remained stable. The remaining three unrelated householders were integrated by the traditional practice of extending kinship privileges to nonkin by means of formalized "partnerships" (Chance 1966:86).

It was also important that traditional Eskimo leaders were effective in dealing with the Americans. They were respected by the whites, since much of their behavior was congruent with that valued by whites. The leaders had a friendly manner, were mentally alert and quickly and easily acquired new technical skills. In fact, the Eskimos in general were admired for the same reasons. Commander Roberts of the U.S. Navy wrote:

> The Eskimo of this area by disposition is light hearted and cheerful. He is generally peaceable and not easily discouraged. He has a keen sense of humor. He is trustworthy, honest and a hardworking man. It was, therefore, believed that no problem would arise in utilizing the Eskimo in positions where he was qualified, and to work hand-in-hand with men from other parts of the Territory of Alaska and from the United States. (Chance 1966:87)

Thus throughout the usually difficult process of adapting to rapid change, the Kaktovik Eskimos were able to maintain their autonomy and identity within the context of an economic dependency. Their emulation of the "superior" culture was not as sweeping as in the case of Palau or Manus. It focused on certain material aspects of United States Culture.

RESISTANCE TO CHANGE

Boundary-Maintaining Devices

There are, as described above, various ways in which cultures change. There are also ways in which they do not change. All sociocultural systems have boundaries. These boundaries are frequently given geographical expression, though by no means always. Boundaries are more a matter of recognizing differences between groups of people and make it possible to keep the differences. Various forces work to maintain cultural boundaries, some of which will be discussed below. Ethnocentrism is one of them and it is universal—the belief, often in the course of human history defended to death, that one's own culture is superior to others.

Americans and Germans and others with superefficient technology are not the only ones who consider themselves superior, possessing the only "right" way of thinking about the world and of coping with their environment. Likewise most primitive peoples, before extensive contact with the Western world, were extremely ethnocentric, thinking that they were *the* people and their ways the only correct ones for dealing with the environment. These feelings make people unreceptive to the ideas and methods used in other cultures to solve problems. Extreme ethnocentrism is a boundary-maintaining mechanism which protects the group from outside influences. A Latin high school teacher summed up what she believed to be the ethnocentric attitude of Anglo-Americans in south Texas:

> The Anglo-American sees himself as the most important being that ever lived in our universe. To him the rest of humanity is somewhat backward. He believes his ways are better, his standard of living is better, and his ethical code is better although it is of minor importance. In fact, he is appalled to find people on the face of the earth who are unable or unwilling to admit that the American way of life is the only way. (Madsen 1964:7)

The term for Eskimo, *innuit*, means "the people," as does the word *denè* used by the Navajo to describe themselves. Hart and Pilling likewise describe the ethnocentrism of the Tiwi:

> Thus, the word "Tiwi" did not mean "people" in the sense of all human beings, but rather "we, the only people," or the chosen people who live on and own the islands, as distinct from any other alleged human beings who might show up from time to time on the beaches. This exclusion of outsiders from real "us-ness" and hence from real "human-ness" was continued when the Europeans began to arrive in the early nineteenth century, and certainly as late as 1930 the Tiwi continued to call and think of themselves as Tiwi, *the* people, and to use other words for all non-Tiwi, whether they were mainland aborigines, Malay fisherman, Japanese pearl-divers, French priests, or British officials, who penetrated into their exclusive little cosmos. (Hart and Pilling 1960:10)

Ethnocentrism coupled with geographic isolation makes a rather effective barrier to change, but geographical barriers are not essential to boundary maintenance.

Nilgiri Tribes

The tribes of the Nilgiri Hills in South India furnish examples of the kinds of barriers to change that can occur as a result of boundary-maintaining devices. The tribes live in constant and close contact with each other and yet have little or no effect on each other's culture. How can this be? The tribes themselves were isolated for centuries from the Hindus of the lowlands due to the steepness of the hills and the climate of the plateau. So the Nilgiri folk, made up of four separate tribes, formed an isolated group living in economic and social symbiosis. The Todas were a pastoral people, the Badagas agriculturalists, the

Kotas artisans, and the Kurumbas food gatherers and sorcerers. David Mandelbaum, who lived with and observed the interaction of the groups, offers several reasons why so little mutual acculturation went on among these people. For one thing, he writes, ". . . all of Toda life had to do with the buffalo herds. Kota religion and interest centered about the smithy. Badaga life was engrossed with the welfare of the crop. Each group had a different focus of interest to which the other societies could contribute little" (Mandelbaum 1941:12–20). But it is the nature of the social intercourse, he continues, that forms a strong barrier to acculturation and borrowing between members of the separate tribes:

> Perhaps more important is the nature of social intercourse. Kurumbas are often called from the jungle homes to minister to Kotas and Badagas. Their magical services are indispensable. In the practice of their profession, Kurumbas may have occasion to call on their Kota clients several times a week. Yet whenever a Kurumba comes into view, the word flashes through the village, women and children run for the safety of home, cower inside until the Kurumbas have gone. All transactions between Kota and Kurumba take place outside the village limits, rarely is a Kurumba allowed within the home confines of another tribe.
>
> In like manner, Kota musicians have to be present at all major Toda ceremonials; yet if the band comes too close to a dairy, the place is polluted and can only be resanctified by elaborate purificatory rituals. Although contact was frequent, social intercourse was confined to a fixed number of narrowly defined activities. Any intimate contact, of a kind which would allow members of one group to mingle freely with another, was stringently tabooed.
>
> A third barier to intertribal diffusion is the matter of prestige symbolism. A unique tribal trait tends to be interpreted as a symbol of group status. Any attempt to imitate it by another group is violently resisted. For example, Badagas wear turbans, Kotas do not. When a few Kotas took to wearing turbans, the Badagas felt that the Kotas were getting above themselves. Some of the Badagas ambushed and beat up the Kota offenders, tore off their headgear, and effectively blocked the borrowing of this trait. (Mandelbaum 1941:20)

The boundary-maintaining devices used by these tribes were effective: the spreading of fear of the sorcerer, as in the instance of the Kurumba magicians (members of the outgroup); the emphasis on symbols of prestige for each group with controls exercised against the "imitator," as in the case of the beating of Kotas for wearing Badaga headgear; the pervasive limitations on social intercourse; and the use of rituals to keep outsiders from polluting the sacred dairy. Though the means employed by the Nilgiri Hill tribes were relatively extreme, they are by no means singular to them. Symbols of prestige, various forms of sorcery or magic, constraints on social intercourse, and religious rituals are in various combinations and degrees of intensity very widely used in human communities as boundary-maintaining devices.

Gypsies and Hutterites

Some groups self-consciously remain apart from the larger societies in which they live. They use some of the boundary-maintaining processes described, and others as well. Two of these groups, the Gypsies of Spain and the Hutterites of

the United States and Canada, are good examples. They have been so successful
in maintaining their identities that they (especially the Hutterites) are often
used as models for others, including some modern youth who are attempting
to set up alternative societies.

The Gypsies have been able to survive as a cohesive group, flouting the
laws of their host country and accepting only new ideas or artifacts which
serve their interests. After being banished by state authorities and excommuni-
cated by the clergy of central Europe, France, and Italy by 1447, they migrated
to Spain. Their antireligious attitudes, petty thievery, and methods of duping
the non-Gypsy brought them into disfavor with the general populace. Harsh
laws were enacted against them in Spain but:

> Throughout the long history of sixteenth, seventeenth, and eighteenth century
> law in Spain, it appears that the Gypsies' response to all laws directed at their
> control was marked by characteristic indifference or, at best, by short-lived,
> superficial adaptation to their conditions; the need to outwit the hunter be-
> coming no more nor less than part and parcel of the whole round of Gypsy
> life. Cut off, then, from other European countries which had legislated against
> them, protected by influential friends and the bribable state of Spanish justice,
> sheltered by wild terrain, and developing to the highest degree their own
> capacity for resistance, the Gypsy had yet to be tamed or made captive by
> Spanish law. (Quintana and Floyd 1972:21)

The basic values of a people, which are expressions of how they view themselves, offer clues to their propensity for survival as a distinct group. One of
the basic values held by the Gypsies is their strong belief in their ethnic
superiority to non-Gypsies. In their origin myths, Gypsies claim to be descendants
of kings and dukes (originally from Egypt). Gypsies consider themselves separate from peasants and, like the noble, believe that to work for the sake of
work is to be unworthy of the dignity of man (Quintana and Floyd 1972:45).

> Through his belief in Gypsy superiority—the individual comes to view him-
> self as hero. Although he lives on the fringes of history, he lives there as a
> hero in his own eyes, proud and aloof. (Quintana and Floyd 1972:114)

Another strong value held by the Gypsies is the importance of obeying
Gypsy law, and these laws are all aimed at maintaining the Gypsy culture in a
hostile environment.

> Close examination of these dictates (Gypsy laws) revealed that they stressed,
> in the main, the maintenance of Gypsy separateness from non-Gypsy popula-
> tions. The first, for example, enjoined the Gypsy not to live with non-Gypsies,
> as well as to conform to all aspects of the Gypsy way of life. The second,
> directed primarily at Gypsy women, discouraged marriage with non-Gypsies,
> and underlined the marital responsibilities of Gypsy women, complete faith-
> fulness to their husbands being the foremost among them. (Quintana and
> Floyd 1972:34)

Gypsies who break laws (for example, stealing from another Gypsy, violating
a Gypsy woman, or revealing tribal secrets) are summoned to appear before
the tribunals for judgment of their crimes. The ultimate and most dreaded

Gypsy woman (courtesy of Bertha Quintana and Lois Floyd.)

punishment for breaking a law is temporary or permanent banishment from the tribe.

The Gypsies have self-consciously created an "image" that would affront non-Gypsies in the dominant Western cultures. It includes elements such as petty thievery, begging, claims to occult powers and superiority, plus unconventional dress and life styles. An anthropologist and an ethnopsychologist, who spent large periods of time with the Gypsies of southern Spain, sum up some of the dynamics involved in retaining the Gypsy identity:

> Rejecting values of the urban, technological world (thrift, serious attitudes toward work and responsibility, cooperation, science) he clings tenaciously to his concept of freedom, "alegria," fatalism. . . . Confined as he is to his own closely knit group, he holds the values of the *payo* (non-Gypsy) in contempt and, therefore, is not significantly affected by them. The cohesiveness of Gypsy society facilitates self-acceptance and a strong sense of identity. . . . Highly perceptive, his survival dependent upon accuracy in judgment, the Gypsy has come to excel at sizing up the *payo* in the service of his own interests. Fearful of solitude, he has clung to the society of which he is a product. (Quintana and Floyd 1972:114)

And regarding the Gypsies' attitude toward changes taking place around him, the same authors write:

> Plugged into the changing world, the Gypsy with few exceptions remains traditionally *not* future oriented, looking instead to the present or past for directionality. He rarely asks, "Where am I going?" in the sense of transforming his life style. In many ways he wants to "stay put," borrowing from those around him only those things which he perceives as relevant to the Gypsy way. His materialistic bent tends to be misleading; the television set does not replace face-to-face communication in his society, his world of things remains subordinated to his world of persons. (Quintana and Floyd 1972:109)

The Hutterites, unlike the Gypsies, were separated from the "carnal" world and the medieval Protestant church in the sixteenth century for religious purposes. They were an Anabaptist group, founded in Moravia, which wished to establish a Christian type community where private property would be abolished. They, like the Gypsies, are visibly distinct in their pattern of dress and way of life. Rideman (1950:3) says:

> Hutterites view the world dualistically. The carnal nature is temporal and passing and brings death to man. By contrast, all who are "born of Christ" are ruled by the spiritual nature, which is eternal. . . . The two kingdoms are separate and each must go its separate way. It follows that Hutterites aim to live separate from the (carnal) world with their loyalties rooted in the spiritual. Separation is ordained by God. . . .

Two researchers who lived with the Hutterites describe their religious doctrine of separation from the world as a most effective means for maintaining the group's identity. Concerning their attitude towards those around them, one colony spokesman said: "A good neighbor is one we never see, talk with or help back and forth, or that never comes on the place." Further, the Hutterite colonies are self-sufficient economically, with strong ethnocentric attitudes concerning their way of life. The Hutterites' segregation is viewed as intolerable by the larger society. It aids in the spreading of myths and falsehoods about their communal life but "the persecution and dislikes expressed by outsiders tend to strengthen the internal cohesion of the colony" (Hostetler and Huntington 1967:96).

Aside from disliking their segregation, neighboring farmers fear their economic competition and rapid expansion in an area. In some areas, these fears have led to restrictive laws regulating the acreage and location of the colonies. In one area province in Canada a control board must decide whether or not it is in the public interest to permit the sale of land to Hutterites.

Throughout history, persecutions of the Hutterites, like those of the Gypsies, have been long and continuous. In 1557 Hans Kral, an imprisoned Hutterite preacher, placed in the stocks for 37 weeks in Tyrol, wrote:

My shirt decayed on my body. There was not a single thread left of it except for the collar. I did not see the sun for one and a half years. In the dark and awful dungeon I no longer knew the difference between day and night. All of my clothes rotted so that I was stark naked. The insects and the worms ate my food as soon as they smelled it. (Hostetler and Huntington 1967:8)

When Kral later escaped he became a leader and, after his death, a martyr.

Persecutions in 1918 of a group of young Hutterites from South Dakota who were conscientious objectors, were just as barbaric as those described in 1557. The young men were chained in a "dungeon" on Alcatraz with the warning from the guard: "There you will stay until you give up the ghost—just like the last four that we carried out yesterday" (Hostetler and Huntington 1967:9). After many beatings, standing nine hours a day with hands tied and stretched through the prison bars with their feet barely touching the floor, they were taken out dead. The Hutterites had been uncompromisingly loyal to their community and faith. Death to them was a release from the "Valley of Tears." This basic philosophy is intimately related to the ceaseless hostility directed at them from the outside world. As Hostetler and Huntington wrote (1967:95):

Hostile acts from outsiders are taken for granted and are built into the world view. When acts of hostility do occur, they tend to function as a cohesive force, thereby integrating the structural relations of the society. When there is no "persecution" or anti-Hutterite sentiment, Hutterite leaders acknowledge a tendency toward internal disruptive patterns.

It is clear that the Hutterites intentionally separate themselves from the rest of society, that they prize this separation, and that persecution is not only anticipated but plays an important role in their cohesiveness. Such a relationship with the outside world and to the group is costly to the individual. What makes a person want to pay the cost, and able to pay it? The socializing process which each member experiences from birth until death is an important part of the answer. It begins with the infant:

In infancy the child learns to enjoy people and to respond positively to many persons. After age 3 he is weaned away from his nuclear family and learns to accept authority in virtually any form. He learns that aloneness is associated with unpleasant experiences. During the school year he is further weaned from his family, learns more about authority, and acquires a verbal knowledge of his religion. He acquires the ability to relate positively to his peer group and to respond to its demands. As a small child his universe is unpredictable, but as he matures in his peer group and takes part in colony life his universe becomes highly predictable. He learns to minimize self-assertion and self-confidence and to establish dependence on the group. As a member of a categorically defined age set the young child learns explicitly when and whom to obey. (Hostetler and Huntington 1967:112)

The "community" in a sense becomes reified:

> The community is more important than the individual and governs the activity of the individual, and the corporate group has the power to exclude and to punish, to forgive and to readmit ... self-assertion by the individual against the group is not permitted. (Hostetler and Huntington 1967:12)

What happens if an individual balks or questions the system?

> Disobedience to the community means forsaking the commandment of God, and sin must be punished in proportion to its severity. Unconfessed sins will be held against the individual on the day of judgment and punishment will be meted out in the afterlife. (Hostetler and Huntington 1967:12)

The individual Hutterite is therefore socialized to want to be a member of the community and in fact is taught to be almost totally dependent upon it for security. The fear of being excluded from the protective group and of being given some unknown punishment in the afterlife prohibits most from committing the sin of disobedience. Martrydom is endured. Persecution only strengthens the community because it demonstrates each time it occurs, that the individual and the group are inseparable. And the group continues intact.

Some minority populations within larger, dominant societies resemble the Gypsies and Hutterites in their desire to retain a recognizable identity and a certain degree of separateness. Few are as successful in maintaining their boundaries, and are subject to changes in some areas of life while retaining their traditional character in others.

Ixtepejans

A different kind of boundary restricts the Ixtepejans of Mexico, an isolated group living in the mountains in a harsh environment. The world view of the individuals is so restrictive and limiting that change cannot readily occur. The people focus on the present and hope only to secure enough to eat from the semibarren soil. In contrast to Western man, Ixtepejans are submissive to their natural environment. Their world view is fatalistic. They live only in the present and the past. Since their history is marked by violence and destruction, they are pessimistic about what the future may bring. They fear change, thinking it can only bring something worse than they have. They even fear looking happy or successful in any way, as evil spirits may be used against them by envious people. It is, under the circumstances of their belief system, impossible for the Ixtepejans to understand the Western concept of progress and change. The anthropologist Michael Kearney who lived and worked with these people writes:

> Here there is an inversion of the predominant Anglo-American positive value on the future and the belief that change itself is desirable. Ixtepejanos believe

that there are minor fluctuations in an overall tendency which will culminate eventually in the destruction of the entire world—the ultimate catastrophe. But these fluctuations are the result of capricious change, or luck. This belief in chance is in accord with the capriciousness they attribute to the powers directing individual and group destiny. (Kearney 1972:123)

Kearney continues:

> Extensive plans are not made for the future because there are problems enough in the present, and then of what avail are plans if the future is essentially indeterminate? There are, for example, no fortune telling techniques except ones that forebode bleak futures. Speaking subjectively, there seems to be a strong desire to somehow immobilize the present, to affirm the moment that forever has the potential to transpire into sudden disaster. . . ." (Kearney 1972:124)

Navajo and Zuni

The Navajo and the Zuni Indians, living in the southwest area of the United States and sharing the same natural environment, reacted in sharply contrastive ways to the same stimuli from Anglo society. Their reactions were consistent for all new things and ideas stemming from contact with the Western world. Whereas the Navajo were receptive to the new, the Zuni used effective strategies to maintain the *status quo*. Both tribes had veterans returning from World War II. Each group reacted differently to the innovations brought back by the veterans, and the problems faced as they reintegrated into their home communities were strikingly different.

The Zuni, in attempting to restrict the influence of the outside world upon their culture, requested many deferments for men in religious offices when the draft began; and when the draft board asked that deferments be requested only for men who held these offices for life, the Zuni filled lifetime offices that had not been occupied for years and revived ceremonials that had become defunct. When the Zuni veterans returned, they were met with a solid front of conservatism and strong pressures were used by the priests and others to make veterans conform to the traditional Zuni norms and reintegrate into the traditional statuses and roles provided by the Zuni system. The veterans who could not conform left the community. The anthropologists John Adair and Evon Vogt, who did the research on this problem, write:

> Some of the processes whereby the Zuni veterans were integrated into the social framework were gossip, rumor, and ridicule. An older veteran who belongs to one of the most acculturated families wanted to establish a branch of the American Legion in Zuni. It was not long before gossip to the effect that he was going to use the money collected in dues for his own ends grew into a rumor campaign. After a few meetings, indifferently attended, the project was dropped. Terminal leave pay which could be collected upon application to the War Department was rumored by some of the elders to be a method of getting Zuni men into debt to the government, and would have to be paid off by more military service. One of the veterans was seen in the village dressed in a double breasted suit. Members of the community ridiculed him and accused him of "trying to be a big shot, trying to act like a white man."

The most dreaded of all rumors is to be labeled as a witch. Peculiar behavior and aggressive action which makes the individual stand out from the community may elicit this rumor. In Zuni belief conspicuous conduct is also to be avoided because it attracts the attention of witches and their malevolent action. Witches are believed to be jealous of those with wealth. An informant said that he had considered opening a store in the village but had not done so because he was afraid of those "jealous people." (Adair and Vogt 1949:550–551)

We can see the use of boundary-maintaining mechanisms in the form of social control—the effective use of gossip, rumor, ridicule, and of the dreaded label "witch."

In contrast to the Zuni, hundreds of Navajo males enlisted, few deferments were requested, and there was no increase in ritual activity to keep newly made religious functionaries at home. Clyde Kluckhohn and Dorothea Leighton, who did extensive field work among the Navajo, commented that the Navajo did not exhibit the same reluctance to go to war as did the Hopi, and that there was interest on the part of the Navajos in the events in Europe and Asia even before the United States actively entered the war. Navajos, who read no newspapers and spoke no English, would constantly ask: "What is happening in the war?" "Who is winning, the Germans or the English?" (Leighton and Kluckhohn 1947:103).

When the Navajo veterans returned, they were greeted with interested curiosity. Pressures on them to conform were not intense; and some have become active innovators in their culture since then. One of the conservative Navajo leaders remarked: "The way I feel about these soldier boys is that most of them can already speak English and write. It looks like they should go on with the white people and learn more and more and then lead their people" (Leighton and Kluckhohn 1947:104).

Whenever the social scientist is attempting to explain why a group of people do or do not change when they come in contact with another independent group, he must take into account the type of cultural system of each group as a variable of extreme importance. The Zuni have resisted change for centuries. Their system is tightly organized, inflexible, and with strong emphasis on cooperation; the community presents a united front. The Navajo, in contrast, have adapted to new environments and peoples in their history of migration from the north to the southwest. Their system is more flexible, more loosely organized. And the Navajo are individualists, with each household living separately and with considerable distance between it and the household of its nearest neighbor. Clyde Kluckhohn, in analyzing Navajo values and themes and integrating principles underlying the cultural system, has described Navajo social relations as being premised upon a "familistic individualism" which permits a relatively large area of freedom for the expression of individuality in Navajo society (Kluckhohn 1949:367). By contrast, Ruth Benedict describes Zuni culture as one with strong communal orientations which demand a high degree of social and cultural conformity on the part of the individual (Benedict

1934). It becomes rather clear that a better understanding of the cultural system of a people and of the personalities in the system could enable one to predict better what the attitudes toward innovations might be.

Jigalong Mob

Robert Tonkinson (1974) describes the adaptation of the Jigalong Mob, a group of Aborigines living around the Jigalong Mission Station in Western Australia, to the impact of Anglo society as mediated in part by missionaries. The mutually unfavorable stereotypes of the missionaries and Aborigines played a role in boundary maintenance. The Aborigines had lived in the traditional fashion, hunting and gathering and moving about in pursuit of game and in search of roots and fruits. They had, of course, carried on their complex religious ceremonies without interference. While their sedentarization at the mission station and the adoption of some wage work led to modifications in their local organization and economic life, they have not suffered any serious breakdown in their kinship system or religious life. This situation is in sharp contrast to the rapid postcontact collapse of Aboriginal culture in most of the other areas of Australia. Not only did the Aborigines at the Jigalong station maintain their traditional belief system and religious practices, but they developed a sense of group solidarity and self-conscious ethnocentrism.

The behavior of both the missionaries and the Aborigines was related to the clearly defined and mutually unfavorable stereotypes held by both for each other. The Aborigines associate "christian" with the absence of smoking, drinking, swearing, sexual joking, and a strong desire to change many aspects of Aboriginal culture related to religious activities. The Jigalong fundamentalist missionaries fit this stereotype. From their viewpoint, the Aborigines were children of the devil and Aboriginal culture the work of the devil. They ascribe laziness, lying, and depraved sexual behaviors to the Aborigines. Therefore, the missionaries agreed that the aboriginal "Law," or belief system, had to be destroyed and replaced with the christian way of life. When the missionaries were not succeeding well in converting the Aborigines, they blamed it on what they described as the particularly low intelligence of the Jigalong Mob. Communication was at a minimum between the two groups, brief and confined to the business of the moment (Tonkinson 1973:125). Missionaries rarely, except for prayer meetings, visited the Aborigines' encampment, and Aborigines rarely entered missionaries' houses.

The relative isolation of the Jigalong Mob enhanced the members' feelings of group solidarity. The members shared common forms of social organization and rituals and a unique cultural heritage. The members have taken care to exclude almost all whites from witnessing most of their ritual activities, and the camp is usually avoided by visiting whites. The laissez-faire attitude that has existed in rural Australia concerning the activities of the Aborigines, outside the work situation, has given the members of the Jigalong Mob a seemingly autonomous control of their activities.

Mutual exploitation is also a pronounced feature of the employment scene

(Tonkinson 1974:144). Whites pay as little as possible and usually in kind rather than in cash. And the Aborigines expend as little effort as possible, as work is merely a means for satisfying their wants. Some young men, however, are enthusiastic about stock-handling. Parents find it convenient and satisfying to be able to remain at the mission near their school-age children and to participate freely in their traditional "law" activities. Elkin terms the coping strategy of the Jigalong Mob "intelligent parasitism" (1951:164–186) and Berndt considers it as "the exploitation of all the available avenues through which a livelihood can be obtained" (1957:77).

Because of their isolation, the Jigalong Mob has not been subjected to many of the overt prejudices that have inculcated strong inferiority feelings among Aborigines in many parts of Australia. Thus through their special defensive strategies—supported by their adherence to their traditional beliefs and practices and their ability to keep a special distance between themselves and the missionaries, the Jigalong Mob has been particularly successful in coping with the impact of Anglo culture.

INTRODUCING CHANGE

Forced Acculturation

In most situations where a technologically superior group dominates a non-literate, technologically inferior group, the acculturation process is implicitly or explicitly "forced." When the "forced" aspect becomes too intense, the possibilities for revolt or rebellion are great. The Cuban revolution and the Peoples' revolution in China are examples in the sense that there was rejection of foreign domination as well as a revolt against indigenous elites. The revolt among nonliterate groups often takes different forms. As described previously, Wovoka, the Paiute Indian, thought he could make white men disappear by performing a ritual dance. Instead this "nativistic" or "revivalistic" movement culminated in the "battle" of Wounded Knee, where the infamous massacre of the Indians occurred. The psychological implications of these kinds of "revolts" will be dealt with under the Psychocultural Mini-Models (see p. 87).

Indians of Brazil

In some cases "positive" change in terms of Western culture has resulted when representatives of the technological superior culture were sensitive to cultural differences. An example of this occurred when the Indian Protection Service in Brazil attempted to establish peaceful relations with the Umotina Indians, who thought of the whites as ferocious enemies to run from or attack. Of course the Indians of Brazil have a reality basis for such an image, for they have been harassed and often murdered by whites. But this image evolved over the years, due in part to a series of cultural misunderstandings. White men did not understand that the polite way to approach any groups of strangers is to simulate an attack with drawn bows and arrows. And these gestures were misinterpreted by whites.

The pacification teams had to break down the stereotype the Indians had of them. They did this by establishing armored posts in Indian territory and by enduring attacks without fighting back. They were then able, slowly, to establish good relations with the Indians. However, the Indians thought that *they* had done the pacifying. An anthropologist with the Protection Service pointed out that the Indians for the first time were able to behave by their own rules of etiquette without experiencing injury at the hands of the whites (Ribeiro 1962:330).

Tiwi

Another case of "positive" forced acculturation occurred when Father Gsell, a Catholic priest working among the Tiwi of northern Australia, thought of an ingenious method of saving female infants from the barter system to which he was opposed in principle. The currency in Tiwi society is women. Men compete for prestige and influence through their control over women. Old, wealthy men buy newborn female infants and speak for female infants before they are born. Thus in most cases a man is unable to have a wife until he is past middle age and has acquired enough material wealth to buy one. Father Gsell, realizing that many of the aspects of the old pattern of Tiwi life had to be abandoned before he could make the Tiwi into Christians, decided to enter the system, observing the rules of the game, and "acquire wives" for himself. The following is the account of what happened:

> To the missionaries, polygamy was sinful and could not be part of the new Tiwi life. Prenatal and infant bestowal had to be abolished. Marriages should be between agemates and should be arranged freely and solely by the couple involved. Such changes were the crux of Father Gsell's program, and the story of how he went about it has run in many a Sunday supplement in the cities of Australia under the title "The Bishop with 150 Wives." Father Gsell did not try to convert or drastically change the behavior of the older Tiwi; he believed that they were too set in their ways. Rather, he built toward a distant day by working among the younger generation. When infant girls became widows, he purchased them from their fathers. Men with young widowed daughters and those with spare young wives sold such girls for axes, flour, tobacco, cloth, and trinkets. Such "Blackies," as they became affectionately called, lived in the convent with the French (and later Australian) sisters. When such a girl reached the age of 18, she was asked to choose one of the young single men for her husband. For his part in this excellent deal which provided him with a wife long before he would get one under the old tribal system, the young man had only to promise that he would never take another wife. Such a wedding was not a Mass, for neither party was Catholic. However, the children born of this new union were baptized and reared as Catholics. Later, a few of the girls who had been sold to Father Gsell before they were ten went through confirmation as did their youthful fiancés. The first nuptial Mass between two such Tiwi took place in 1928. (Hart and Pilling 1960:102)

Unlike the introduction of the steel axe to the Yir Yiront of Australia, described earlier, this innovation was not abruptly disruptive.

Attempts to Secure Support from the People

Swazi

Change agents sent out by a country that is interested for one reason or another in helping to shape the future course of events for people in another land have learned by bitter experience that the only kinds of introduced changes that become effectively incorporated into a culture are those that have the support of the people themselves or their recognized representative. The use of the King of Swaziland (Sobhuza) is an example of how changes can be more easily introduced by using recognized channels of communication and control.

> . . . the position of the Swazi king *cum* paramount chief has long been the focus of opposing systems. In the first period of contact the whites exaggerated his rights and powers to obtain concessions for themselves; later, they curtailed the substance of traditional authority but used the king indirectly to act as the primary agent in bringing about his people's acceptance of innovations. At present, Sobhuza is still expected to be the first to improve his stock, use new agricultural techniques, employ demonstrators, encourage creameries and dairies, patronize schools and hospitals, and so forth. Until the early forties, he alone had regular and formal contacts with senior members of the white administration; these gave him a greater semblance of power than he actually wielded, with the result that his subjects tended to blame him for legislation for which he was in no way responsible and about which he was sometimes not even consulted. He and his mother were the only two members of the traditional hierarchy who were paid by the administration. He received 1250 pounds sterling (approximately 3000 dollars), which amount was obviously inadequate for any national undertaking but described by some Swazi as an attempt to "buy the kings." (Kuper 1963:40)

As can be seen in this example, even when administrators seek the support of the people in introducing change, many complex problems can arise. In this case the administrators in working through a figure of high status such as the Swazi king, inherited a myriad of problems inherent in the system itself. Many people who had long been dissatisfied with the system now had the courage to criticize the king who had lost some of his powers. So the attempt to co-opt the support of the people through the office of the king was only partially successful. This process of "indirect rule" was used by the British as a technique for keeping the colonies under control. The objective was to introduce some change, such as agricultural improvements, without causing too much change, or change of a revolutionary character that would be disruptive to colonial rule.

Lugbara

"The New People" of the Lugbara of Uganda illustrate another method of introducing change by working in and through the system itself. Government officials and missionaries have made it possible for young men to attend schools, live in Western houses, and adopt a Western way of life. And yet these men still retain their strong ties with Lugbara society.

> Labor migration and cash-crop growing, together with the appearance of chiefs and traders, have led to the last development, that of an incipient new class of people who gain their livelihood by earning wages or selling produce instead of by traditional subsistence farming. These are the "New People" (*'ba odiru*). The more important New People are the educated and semieducated protégés of the government and the missions, and the wealthier traders. They are men who come into contact with Europeans and other foreigners. They attend the same schools; they live in brick houses and adopt a Western way of life; their families intermarry and many of them have ties with similar people outside Lugbaraland. These men are Lugbara and therefore have intimate ties with Lugbara society, but as New People their loyalties are to members of their class, as well as to members of their own lineage and families. The leaders of this class provide a new example for the aspiring younger men who can earn money from labor migration or cash-cropping. The traditional idea of slowly becoming a respected elder by merely growing old and acquiring lineage seniority, a necessarily slow process, is giving way to that of acquiring power and position outside the lineage system. To achieve this a man needs wealth, education, perhaps a job with the government or missions, and a willingness to deny many of the traditional ties with lineage and family. Many—perhaps most—of these men have seen southern Uganda as labor migrants, and the elder among them were soldiers in the second world war and saw countries outside East Africa. They consider themselves to be the vanguard of social and political progress. The older people who see modern developments in a different light—as stages in the progressive and regrettable destruction of Lugbara culture—call them *Mundu* and bewail their growing importance. But the older people are dying out and the New People are clearly the men of the future. (Middleton 1965:91–92)

These New People are paving the way for a transition from old to new. They have successfully bridged the gap between Lugbara society and the new Western-type social order and have *realized the rewards* of the new society. Thus they furnish a special kind of example for the Lugbara youth. This situation prevailed until 1965 at least, when anthropologist John Middleton wrote the words cited above.

5

Modernization-Urbanization Mini-Model

INTRODUCTION

Although "urban anthropology" has recently become a popular area for study, anthropologists have focused for many years on the adaptive changes occurring among preliterate groups and peasant peoples as they are influenced by urbanites. Certain broad generalizations can be made about this process. Archaeological and written records indicate, for example, that when preliterates and peasants went through the transition from precivilized villages to urban centers, certain changes were found in all cases. All acquired writing, architecture, taxation, development of sciences, trade, and art. Aside from this base, many varieties and types of adaptation have occurred.

The Modernization-Urbanization Mini-Model deals with technologically simple sociocultural systems (peasants usually but tribal people sometimes) adapting to technologically complex sociocultural systems (represented by the city and through direct contact or by communication systems). The process usually occurs between peasants and urbanites sharing a core culture. Early models and hypotheses that were applied by anthropologists (Redfield 1947, 1953) to modernization and urbanization processes in Central America were found to be insufficient for describing the situation in other parts of the world. The earlier researchers posited a continuum of development from primitive to peasant to secular and urban, but it was later found that some preliterate groups never experienced a peasant stage. They also predicted that the process would mean the isolation of the individual, the breakdown of kinship relationships, and result in superficial social relationships. These predictions were not always fulfilled either.

The contemporary Modernization-Urbanization Mini-Model does not posit specific sequences of development but focuses on individuals as members of preliterate or peasant sociocultural systems adapting to the influences of the city—through direct contact or through the influence of change agents. When contact is direct, the model includes the special kinds of relationships existing between individuals in the country and those in the city which serve special functions for them (see social networks analysis below).

Some preliterate groups are becoming modernized without passing through a peasant stage. Nevertheless, most of the world's population has gone through such a stage where the people were marginal participants in the complex society of which they are a part. It is surprising to find that more than half of the world's population today can be said to be peasant and another 20 percent or more may be recently "post-peasant" (Gamst 1974). It is not surprising that many anthropologists are studying change among peasant groups.

Modernization does sometimes occur without urbanization when groups of people living apart from cities learn (through mass media and government agents) how to become technologically "modern."

As was the case for the Acculturation Mini-Model, the Modernization-Urbanization Mini-Model relates to all three of the levels of the Grand Scale Model (Figure 1) and can be analyzed with focus on one level (individual, social interaction, or cultural) or all three.

After a discussion of the history and importance of "the city" and "peasantry," a wide variety of examples of cases will be presented to illustrate the unique kinds of adaptations made by peasants to the influence of the "city."

THE CITY

Peoples throughout the world have been urbanizing for more than four thousand years, when the first complex cities sprang up in Mesopotamia, and then in Egypt and the Indus Valley. Later, about 3000 years ago, cities appeared in Mexico and Peru. These earliest urban centers conformed surprisingly closely to the model later developed by social scientists for the "city." These all had large populations, supported by a predictable supply of food derived from improved agricultural techniques; there were experts and specialists; society was stratified—people were ranked according to the kind of work they did or the family they were born into; and a strong central government and governing elite guaranteed safety for the lives and property of the common man, with armies that would be used against enemies. Today these early cities, with their monuments, written records, works of art and science, lie in ruins, due mostly to an inability of their inhabitants to adapt successfully to the environment. Overpopulation, pollution, destruction of forests were threats then as now. Although the ancient cities died, the basic model for "the city" survives. The ancient cultural systems contributed to the development of new systems. The Indus civilization, for example, led to the rise of the new civilizations in the Ganges Valley, which persist today, having changed and adapted continuously through the centuries.

The "new" kind of city that arose after the Industrial Revolution in Europe, and is in most respects the city of today, probably shares a great deal in structure and interpersonal relations with the original old cities. Large concentrations of population in a limited geographical area, the centralization of authority, religious, commercial and particularly priestly functions were among the shared features. The "new city," however, is of heterogenetic rather than homogenetic origins. It is built upon a variety of life styles and, above all, "rationality" (a combination of efficiency and pragmatism). One modern writer, typical of many, encapsulates the rationality of the modern city as follows:

> It is a massive and mobile form of community life in which social values are rational and instrumental. Pragmatic truths are valued over group solidarity and social securities. Social relationships here are disproportionately specialized, instrumental, and limited in content and duration. New groups arise to serve community functions. (Ryan 1969:316)

Interpersonal relationships become depersonalized, due in part to the complicated exchange systems (money, interest, stock market, etc.), to a highly developed technology emphasizing "mass production," and to a dependence on specialized communication networks, rather than on the personal, social, and kin-based set of relationships found in small communities. In place of the traditional, extended family, the small nuclear family (husband, wife, and children) arises as more flexible and adaptive in the new milieu. Varieties of special interest associations came into being to fulfill functions performed previously by small primary groups. In the new city, time, efficiency, and quantities of material goods and comforts are especially important.

In today's urbanized society decisions are increasingly made on the basis of pragmatic efficiency, of what "works," rather than on the basis of ethics, values, or justice. The accelerated pace is geared to "progress" and rapid achievement. In a depersonalized, technological order, it is difficult to keep the social environment for the individual secure and meaningful. Impersonal bureaucracies tend to take over functions to such an extent that they become uncontrollable. As one author writes:

> In many modern societies, the life of the individual is governed not by small cultural units such as the family, or neighbors, or religious organization, but by faceless bureaucracies. In modern states and cities, such bureaucracies contend against each other for resources and seek to increase their size and influence. Whether seeking to grow or to control their clients, bureaucracies formulate new rules and employ more persons to enforce them. The individual is governed now, not by the cultural traditions of his community, but by the countless and inexplicable rules of the innumerable bureaucracies with which he must deal in order to survive. On the other hand, with the evolution of larger and larger cultural systems, and the increasing inclusion of mankind within a single world order, perhaps all of this is necessary, but perhaps it is time to consider what has been sacrificed upon the altars of modernity and efficiency. (Haviland 1974:566)

There are many exceptions to this rather one-sided picture. As we will see, people do not give up their relationships easily and they try to create a human environment wherever they are. But what has been described will serve as a starting point for our analysis.

PEASANTRY

Because the city plays such an important role in modern times, there is the impression that most peoples are or will soon become urbanized. This impression may or may not be correct. At present, between one-half and two-thirds of the world population of about 3.6 billion people may be considered peasants (to be defined), and by far most of the human beings who have ever lived may be so considered. Peasantries are found in vast areas of South America in the New World and in most of the Old World; they extend from Scandinavia through Morocco and across Europe, Northern Africa, Southwest Asia, Central Asia, the Indian subcontinent, and the Far East, terminating in Japan and Indonesia. Thus, in discussing modernization and urbanization processes, what is happening to peasant communities is of the first order of importance.

According to a pioneer student of peasant societies, Robert Redfield, the course of man's life on earth has gone through three important stages. They are the "primitive," the "peasant," and the "secular-urban." When the tribal peoples in the Middle East became agriculturalists, written language and cities soon developed. The very earliest cities were not truly urban, however. Those described in Mesopotamia and Egypt were mainly religious and political capitals, but they were centers of heightened activity and expression for the folk culture of the countryside. They were the centers toward which the peasants in the nearby countryside first oriented their lives. The city of Benares, India, was and remains just such a folk city, where Hindu folk culture is expressed and preserved.

When the "new" city developed, the schism between the world of the peasant, deriving his living directly from the land, and that of the urbanite, became insurpassable. This is understandable when folk (peasant) society is contrasted with urban society. As Redfield characterizes the former it is

> . . . small, isolated, non-literate, and homogeneous, with a strong sense of group solidarity. . . . Behavior is traditional, spontaneous, uncritical and personal; there is no legislation of habit or experiment and reflection for intellectual ends. Kinship, in its relationships and institutions, are the type categories of experience and the familial group is the unit of action. The sacred prevails over the secular, the economy is one of status rather than of the market. (1947:293–308)

To the extent peasants have knowledge of the city and the way of life within it, they see themselves as inferior. Attitudes of hostility, suspicion, and self-denegration are reinforced. George Foster, in working with modern-day peasants, describes their world view as characterized by an image of "limited good." The peasant views his world "as one in which all the desired things in life such as land, wealth, health, friendship and love, manliness and honor, respect and status, power and influence, security and safety, exist in finite quantity and are always in short supply" (Foster 1965:304). Other students of peasantry also emphasize this trait (Rogers 1969:40). Many anthropologists have noted in contemporary peasant societies that there is competition for friendship and love, preoccupation with health and illness, and often emphasis on manliness and honor. With this view of "limited good" the contemporary peasant almost seems borderline paranoid about the prospect of others getting too much or that others might suspect one of doing too well (see Kearney 1972). And the peasant is described by Kearney and others as subject to the evil eye and the workings of witchcraft and magic.

J. Acheson (1972) feels that the concept of "limited good" is too simplistic. He believes that Foster failed to emphasize economic blocks to individual responsiveness and other factors motivating individuals to take advantage of special opportunities.

At this point the reader might ask, "What is a peasant?" Most anthropologists define peasants as peoples with an agricultural mode of life, usually emphasizing subsistence farming and dependent upon the products and markets of the wider society whose center is represented by the city. Peasants are marginal participants in the social and political life of the nation or area of which they are a part. Yet they are a part of a society more complex than their own could be by itself and cannot be understood apart from this complex society. Professor Gamst elaborates this skeletal definition of peasantry. He writes that categorical considerations of a peasantry would include the following:

> Basic is small-scale, rural agricultural and sometimes craft production, using preindustrial equipment and techniques on a subsistence level. The family is the central social unit of production, and when the peasants are agriculturalists—as they are most often—the family is the land-using unit. Cultivating peasants may be considered as "tied to the land." However, holding of land, although common, is not necessary for inclusion of subordinated cultivators under the rubric of peasantry. Because the peasant family is not entirely self-sufficient, it usually sells some part of its production in a market system of exchange and purchases certain essential goods there. It also surrenders some part of its production to members of an elite, because of their superior claim to this production, a claim based upon authority received from the state. (Gamst 1974:13)

These elements may define peasantry but hardly assist in defining the actual peasant condition. Eric Wolf comments on this:

> .... peasants are rural cultivators whose surpluses are transferred to a dominant group of rulers that uses the surpluses both to underwrite its own standard of living and to distribute the remainder to groups . . . that . . . must be fed for their specific goods and services . . . (Wolf 1966:3-4).

Another anthropologist, May Diaz, comments on the peasant's condition:

> Peasants live in a social world in which they are economically and politically disadvantaged. They have neither sufficient capital nor power to make an impression on the urban society. But they have no illusions about their position. Indeed, often they have no notion at all of that imaginary world which offers social mobility, entrepreneurs . . . (Diaz 1967:56).

When, in the course of cultural evolution, the "state" evolved and the population became divided into the elite and the commoners, peasants were among the commoners.

Peasants have been struggling against oppression for hundreds of years. Especially in the twentieth century peasants have been struggling for social revolutions that will give them land and freedom from oppression by the landowning classes—in Guatemala, Nicaragua, Colombia, Paraguay, Argentina, Bolivia, Peru, Brazil, Indochina, and the Philippines. Peasant rebellions have seldom become successful revolutions without a group of leaders from urban centers. Peasants lack acquaintance with the complex operations of the state. Usually when a revolution was successful it did no more than change some conditions in the immediate countryside but did not affect the cities which had real power. The peasants suffering most from oppression are least able to muster sufficient resources to challenge their overlords. A comparative study by Eric Wolf (1969) of the revolutions in Mexico, Russia, China, Vietnam, Algeria, and Cuba where peasants played a central role showed that those peasants likely to revolt successfully were not the poorest and landless but the "middle peasants" who had enough control or leverage over their own resources to overcome powerful landowners.

DEVELOPING SOCIETIES

Most of Asia, Africa, and Latin America were unaffected by urbanization and secularization until about the mid-twentieth century. But by the 1950s most traditional societies had become transitional. Not all societies today are passing through a peasant stage, however. Many tribal societies in sub-Saharan Africa, for example, are beginning modernization toward an industrial level, never having experienced the agrarian peasant level. Most developing societies exhibit some of the same features, but each represents a unique development, expressing the cultural traditions of a particular area in varying degrees. Modernization means for all an increasing scale in social relationships—a wider range of contacts, expanded dissemination of information, development of bureaucracies—and for most members of transitional societies, the introduction of standardized machine products, to the detriment of the traditional arts and crafts.

Although the city furnishes models and is the center for formal leadership in development, industrialization and modernization do not require its subjects to live within the city confines. All peoples in small communities are influenced by the dynamic city and all of the countryside is affected by it. In most areas the urban influences are first felt through the migrants to the city, but everywhere channels are open to the countryside and include the many urban workers who return to their villages. Ryan comments on this relationship.

From the "new" city goes direction and coordination for educational institutions in the hinterland; from urban-centered educational centers flow the teachers themselves. In the city is the radio station with news of the political and scientific worlds given in regional dialects along with advice to farmers and housewives and health counsel. Newspapers circulate outward as do the orders of governments. The regional metroplis does not create all of this knowledge, but for the peasant it originates interest and mediates the knowledge coming from the world beyond. International wire services, air freight lines, consulates, embassies, technical aid experts, politicians, and professors are all engaged in diffusing news of the world in the broadest possible sense. (Ryan 1969:420)

MODELS FOR MODERNIZING

Contemporary groups with a distinctive culture of their own and wishing to modernize do not necessarily want to become "Westernized." Many groups have successfully maintained their ethnic identity (Muslims, Bantus, Bontok, etc.). Modernizing groups embrace the material achievements of the West and some adopt social values, such as emphasis on individualism in achievement and an emulation of the "rational" social order. Different groups select different models for different reasons. The United States represents a fuller attainment of technological efficiency and industrialization, but Russia, representing rapid development, serves as a model for many weak new nations. Some South Asian traditionalists want the advantages of the West without the emphasis on "Western" materialism. Others want political democracy while still retaining caste privileges, or at least the elite do.

It is interesting to see that modernization need not lead to the destruction of traditional institutions. Sometimes traditional institutions facilitate rather than impede the social changes consequent to modernization. Some social scientists, for example, feel that Buddhism may be a positive force for modernization in South Asia (Ryan 1969:409). The good Buddhist may use all material benefits of technology without losing his religion or challenging any of its philosophical assumptions. Often a "dual society" evolves such as in Latin America and Spain where a modernized sector exists side by side with a traditional one. A Rolls Royce or a Volkswagen might be seen parked next to an ox cart. The groups with money often enjoy the material items without subscribing to the value system of the modern city. In the modernizing Yoruban (Africa) city of Ibadan a nonmechanistic, preindustrial African tradition converges with a technologically oriented European tradition (Mabogunje 1967). Sometimes peasants in developing countries become modernized in political attitudes and remain traditional in agricultural attitudes and technology. There is no fixed pattern or sequence in the modernization process. Much of the rest of this section will be devoted to examples of the varieties of ways in which contemporary peoples modernize and urbanize.

POSTPEASANT STABILIZATION

Fred Gamst adds a rather sobering note to the discussion of urbanization and modernization. He writes that, due to lack of sufficient resources, large parts of the peasantries of many countries will be arrested in a postpeasant stage, focusing on individual family labors and cultivation. The "rational" city model has not been able to deal with the life and death problems of over-population, pollution, and depletion of critical resources. This "rational" model may therefore ultimately prove to be nonrational, and when and if urban civilization again collapses, Gamst (1974:71) comments that the postpeasantries will still be around to constitute the supportive sector of the new postindustrial civilization.

NETWORK ANALYSIS

Anthropologists have, as described in the Acculturation Mini-Model, had to be eclectic in their use of theories and techniques while studying acculturation, modernization, or urbanization processes. Anthropologists studying complex societies have found that the customary model of anthropological fieldwork, using mainly participant-observation techniques by one or two workers is not sufficient. They have used sociological survey techniques (questionnaires, etc.) and concepts in conjunction with anthropological strategies to great advantage. Many anthropologists have found "network analysis" useful for exploring the relationships between individuals in a village and, of more importance, the relationships between individuals in a village and those in the nearby city. As Barnes, one of the originators of the method notes, "network analysis" has become a rather "trendy" term (Barnes 1972:2) with many meanings and should be used with caution. It is not a theory and can be used with many theories. It is simply a convenient way of studying social relationships and the relations between relationships at a distance. Most people are connected to others by complex networks of social relationships. When a village begins to modernize it is important to understand the kinds of networks established between villagers and city dwellers. They are usually ties of kinship and friendship, called first-order contacts, and the anthropologist can trace them from the viewpoint of selected informants. Second order contacts are also extremely important as villagers extend their relationships with city dwellers. For example, if a villager needs legal assistance and is related to a city dweller who has a lawyer friend, the contact can be crucial to him.

In a small community, the same person plays many roles in relating to others. To any one other person he might be a neighbor, a relative, a member of the same religious and social groups, and a coworker. These would be called "multiplex" or "many stranded" role relationships. On the other hand, in large-scale, industrial, urban societies, single-stranded role relationships are typical.

An individual relates to another person in terms of one role, such as the doctor, the butcher, the storekeeper, the electrician, the plumber, the milkman, a neighbor, a coworker, etc. Whether anthropologists choose to study the smaller systems and institutions of a complex society represented by a large city or to begin with the villages and work outward, they are inventing and using various methods and techniques of study such as the network analysis just described.

VARIATIONS IN COPING

The urban-modern models are available to most groups and individuals in the world today—either by mass communication techniques (radio, television, movies) or by direct contact with cities (with improved transportation) or indirectly through contact with others who are familiar with "city ways."

While there are some generalizeable and rather predictable kinds of processes, such as the depersonalization, rationalization, and isolation of individuals just discussed, that occur when modernization and urbanization take place, each community generates unique ways of responding to the challenge of adapting to new stimuli. Variations are often due to the larger system to which the villagers are adapting. The ecology and natural environment can also play important roles. In Swiss villages such as Kippel, to be discussed later, the mountain environment has a decisive influence (J. Friedl 1974). Sometimes chance factors account for variations. In the village of Orašac (Serbia), the fact that mines were developed nearby, requiring only intermittent labor, had important repercussions in influencing the "modernization" process (Halpern and Halpern 1972), as will be dealt with in this section. And sometimes a group of people will objectively assess the costs involved in modernizing and decide to reduce them, as will be seen in the case of the inhabitants of Almonaster, Spain (Aguilera, n.d.).

Following are brief case studies representing important variations exhibited by communities and populations experiencing modernization and/or urbanization. They do not illustrate a single theory of culture change, or even consistently interrelated parts of a theory. Anthropological understandings of urbanization and modernization have not arrived at the point where systematic statements of an encompassing theory are possible. The cases included below illustrate a wide range of the consequences of modernization and urbanization and are the kinds of data from which generalizations and theory will emerge.

The New Wind in Gopalpur

The new wind blows in Gopalpur (South India), though fitfully, and its effects are sometimes surprising. The government officials, charged with bringing the new wind of modernization to Gopalpur, work honestly and efficiently, insofar as it is possible for them to do so. At the same time, many changes which could be made are not being made. Government officials tend to lay the blame for lack of progress upon the people of such villages as Gopalpur, who in turn tend to lay the blame upon the government officials. Both groups feel helpless and apathetic. The new wind blows in an unchanneled and undisciplined way, stirring up new problems for every one solved. The source of the difficulty seems to lie in the government officials' failure to perceive the interrelationships among the things they are trying to change. The culture of Gopalpur is an organic whole; its religion and its social organization are adapted to the economic tasks traditionally carried out in the village. The reform programs stimulated by the new wind are not organic wholes. The new wind offers some hopeful and some frightening prospects, but it does not offer a way of life. (Beals 1962:83)

The new wind, "Navira" as the people of Gopalpur call it, is being felt in small villages throughout the world in much the same manner as it is in this small South Indian village. It is born of new scientific and technical knowledge —advances in medicine and experimental agriculture, for example—and is a product of the urban environment.

After many centuries of coping with and adapting to the environment, Gopalpur has attained a state of equilibrium, where the checks and balances are finely equilibrated:

The traditional culture of Gopalpur contained the answer to every problem. The fathers and forefathers of people in Gopalpur weathered flood, famine, pestilence, and war and built great cities on the fertile plain. As the new wind blows, feelings of pride and greatness are replaced by feelings of poverty and helplessness. (Beals 1962:76)

If a Gopalpur farmer decides to adopt new agricultural practices, he does so at the risk of threatening significant social and economic relationships. This is one of the deterrents to modernization noted by anthropologists in studies elsewhere.

To purchase improved agricultural equipment, the farmer must sever his traditional relationship with the Blacksmith and Carpenter. This is more than an economic relationship. Not only are the Carpenter and Blacksmith neighbors and friends, but they have religious functions that make their presence essential on such occasions as birth, marriage, and deaths. The Carpenter and Blacksmith offer an integrated set of tools and guarantee repairs. Under these circumstances, the purchase of a moldboard plow, or any improved equipment, becomes a tricky and difficult business. On their side, the Carpenter and Blacksmith receive a fixed quantity of grain at harvest time. If they were to improve their product, they would find it difficult to raise their prices to cover its greater cost. The benefits of improved agricultural techniques have not been demonstrated, and their use is attended by great economic and social risk. In refusing to adopt new methods, the farmer of Gopalpur shows common sense, not conservatism. (Beals 1962:79)

Other changes proposed by government officials in village religion and social organization threaten the basic patterns of cooperation and competition necessary for the economic life of the village. Government officials and missionaries are opposed to such practices as human or animal sacrifice, institutionalized prostitution, arranged marriages, gambling, meat eating, drinking, concubinage, divorce, quarreling, landlords, and time "wasted" on rituals and ceremonies. The condemning of these practices reveals a lack of understanding of the system as a finely balanced functionally related whole, for the patterns of cooperation and competition that make the economic life of the village possible are interlocked, within the system, with the condemned practices. Each of the two opposing groups believes itself to be more moral than the other, but this is not the problem. The real problem is finding substitutes for these condemned practices. As Beals writes, "People in Gopalpur do not know what to do *instead* of meat eating, animal sacrifice, and ceremonies, nor do they know of any advantages to be gained by renouncing them." (Beals 1962:82). But while the government officials and merchants of the nearby town are debating among themselves the desirability of change, it is pressing in from every side.

The villagers of Gopalpur are finding the forces for change extremely disruptive. This is due in part to the strong emphasis on and retention of a caste system, which is antagonistic to the pragmatic emphasis on social relations and a trend toward egalitarianism. Further, as described above, government officials and agents of change are unaware of the interdependent, interrelated parts of the sociocultural system found in places like Gopalpur. And the villagers of Gopalpur are suffering from a loss of self-respect. As Professor Beals writes:

> Whether or not Gopalpur is, in fact, richer or poorer than it was a hundred years ago, the new wind has brought its people the sudden realization that they are now second-class citizens of the world. Only a few years ago, people felt that they were part of a great civilization and that most of the other people in the world were dirty, uncouth, and barbaric. Now the coin is most bitterly reversed. City people who come to Gopalpur descend from their jeeps slowly and cautiously, as if the very soil were defiling; they seem to detect some noxious odor in the village. (Beals 1962:76)

A Case of "Lagging Emulation" in Vasilika

In the Greek village of Vasilika, Ernestine Friedl found the "modernization" process occurring at a very slow rate. One of the main reasons for this is what she terms "lagging emulation." She writes:

> The emulation in question is the process whereby social groups of lower prestige, upon the acquisition of new wealth or other forms of opportunity, imitate and often successfully acquire what they conceive to be the behavior of those with greater prestige; the emulation "lags" in that the behavior imitated is that which reached its acme as a prestige symbol for the higher social group at an earlier period in its history, and is now obsolescent. Lagging emulation occurs, then, under conditions in which the groups which constitute the traditional elites or which are otherwise considered worthy of emulation are themselves acquiring new ways at the same time that the traditionally less advanced groups are enabled to alter their previous patterns of life. (E. Friedl 1964:569)

The kinds of situations referred to are those where the people are never quite able to catch up. Friedl gives an example of lagging emulation related to attitudes toward time:

> Most business or official transactions are preceded by the drinking of a cup of Turkish-style coffee and some extended general conversation. The postman on his rounds of the village stops at the coffee house to accept the sweet or drink offered him by the village host. Such uses of time, including a much wider latitude for the keeping of appointments, are entirely expectable in any rural community. But the leisurely pace, with time always available for amenities, even as part of what are otherwise exclusively business or official transactions, was part of the pattern of the relations between people of influence in the Athens of several decades ago. (E. Friedl 1964:577)

Vasilika is thus really out of step with modern urban industrial society. It is more congruent with the atmosphere of contemporary Athens than with New York City, to be sure, but even Athens is adopting the rigid schedule and clockbound routine of the city, "with more brusqueness and what Americans would call a more businesslike attention to the matter in hand" (Friedl 1964:577–578).

The villagers are caught in a bind. They feel strongly motivated to keep up with their neighbors, who are not themselves keeping up with the times.

> However, if a village household adopts at least some of the new traits, it is only partly because of the respect which it pays to its urban kin. A more powerful influence is often the strong sense of competition which the rural household feels toward other village families, on which it hopes to score a point by showing superior sophistication. Those village families which have no urban relatives gradually try to copy the behavior of those which do. (E. Friedl 1959:35)

E. Friedl poses the question: Why should rural populations imitate outmoded upper-class behavior rather than strive to acquire the newly emerging forms with which those in the forefront of national development identify? Her answer to this question is related to the models available to the villages. The immediate contacts of the villagers are usually with persons from the city who are not themselves at the forefront of change. The city relatives of the villagers—members of the civil service and the local professionals—are not of upper or even upper-middle rank in power or culture. The villagers who are attempting to better their lot find that following the outmoded urban models of high position gives them the prestige they seek in their local community (see E. Friedl 1962).

Again, as in Gopalpur, the self-esteem of the villager has been threatened by the image of the urbanite. And the weak attempt of the villagers to look modern would be ridiculed by urbanites in Athens belonging to the new power elite. These kinds of consequences of modernization appear to be widespread.

Worker-Peasants in Kippel

The modernization process, as described by John Friedl for the Swiss alpine village of Kippel (1974) is proceeding relatively slowly and at an uneven rate. And for some of the residents this has meant an easier transition period.

Major changes in the village of Kippel have been due primarily to shifts in the economy from subsistence agriculture to industry, with a new reliance on cash rather than on the subsistence orientation. However, changes in the economy have occurred more rapidly than in religious or political activities, basic values, or in agricultural practice. J. Friedl (1974:7) writes:

> . . . rather than apply modern ideas to turn it into a productive occupation under today's market conditions, the villagers have left agriculture for jobs in industry. Furthermore, agricultural conservatism is to a great extent determined by the limiting ecological factors present in this and other alpine valleys. Finally, a tendecy to hang onto the past through agriculture (and thereby the old values and traditions) exists as a force counteractive to the rapidly changing village life, and this tendency proves to be an inefficient luxury rather than a rational economic activity. Agriculture today is a symbolic activity directly related to subsistence and the security it brings to the older members of the village. It is practiced by each household independently and does not relate to a wider market. In this sense it can coexist with a rapidly changing economic order.

Because the villager is able to commute to nearby industrial plants and earn wages, he is able to maintain his land and continue with his outmoded

Cultivating with traditional implements in Kippel (courtesy of John Friedl).

agricultural practices. He has become a worker-peasant. The failure to mechanize, as J. Friedl explains, may be due in part to the terrain and the quality of the soil, which do not justify large investments. However, the refusal to modernize agriculture is related to a way of life and traditional values that have deep meaning for the villagers. J. Friedl calls the maintenance of a traditional agricultural system while adopting the new techniques of industry an "autarky complex," or a self-sufficiency complex. It refers not only to material aspects of agricultural practice but to the total set of values and attitudes held toward the world. A social scientist familiar with the situation wrote:

> The worker-peasant still tends to think of himself primarily as a peasant rather than a worker. He schedules his vacation to coincide with harvest time, he stays away from work to watch over the birth of a calf, he loses sleep to work in the fields, and he still refers to himself unashamedly as a mountain peasant, a *Bergbauer*. He retains his system of partible inheritance, to assure his children a viable agricultural holding to support their households, as if they were going to return to the land. And the agricultural work that he performs is still oriented toward consumption by his own household, rather than specialization for the market. He defends this by asking, "What should we eat in the winter if we plant our potato and grain fields with strawberries in the summer?" (Niederer 1969:292)

There are many deeply ingrained beliefs and guiding principles that accompany the villagers' identity as peasants. A fatalistic attitude still pervades the thinking of the worker-peasant and his family.

> Little value is placed upon preparation, preventive measures, and regularity in social obligations. Foresight has so often been negated by the harsh climate with its frequent catastrophes that the local population has become hardened to the futility of planning ... *ad hoc* events are much preferred, and the placing of a date and time on an event is often seen as an intrusion upon people's lives. (J. Friedl 1974:120–121)

This kind of view of the world and set of attitudes has made the merchants and others serving tourists coming to Kippel less successful than they could be.

Young people are changing but at a relatively slow rate. As part-time workers in industry they are becoming economically independent at a younger age. Contact between sexes is no longer supervised. Young people are still religious but do more independent interpreting. Most important is the fact that large numbers are not leaving the village, as they are in so many other places. Many are involved with the tourist trade and many have small home operated endeavors, such as a small watch factory.

Friedl has some important observations to make about the relationships between industrialization-urbanization-modernization. His study would seem to contradict some of the assumptions frequently made about modernization and industrialization. He writes (1974:90):

> First of all, industrialization need not coincide with urbanization, for as we have seen, the economy of the village and the life style of the villagers became industrialized without transforming Kippel into a large metropolis or a seat of rural industry. The men and women commute to work, and even the towns

where they work are small and in many ways rustic. Secondly, we find that industrialization and modernization are not the same thing, and they do not necessarily occur together—one might question whether in fact they ever really occur together. Industrialization in Kippel is a process that began shortly after World War II, the initial stages of which lasted between 10 and 15 years. Modernization, or, as I see it, the adaptation of basic social institutions to an economy based upon the secondary and tertiary sectors (industry and services) rather than agriculture, is a process which in Kippel has only really begun on any meaningful scale in the last decade, well after industrial employment had firmly established itself with the villagers. But the economy has not stood still while Kippel caught up with it. The economic base of the village has already begun to change again from industry to tourism, and the worker-peasant has had to yield to the specialist, the trained and educated man of tomorrow.

Such observations are important if we are to separate out the effects of industrialization, urbanization, and modernization. Many studies fail to make this separation as clearly as has Friedl in his study of Kippel.

Peasants in a Newly Developing Socialist State

The Halperns, who studied Orašac, a Serbian village in Yugoslavia, demonstrated the reciprocal influence of the city on the rural village—the "urbanization of the village"—and of the rural peasantry on the city, a sort of "peasantization" of the city. The Halperns were the first Western students to do anthropological research in postwar Yugoslavia. They found some special emphases in the modernization process in this slowly evolving socialist state. Unlike other communist countries, the authority of the state in Yugoslavia is minimal and there is a surprising degree of flexibility. The Halperns write:

> ... with its flexible ideology, permitting emphasis on local autonomy, market economy, workers' councils, and limited private ownership of both land and small-scale enterprises, certain of the details of the workings of its internal life as they have recently evolved are not too distinct from those of its non-communist neighbors. Contemporary Yugoslav society, with its continuing socialist commitment, is also an open society with vital links to the West in intellectual terms as well as in trade and tourism. (Halpern and Halpern 1972:29)

As in the case of Kippel, the villagers of Orašac can also be peasant-workers if they choose. Work in nearby mines and quarries is compatible with a traditional way of life. The worker can commute and still work his agricultural holdings. Further, work in the mines was often seasonal or intermittent for a few years.

Whereas between 1949 and 1960 one-ninth of the population of Yugoslavia moved from rural areas, this did not represent an abrupt change in life style. The separation of towns and countryside occurred during the nineteenth century but without a complete division between the two. Towns included many farmers and many townsmen had agricultural holdings in their villages. Trades and crafts did not die out in the villages. "The towns existed almost

Persistence of traditional agricultural methods (courtesy of Joel Halpern
and Barbara Halpern).

exclusively to facilitate agricultural trade and to service the rural population"
(Halpern and Halpern 1972:66).

The same general processes occurred in Yugoslavia in the 1960s. There
were no established urban models to follow. The Halperns found a situation
they described as a simultaneous "urbanization of the village" and "peasantization of the town." They found the rural influences on town life to be more
extensive than social scientists had heretofore described. The villagers moving
into town are often building private homes on the outskirts, which they usually
consider to be their residences for life (Halpern and Halpern 1972:75). The
outward appearance of the homes and the household furnishings are similar
to those found in the villages. The Halperns write:

> . . . the kitchen, with its wood stove, is the focal point of the home, especially
> in winter, for it is usually the only heated room. Most household activities
> take place here; the other rooms tend to be used for sleeping only. As in the
> village pattern, often a bed in the kitchen is used by an older relative or by
> children. Similarly, the so-called guest room is set aside, as in the village, to
> display choice items of handiwork, and the walls are adorned with photo-
> graphs of relatives, dominated by large portraits of ancestors. Occasionally
> there is a colored lithograph of the family's patron saint. Most of the recent
> arrivals are relatively young, and many are politically active, factors which
> would tend to lessen the occurrence of overt religious display. (Halpern and
> Halpern 1972:75)

There is usually no indoor plumbing and water is usually supplied by a
well in the yard. Chickens may walk in and out of the kitchen and there may
be a pig in the courtyard. Often there is a small vegetable garden and a few
fruit trees. Villagers moving to town are very involved with their new homes.

The owners of such homes emphatically say that they could not think of "living with strangers," that is, in an apartment house, even if a flat were available, despite the fact that multiple dwellings usually have piped water, indoor toilets, and tile stoves for heating in all rooms. (Halpern and Halpern 1972:76)

A worker is likely to use his annual vacation time to improve his new house and yard. Factory managers are dismayed to see the new migrant putting forth his best efforts in nest-building rather than on his job. Unlike the American suburb, these are settlements of village migrants seeking to join the town rather than of prosperous urbanites seeking to escape it.

The "urbanization of the village" is noted in new patterns of conspicuous consumption of material items, linked with prestige. Cars are commonplace and afford one status. The emphasis on cash and part-time jobs has grown. The restricted role of the church and increasing equality of women is due both to the impact of communism and to the role of modernization. Government coercion is minimal. However, the socialized sectors in industry or agriculture have economic support, advanced equipment, and professional staffs.

The village and the town have influenced each other in a reciprocal fashion. The urban Yugoslavians, as those in other nationalist movements, have turned to the village cultures in attempting to understand what has made them distinctive in the modernizing world. The prewar values of the peasant persist even in the context of a socialist state (Halpern and Halpern 1972:138). Kinship ties remain important and afford a means for villagers to migrate temporarily or permanently to town. City people also can return to the village in time of war or to vacation in summer or to retire in old age. The fresh air and peace of the countryside are causing the city dwellers to build small weekend homes in the village where they can grow plants and have pet animals.

There is also a notable influence of peasant culture on urban tradition in the form of literary themes, folk song and dance, crafts and rich museums. Much of the decor in the buildings is borrowed from romanticized folk art.

The Halpern case study contributes special insights into urban-rural relations. The reciprocal relationship described in this study is probably to some extent universal, though it seems more marked in Orašac than in most communities studied by anthropologists. The Spanish cases following seem quite different.

Two Modernizing Spanish Villages

"Modernizing" processes are sharply contrastive in two separate villages in Spain. The village of Benabarre in northeastern Spain is suffering from the commonplace "rural exodus" to the city (Barrett 1974). In contrast, Almonaster la Real in Andalucia (southern Spain) is modernizing without secularization and successfully combatting out-migration (Aguilera, unpublished ms.).

Spain has been transformed in twenty years from a nation of pedestrians to a mobile population on wheels. Mechanization arrived abruptly in the countryside. As a consequence of industrial expansion in urban areas and lack of means for making a livelihood in rural areas, massive emigration to the cities has occurred, often depopulating entire communities. Emigration seemed to be the only solution in many cases. Those remaining had a higher standard of living which would have been impossible with increased population.

Benabarre was severely affected by emigration. Usually just parts of families moved to the city. Young people are attracted by the employment possibilities and the exciting environment of the city; some were forced to leave, as they could not make a living; small proprietors and craftsmen could no longer compete with mass production and chain stores. The peasant householders that once formed the backbone of the community found themselves with no heirs. The situation was unattractive to young males. Usually there was insufficient land to support mechanization, which is extremely costly. And without mechanization it was impossible to compete in the market. The households in Benabarre were unable to satisfy their new consumer demands with their limited resources and traditional agricultural subsistence techniques. Thus the young quickly became disenchanted. As a young Benabarre girl remarked:

> I've lived this life [in a peasant household] and I don't like it. One of my sisters is married to a factory worker in Monzón [a large provincial town] and lives in an apartment there. She doesn't have to feed pigs or go around in sloppy work clothes all the time like we do around here. She dresses up every day and spends afternoons walking the children and promenading (*de paseo*) with her friends. That's the kind of life I want too. (Barrett 1974:53)

The emigration from Benabarre has its positive aspects. Those remaining have been able to maintain a higher standard of living as a consequence of the reduced population and to expand possibilities for obtaining goods and making life easier. As in the case of Orašac, city life has become "personalized" through complex sets of interpersonal social relationships. Since most emigration has consisted of children of households which continue in Benabarre, many individuals have immediate relatives who live and work in the surrounding towns and cities. Aside from relatives, the villagers have many friends and friends of friends who can often help them in dealing with legal matters, providing their children with secondary education and finding jobs for their family.

Richard Barrett makes use of a "network analysis" in interviewing, tracing both first and second order contacts. He found what he termed a form of "exchange relationship": villagers provide certain rural products and hospitality, while urbanites accommodate villagers when something is required of the cities. The exchange is based upon the principle of reciprocity. A villager can expand his contacts by placing one's personal contacts at the disposal of friends. In network analysis this has been termed the "friend-of-a-friend syndrome." An illustration of this is provided by a former mayor of Benabarre who lives in the provincial capital and owns a bar-cafe where villagers gather while visiting. Dr. Barrett describes the situation:

Small shop in Benabarre (courtesy of Richard Barrett).

The owner is not a man of great influence in the city, but he is acquainted with many of the important men of Huesca who frequent his bar. Consequently he is able to aid villagers on occasion by putting them in touch with officials or administrators. An informant explained to me that he once needed some papers approved on a social security matter. The application was submitted to the proper office in Huesca but then weeks passed with no response. The next time he journeyed to the capital he mentioned his difficulty to the bar owner. The latter told him to return to the cafe at half-past two that afternoon when the social security section chief (*jefe*) would come in for his daily cognac. That afternoon the bar owner introduced my informant to the *jefe*, providing him an opportunity to explain his problem. The section chief said he would look into the matter immediately; and true to his word, the papers were received in the mail three days later. As a former villager and onetime mayor, the bar owner is disposed to mediate ties for almost anyone from Benabarre. (Barrett 1974:87)

The major reciprocal contribution of villagers is the hospitality they offer during vacations and holidays. Village homes are spacious and extra rooms are converted into sleeping quarters for visiting families, who are treated as guests.

Aside from the social ties furnished the villagers by the emigrations to the city and a higher standard of living, a new middle class has emerged. The former notables in Benabarre, who encouraged sharp class differences, have withdrawn and lost their power. Instead the new leaders are successful merchants, livestock dealers, and entrepreneurial farmers who can deal better with the "modern" Spain.

In Almonaster la Real Andalucia, another underdeveloped region of Spain, "modernizing" has meant something different. Almonaster, with sixteen neighbor communities, was able to become part of a multicommunity better able to cope with economic, political, social, and religious conditions in a way that could insure control over many of the basic institutions (Aguilera, n.d.:7). The villagers of Almonaster were able to control emigration and to modernize in the economic sphere while retaining in large measure their traditional way of life. It is clear again in this case that earlier models of modernization, inferring that peasants became urbanites in a total sense, are not valid. Modernization need not be equated with total destruction of tradition.

Due to rough terrain and limited land the villagers of Almonaster could not fully mechanize, modernize, and compete on the market with their traditional grain crops. They had two choices. One was to concentrate on those traditional activities that could be competitive (focusing on pulpwood, pigs, or tourism) and experience a loss of population. The alternative was to maintain a locally determined standard of living, at lower than "modern levels," using available cash for the most desired consumer goods and services. They chose the latter. The traditional emphasis on each household's subsistence activities in addition to its money-earning ones has meant that only a small increase in consumption has taken place. The area has maintained its level of population, allowing for the survival of traditional ritual and social systems (Aguilera, n.d.:15). This difficult job of placing a ceiling on consumer consumption was accomplished by a well-organized corporate community culture, which was part of the old tradition. The modern consumption pattern on the part of the rich is also constrained by the agreed upon inventory of the community as a whole. Modern furniture and most appliances, for example, are not bought by even the rich.

The inhabitants of the multicommunity, of which Almonaster is a part, are well aware of the choice they have made. And most are highly in favor of living at home and limiting consumption. As one member of the community remarked:

> Here we are poor but happy, clean and proud; there (in the city) they have good money but they are unhappy, the children and the homes are dirty and they become sullen. (Aguilera, n.d.:25)

This example of coping with the sometimes disastrous demands made upon a social group and culture by a need to modernize represents a unique and creative solution. As Aguilera remarked: "Rather than a secularization of the 'peasants' there is only the smooth operation of the multicommunity process as it adapts to a changing environment" (unpublished ms.:25).

The contrasts between Benabarre and Almonaster, communities in the same country, but in different regions, show how difficult generalization about the effects and processes of modernization is. Nevertheless, it is important that the same processes of secularization and population loss threatened both. It was the response to these threats that differed.

RESISTANCE AND PERSISTENCE

The Toba Batak of Sumatra

While working in Sumatra, Edward Bruner also found that the earlier theory regarding urbanization developed by Redfield (1947) scarcely applied to the transition of the Toba Batak in the city of Medan from rural to urban living. The predicted isolation of the individual, the breakdown of kinship organization, and the development of impersonal, superficial social relationships did not occur here. As Bruner describes the situation:

> The kinship and ceremonial practices of the government official in Medan (the city to which the villagers had migrated) were found to be basically similar to those performed by his uncle in the village. Batak urbanites have become increasingly sophisticated and cosmopolitan, but the traditional basis of their social life has not been undermined. Kinship has remained the major nexus of interpersonal relationships in the urban Batak community, the patrilineal descent group is intact and flourishing, and the village life crisis ceremonies are performed in the city with relatively little modification. Of course, Batak culture today is not the same as it was a century ago, but comparison of the social and ceremonial organization in *contemporary* rural and urban environments indicated that no major differences existed. . . .
>   The people themselves are well aware of the retention of village ways within the urban center and say that all Batak, wherever they may reside, follow essentially the same "adat" (custom). (Bruner 1961:508–509)

Bruner makes some suggestions as to why the Toba Batak social and ceremonial organization has been maintained in an urban environment. One explanation lies in the fact that the urban Batak do not assimilate the national Indonesian superculture since a national Indonesian culture does not yet exist. Indonesia is a nation of 90 million people fragmented into many diverse ethnic groups. Since the Japanese occupation and the creation of the New Republic of Indonesia, it is no longer necessary for any Toba Batak to renounce his ethnic identity. In the city of Medan there is no population majority and no locally dominant culture to serve as a model. Ethnic groups compete with each other for economic and political power, relationships between groups are tense, and thus each ethnic group tends to encapsulate itself (Bruner 1974:269). This leads to a great retention of ethnic customs and values.

Another explanation for persistences among the Toba Batak is that "the rural and urban Batak are linked through a complex communication network in which Western goods and ideas do flow from city to village, but the flow of people and of the moral support and vitality of the *adat* is primarily in the other direction" (Bruner 1961:515). A brief description of a modern Batak wedding among the urban elite illustrates the persistence of traditional forms:

> In the morning a Christian service is conducted by a Batak minister in the Batak language. In the afternoon adult Batak men participate in a ritual which symbolizes the kinship organization and the relationship between the patrilineal descent groups, and they discuss, in Batak, the meaning of the adat

[traditional] ceremony. In the evening brief congratulatory speeches are given in Indonesian by business associates, women's organizations, and youth groups. (Bruner 1961:517)

The important point to note here is that the wealthy city dweller has not modified his village *adat*; he has merely added on the Western reception.

The Qemant of Ethiopia

The Qemant, a pagan-Hebraic peasantry of Ethiopia, furnish an important example of a sociocultural system essentially unaffected by modernization. The anthropologist Frederick Gamst who lived with this group writes:

> Until the present they have been essentially unaffected by the global processes of change. Only a few trade goods made by machine are now found among the Qemant: glassware and metal kettles for drinking and serving beer, umbrellas, some items of male clothing, and a few hand tools. The diet of the Qemant remains unchanged and appears to have changed little during the past several centuries. A rare handful of Qemant have abandoned agriculture for government employment and residence in Gondar. A limited number of children in a few communities now attend schools, the largest and best of which are in Gondar. Only a few dozen or so Qemant of the last generation were formally educated, and they are no longer rural residents. Attitudes toward mechanical devices may be summed up by recounting the belief that machinery, which is always associated with Europeans, is powered or driven by *Saytan*. (Gamst 1969:123)

The Qemant were the original inhabitants of northern and central Ethiopia. Their religion is composed of syncretized pagan and Hebraic elements, with a few Christian features. What is most remarkable here is that the Qemant peasants have been able to retain their social identity from 1000 A.D. to 1960— A.D. in spite of being subjected to the Amhara rulers of Abyssinia and to a program of forced acculturation, as a result of which only a few Qemant became Christianized. Several things favor this persistence. One is the fact that the Qemant live in remote, rather inaccessible areas. More important to note, however, is that the Qemant religion has important built-in boundary-maintaining mechanisms. All of the important rites connected with birth, death, and marriage were carefully carried out according to ancient custom. The strict marriage laws, taboos concerning menstruation and childbirth, and the belief that neighboring peoples are ritually polluted and must, therefore, be avoided, afforded the Qemant a sense of group solidarity which was virtually impossible for an outsider to penetrate. The Qemant submitted to their Amhara rulers outwardly (by paying taxes, giving tributes, etc.), yet they retained their strong cultural and religious identity.

The city *per se* is not playing an important role in the industrialization of Ethiopia. Industries themselves are separated and situated remotely from one another. As Gamst writes:

. . . in a developing country such as Ethiopia, industrialization does not necessarily mean massive concentration of industry in urban areas. Instead, the industrial wellsprings of modernization in Ethiopia may be geographically remote, situated in other nations, but the influence toward cultural change may be forceful and near at hand as the result of modern forms of communication and transportation. (Gamst 1969:123)

The disseminating source of modernizing influences for Ethiopia will for the rest of this century be places such as Europe and North America. The process will be speeded up as forms of communication and transportation become more modernized. And, as in other examples of industrial urbanization:

The very nature of industrial urbanization creates a new order of sociocultural change in which every ethnic group will in some way produce for and be dependent upon the world market. It is also an order of change in which the boundaries and identities of many groups, including some of those in Ethiopia, will fade and become lost. (Gamst 1969:123)

Zinacantecos: A Mexican Peasantry

The modern Mayan Zinacantecos of Mexico are another example of a peasant group which has been able to maintain its special identity in spite of the effects of modernization. The highly ceremonialized religious system of the Zinacantecos has persisted despite the change from independence before the European invasion to status as a conquered people. It has survived Christian Catholic proselytizing and, in fact, has been enriched by it, for example, by borrowing religious figures and fiesta days. As Evon Vogt (1970) reports, this belief system defines, explains, and defends everything about the world for the Zinacantecos. It serves as a philosophy, cosmology, theology, code of values, and science. Thus, as long as the individual remains within this belief system and his external conditions do not change too drastically, nothing else need be "known."

Why has the Zinacantecos' belief system persisted with so many odds against it? The system requires a great deal of money. There are thirty-four religious fiesta days and each requires extensive funding. Each time a man assumes a new position in the hierarchy of religious statuses (cargos), he must raise money (up to 14,000 pesos). And each time a curing ceremony is needed, money is necessary. Thus the economic values of the Zinacantecos converge rather neatly with those of the Ladinos and urbanites, perforce. The Zinacantecos leased land from Ladinos and became entrepreneur-type maize farmers. They also became money lenders. The one important difference, however, between the economic behaviors of the Ladinos and those of the Zinacantecos is that the Zinacantecos do not use their surplus money for personal reasons. They pour most of their money into the ritual system. The needs of the system supersede those of the individual, and the system continues to thrive (Vogt 1970).

A German Peasant Tradition

The *Bauern* (farmers, or peasants) of Burgbach, Germany are a class segment of a larger population that contains an urban center—actually a metropolitan capital. They are tradition-oriented and rural, though they have accepted many technological changes such as electric motors, tractors, and the like. They produce through cultivation most of their own food and produce also for a market. Land is largely inherited rather than purchased, and the people have strong ties of sentiment to it. The community is dependent upon it politically and economically. The Bauern of Burgbach therefore exhibit some of the key criteria of the peasant, as listed above, as the concept is used by most anthropologists. In spite of the new influences and pressures for change introduced by the many refugees from former German areas, by commuters from the city, and by the introduction of factories, the traditional way of life of the grape-growing German peasant persists. The traditional patterns coexist with those of modern urban, industrial West Germany. This is a common circumstance in many parts of the world where local traditions are strong and have great time depth. The Burgbach case study shows how and why persistence occurs. The explanations of persistence described below are: the tight functional interrelationships between humans, land, and economy in the traditional system, thus making any single aspect of the system difficult to change; and the process of substitutive change.

In 1961, when G. Spindler first started fieldwork in Germany, Burgbach was a village of contrasts.

The most important structure in the village, as seen from the rim of the valley above, is the ancient Stiftskirche, the Evangelical church, built in 1533 on the site occupied by a chapel probably built in the 7th century. Scattered among the lesser houses are the Grossenhäuser (great homes) of the tradition-oriented Burgbachers—116 of them—occupied on the average by 8 people, 4 milk cows, 15 chickens, 3 pigs and 1 rabbit. In the center of town, in the old market area, are new stores with large plate-glass windows and attractive displays. On the side of the village opposite the Stiftskirche is the new ultra-modern rectangular-spired and triangular-shaped Catholic church. Mercedes-Benz, Volkswagens, and lesser automobiles, most of them quite new and all of them shiny, course the narrow streets. Small noisy, diesel tractors growl along, hauling ancient wagons loaded with manure from the heaping, neat piles in front of the Grossenhäuser. Occasionally a huge oxlike cow does the pulling urged along by a husky Bauer (farmer or "peasant") or his Frau. A walk down the center street will take one past a row of attractive, colorful and very modern apartment houses, a dozen or so Grossenhäuser and as many manure piles, a modern gas station and garage, with an Opel display room . . . [several] high class Gastätte catering largely to the commuters and Stuttgarters, and next to them the butcher, working on the carcass of a huge pig.

The forces for change seem overwhelming and yet many people make their living predominantly or in substantial part from the soil, and live a way of life with marked continuity to the traditional past.

Let us look inside one of the Grossenhäuser. In the first story are the animals—the pigs, chickens, cows—behind large double doors that open to the street. An electric turnip chopper, electric apple masher, wine press, fodder cutter, electrically operated water dishes, all indicate that technical progress has arrived. The diesel tractor, rototiller, and mowing machine, confirm this observation further.

In back of this section is the door of the root cellar. Here are stored the canned fruits, the vegetables, potatoes, turnips, apples, eggs in large crocks, that the family consumes. The Bauern supply virtually all of their own food. They raise all their fruit and vegetables, grind their own wheat for bread and Kuchen, press their own white grapes, and mash their own apples for Apfelsaft. The cows furnish milk, the chickens—eggs, the pigs—the ingredients for Wurst, about the only form of meat the Bauern eat. The Bauern raise all their feed for animals—oats, barley, wheat, corn, turnips, alfalfa, and timothy hay—everything excepting a protein feed concentrate fed as a supplement for higher milk production.

The Grossenhäuser are mostly quite old. Many of them were built in the 16th and 17th centuries. Their remodeling, and the electrical equipment installed in them, is not necessarily symptomatic of the destruction of a way of life, but rather may indicate a reaffirmation of its validity as it adapts to contemporary conditions. (Spindler 1961:4–6)

Ten years later the traditional Burgbacher way of life was still strong. It persisted in part due to a very tight-knit set of functional relationships existing among the various segments of the socioeconomic-cultural system. For example, the traditional, large extended family of the "Bauern" is required for the growing of wine grapes, since it is the familial, wage-free labor of this large family that makes the operation feasible. Manure is essential for fertilizing the vineyards and the only source of manure is the livestock kept in the lower part of the "Great House" of the large family, so this traditional form of house has another function. Baking bread in the bake house is only possible if a person has the necessary bundles of grapevine prunings or twigs from the vineyard land (G. Spindler 1973). Tight-knit systems of this kind tend to persist because no one part can be significantly changed without changes occurring in the whole system, and the whole system is not easily given up or even modified significantly by people who value it and whose ancestors have lived by it for generations.

This traditional, land-related way of life in Burgbach has persisted until the present also partly because the changes that took place were substitutive in nature. Electric motors substitute for human power in pressing fruit juices and chopping beets, and milking machines substitute for the milk maid; a tractor substitutes for the ox pulling the wagon, and so forth. The overall pattern can remain essentially intact, despite these changes. In fact, since these changes increase the efficiency of an essentially traditional operation, they make it possible for the traditional forms to persist longer than they would without the changes. However, major changes, transformative in nature, are occurring. They are changes in principle, not merely substitutive changes. They challenge the fundamental organization of the traditional system. An example is the process (called *Flurbereinigung*) of recontouring the vineyards to combine family plots into large plots. Ownership tends to concentrate in fewer and fewer hands. Hand labor is eliminated because it is no longer necessary on the large, recontoured vineyard plots. Almost total mechanization becomes inevitable. This is part of an overall rationalization of agriculture designed to increase production at the same time that costs are lowered. This programs calls for elimination of the traditional practices connected with cultivating the small family plots. These old, ritualized ways of doing things afforded great satisfaction for the Bauern, including the utilization of extended familial relationships as a source of labor, and contributed to the maintenance of the finely equilibrated system described above. One elderly woman remarked:

> Where our forefathers painfully labored to build terraces to hold the soil and drainage channels to carry off the water during storms, and where they carried the earth washed down the slope back up again on their backs, now all that is gone forever . . . and what is to keep the soil on the hillsides with the terraces gone? (G. Spindler 1973)

These traditional practices connected with growing wine grapes have been a part of her and her ancestors' way of life for centuries and there is nothing to replace them.

The situation in Burgbach illustrates a frequent consequence of the process of economic rationalization. This process may create the conditions for a new rationality that can be dangerous for successful long-term adaptation. The rationalization process occurring in Burgbach is creating a situation where men and women tend to be alienated from the products of their labor, from each other, and from themselves—a situation where impersonal units are substituted for people. Under these conditions social and personal disorganization often occurs. This process may apply to many other comparable situations where people are being forced by new circumstances to rationalize their economic systems and eliminate established, satisfying ways of doing things.

NONREVOLUTIONARY MODERNIZING

The Japanese

The Japanese are considered to be special examples of smooth and effective modernization. Edward Norbeck's study of a fishing village and of urban life in Japan develops this thesis. The quotation from his study, below, focuses on the rapid and almost total transition from a rural village to an urban orientation by a young man born in the village.

> Aki had never visited Takashima and Jiro (a young man from the village of Takashima) had not been there for several years. When Jiro's parents expressed a wish to see their new grandchild, Aki (his city-born wife) said that it was their duty to take the child to Takashima and added, honestly enough, that she would like to make the trip. The visit was brief, and none too comfortable. Aki and Emi were well received, and Aki in her usual way was friendly and gracious. But there was an atmosphere of reserve that was especially evident when they met Jiro's more distant relatives and former

A couple on New Year's day in Osaka (courtesy of Edward Norbeck).

neighbors. Beyond greetings, expressed in the vocabulary of country courtesy, those outside Jiro's family had found nothing to say to the visitors. The trip was Aki's first close contact with country people other than acquaintance with various maids from the country in the employ of her family and the families of friends. Like most urban Japanese, she had thought of rural residents as people apart. She found the scenery beautiful, the houses and farm plots picturesque, the food coarse, and the people quaint and timid but worthy. Jiro's ideas had become much the same, and both returned to Osaka with the secret feeling of a duty performed. (Norbeck 1976:87)

Jiro had been born in the small fishing village of Takashima, yet, by the time he had finished college in the city, he could be considered urbanized. His ideas were then "much the same" as those of his city-bred wife, Aki. Nevertheless, both shared a commitment to the value of duty to one's parents, a basic Japanese value common to peasant and urban dweller alike for many centuries.

Why has the transition characteristically been swift and nonrevolutionary for the Japanese? "A century ago Japan was a nation composed principally of peasants whose way of life conformed in general outlines with that of folk societies elsewhere in the world" (Norbeck 1976:9) states Edward Norbeck, an anthropologist who has studied both folk and urban Japanese. He continues:

In 1941 at the time Japan entered into war with the United States and Europe, profound changes had taken place peacefully in almost all sectors of life. No other nation of the modern world had undergone such drastic and self-sought cultural changes under conditions of internal peace in an equally short period of time. (1976:10)

One of many partial explanations for this peaceful transition lies in the fact that Japanese culture is receptive and flexible. Japan has been ingesting innovations from other cultures for many centuries. Chinese culture had previously brought a flood of new ideas, behaviors, and material items to Japan. Norbeck writes:

> The mode of reception of Chinese and the later Western culture was the same, one of selective adaptation rather than wholesale borrowing, adaptation that permitted innovations to become assimilated without suddenly obliterating the old ways and causing violent social upheaval. Foreign culture that conflicted seriously with established ways was rejected. The Confucian idea that an inadequate ruler should be deposed, for example, was anathema to the Japanese, to whom the continuity of family lines in fixed positions of status was a value of prime importance. When individual members of any social group were incompetent, means other than frank disbarment were preferred, means that preserved social forms and individual and group honor. Throughout, the acceptance of Western as well as Chinese culture resulted in assimilations that had a distinctively Japanese cast. (Norbeck 1976:9–10)

Another explanation of the peaceful transition accomplished by the Japanese lies in the fact that many of their traditional values are compatible with those of Western urban dwellers. High value was placed upon education, and great sacrifices are often made by the entire family to educate a son. Success, competition, and cleanliness were all important. The practice of thrift and industry was commonplace. The ethic of achievement was an integral part of Japanese culture. As Norbeck (1976:20) comments, "Whatever the origin of this ideal, the modern Japanese 'naturally' values industriousness and 'naturally' wishes to succeed."

The relatively easy transition on the part of the Japanese to urban patterns of living does not mean that change, and rather dramatic change, was not imperative. A few of these necessary changes are touched upon in the following:

> In the city, a sentiment has grown against living with one's parents, parents-in-law, or mature children, and the idea is not a total stranger to rural residents. Father's voice had lost a good deal of authority and mother's has gained. Younger sons are often at no disadvantage as compared with the eldest son, and sisters and new brides have lost some of their meekness. To prepare them for an adult life that is likely to take them away from farming, younger sons and even daughters of rural families may receive more formal education than elder sons, who are ordinarily expected to remain on the farm. The mother-in-law who attempts to dominate her son's bride is in danger of being branded as "feudal," a demeaning word. A common postwar saying is that two things have grown in strength since the war, stockings—now of tough nylon—and women. (Norbeck 1976:13)

Jiro's family is a part of a new middle class and shares many characteristics with Western urbanites. They are television viewers and book readers informed on national and world affairs; installment buyers; consumers of instant foods and household appliances; agnostic but favorable to moral education for their children; unconcerned about perpetuating their family line; mindful of parents but rarely living with them; loving children but strictly limiting their number (Norbeck 1976:76). In fact, the entire process of urbanizing and modernizing represented by the case of Japan is universal in many respects and overrides cultural differences.

The standard of living increases, self-sufficiency declines, congestion increases along with industrial pollution, the country is relatively depopulated in favor of metropolitan areas, farming becomes a part-time occupation made possible by technological advances and rationalization, the family shrinks in size but the population as a whole continues to increase, older people live increasingly away from their children and a problem of what to do with and for the aged appears, rituals and religiosity decline or disappear, even though religious movements may occur, voluntary associations increase in number and in functions, the status of women improves, the aesthetic quality of life declines insofar as it is related to the natural world, and everything costs more. Some of these changes appear to be linear, others seem to fluoresce and recede, many may be considered symptomatic of more fundamental processes of change and adaptation that we have no very good ways of describing as yet.

Nevertheless, in spite of these universals, each culture appears to retain certain qualities that distinguish it from other cultures in the very processes of change, even radical change, as we have seen.

A Peasant Village in Taiwan

Groups other than the Japanese have special traditional values that converge with those of the industrializing society. K'un Shen, a Taiwan village, is a good example. The people are receptive to new ideas and respect "science." Norma Diamond, who lived with these villagers for a long period, reports:

> The proverbial conservatism of the Chinese peasantry appears to be absent from K'un Shen, with little in overall ideology to block change and modernization. In many ways, the values held by most people in the community are already in line with the demands of an industrializing society. . . .
>
> Long and hard hours of work are not perceived as something to be avoided . . . and the work ethic is closely related to the individualism evident among the villagers. Life is a constant and often difficult struggle to maintain a small household. Rarely is cooperation extended automatically among kinsmen. The values of the community hold that a man's first responsibilities are to his wife and children and to aged parents without means of support, but his grown brothers should be able to fend for themselves, and feelings of responsibility are even weaker to more remote collateral kin. Values such as these make mobility possible. And as new industries develop in the urban centers, we would expect a relatively painless change in occupation . . .
>
> The transition to the modern world is also eased by the villagers' view of the natural world and man's place within it, particularly the view that man does have some control over nature and can better his life through improved knowledge and skills. The religious beliefs current in the community do not

present a serious barrier to acceptance of change. In the area of health, the system has proved flexible enough to allow the incorporation of new methods of curing and preventing of disease. More generally, scientific knowledge introduced from the Western world is seen as an increment to knowledge rather than a blanket refutation of traditional beliefs. (Diamond 1969:108–109)

There is a strong respect for "science" in K'un Shen which is undoubtedly the result of recent culture change as far as content is concerned, but the ease with which "science" has been accepted suggests an earlier pragmatism and openness to new methods which prove workable. People speak often of looking into "new ways" of doing things as well as learning the customary ways of doing things. "Newness," in itself, is neither good nor bad. . . . (Diamond 1969:28)

Although dramatic changes have not yet occurred within the village, there is an eagerness for certain kinds of change such as improvements in the standard of living, the taking on of new occupations (particularly among the young people), and the learning of ideas that will make the village "modern" or "progressive" when viewed by the rest of Taiwanese society. The word "change," like "science," has also acquired a positive connotation. (Diamond 1969:109)

In spite of great potential for change, it has occurred rather slowly in K'un Shen, largely because economic assistance and opportunities have been less available to the villagers than they have been in other similar situations.

Industrializing in Malta

The villagers of Hal-Farrug in Malta, historic island in the Mediterranean, like those of Takashima, Japan, experienced a simple and gradual period of transition from agriculturalists to industrial laborers between 1871 and 1960. During that period the number of full-time farmers decreased from 77 percent to 15 percent (Boissevain 1969:10). One of the reasons for the relatively painless transition was that, like the Japanese villagers, the Maltans had been adapting to outside cultures (both Christian and Moslem) for many centuries. Until Malta achieved independence from Britain in 1964, the island had been essentially a fortress in the hands of the British naval forces, and before that, except for a brief interlude, had long been the seat of the famed Knights of Malta. As a bastion between the Christian and Moslem worlds, it had been strongly influenced by the cultures of both. Another factor conducive to change among the villagers of Hal-Farrug in particular and Malta in general was that there is a high literacy rate among the Maltans. Also, rather than simply to supply their conquerors with agricultural products, the villagers had provided special services to foreign garrisons for many centuries.

The networks of personal and familial relationships furnished innumerable contacts with urban dwellers and other villagers. Jeremy Boissevian (1969:93) describes these:

> . . . contacts exist between Farrug and other social and geographical areas of Maltese society in each major activity field. The part is in contact with the whole through economic, kinship, religious and political relations. Villagers

work outside Farrug, and outsiders work in the village . . . today 219 of the 296 workingmen travel outside the village daily. Most work in the conurbation surrounding the capital. There, they meet persons from many other villages and towns. They are invited to attend special family celebrations and annual fiestas in other villages. At work, they are in touch with persons from all over the island. They exchange news, stories, and notice slight differences between villages. This is a forum where men, and in ever-increasing numbers, women from all over the island meet one another and exchange information.

CONCLUDING REMARKS

The many illustrations provided in this section on modernization and urbanization illustrate the variety and complexity of the processes. There are no simple unilinear stages occurring from peasant or rural to urban, and modernization often occurs without urbanization. Persistence of established values and patterns of behavior occurs along with transformation. Although we can make some generalizations about the processes, each case also represents a unique and often creative way of meeting the challenge to change.

Many authors have emphasized the negative aspects of the technological revolution associated with modernizing and urbanizing. There are, however, positive ways of viewing the processes. Robert Redfield (1953b) emphasizes some of the creative aspects. He dwells on the changes that have taken place in people's minds as a result of the technological revolution rather than on the technological changes themselves. In the folk society, the technical order is subordinate to the moral order. During the urbanization process, the old moral orders are shaken or destroyed. But there is a rebuilding of moral orders on new levels which results from the thinking of many different kinds of peoples. The kinds of men found in the city—the administrative elite, the literate jurist with opportunities for reflection and cultivation of esoteric knowledge, the specialized artisan—are different from the peasant. They can spend time reflecting and looking inwards; they have a new world view and style of life. In civilization the technical order becomes great but the moral order does not become small; it is simply of a different level. *It is at a level marked by self-consciousness and by conscious creativeness* (Redfield 1953b). It is in the urban environment that intellectuals can construct new and contradictory theories about the social order, that psychiatrists can aid people to become conscious of their motives and the reasons for them. A member of a primitive society rarely has to analyze his thoughts and feelings in this fashion. The traditional formulae for behavior are usually sufficient for his adjustment to his social and natural world. Dangerous, potentially destructive ideas are born in the city but so also are ideas such as the concept of human dignity, freedom from slavery, equality of mankind, permanent peace, and so on.

A contemporary writer comments on what he believes to be coming changes for all of mankind as the world's population becomes industrialized and the technological revolution to which Redfield refers is more complete:

The super-industrial revolution can erase hunger, disease, ignorance, and brutality. Moreover, despite the pessimistic prophecies of the straight line thinkers, super industrialism will not crush man into bleak and painful uniformity. In contrast, it will radiate new opportunities for personal growth, adventure and delight. It will be vividly colorful and amazingly open to individuality. (Toffler 1970:187)

Some interpreters of the modern scene believe that the special self-consciousness referred to by Redfield will assist peoples in finding means for surviving (Reich 1971:82–83). It is paradoxical that without our elaborate technology we would not be *conscious* of our relationships to nature and the moral order.

6

Psychocultural Mini-Models

Psychocultural Mini-Models stem from the third level of analysis represented in Figure 1, with focus on the individual and his or her mentalistic
processes. A person's cognitive processes—the way he or she views, sorts, and
synthesizes things and events believed to exist in the world—are crucial factors
in understanding how individuals adapt to the impact of an alien cultural
system. The individual is forced to think in such a way as to act effectively in
the new framework where the definitions of reality are different. All cultures
provide a cognitive orientation toward the world which aids their members
in interpreting objects and events. This is often called a "world view." Although
this is a "culturally constituted" framework for interpreting the world about
one, nevertheless each individual has his or her own version of it (see Hallowell
1963:106).

Many studies of culture change are made at the "system" level or at the
observable social interaction level. The individual and psychological explanations are omitted. These kinds of analyses hold up well until the established
cultural system begins to disintegrate during rapid change and individuation
takes place, as is happening frequently in the contemporary scene. With only
a "system" frame of reference and no place for attention to individual adaptations, the anthropologist cannot explain why or how disintegration and reinte-
gration are taking place at a personal level. Neopsychological formulations such
as "perception of new alternatives" and "anxiety about the efficacy of traditional
solutions" are often used without reference to known individuals. It is necessary
to go further than that and find out specifically how and what individuals
think and feel during periods of change.

The following mini-models all employ psychocultural concepts and methods
but are so different from each other that they can be only loosely grouped
under one heading. They all share in common, however, special attention to
the individual and his or her mediation of events, whether exhibited in
responses to psychological tests, autobiographies, or in direct behavior. They
also share in common an attempt to relate sociocultural and psychological
processes, though in diverse ways.

INNOVATION

Innovation was dealt with earlier as a special model. It is closely linked with diffusion and acculturation processes. It is mentioned again here as a distinctive psychocultural process. According to Homer Barnett, innovation is the recombination of previously existing ideas into a new idea or *mental configuration*. Changes in ideas are crucial to culture change and Barnett was concerned with how new ideas developed in an individual's mind. The model is used to explain how the innovator first *analyzed* two preexisting configurations, then matched or *identified* similarities in the two and then *substituted* the new idea for the two preexisting ideas. The anecdote about how the first Cheyenne lodge may have been created (see p. 14) illustrates Barnett's hypothesis (1953). The creator first analyzed the preexisting mental configurations of "shelter" provided by their (presumably) existing dome-shaped ones and the conical shape of the leaf in his hand. He then *identified* similarities in the two and then substituted the idea of the new shape for that of the old, resulting in the Cheyenne conical-shaped lodge.

Innovation is not a source of change, as stated earlier, until the new ideas have been accepted. Barnett explains as part of the model that before accepting an innovation, an individual must assign some sort of meaning to it, and it must be advantageous to him or her to substitute the new idea for the old. Barnett believes that a potential acceptor goes through the same processes as the innovator—analyzing, identifying, and then substituting. Barnett argues, however, that the new idea for the innovator is not really the same as it is for the acceptor, since mental configurations of persons are never identical.

The kinds of preconditions necessary for new ideas to be accepted were listed previously but without special focus on the psychocultural process. It is always necessary to relate the individual (in this case the innovator or acceptor) to his social and cultural context as the various parts of the psycho-sociocultural system are closely interconnected (see Figure 1).

It has generally been noted that innovations occur more frequently in the more complex systems with complex inventories of ideas. In many cases it is the "marginal" man, feeling some distance between himself and his own culture, who can more readily see new possibilities to be reworked into new ideas.

It has been recognized that stress and tension states often supply the motivation for change, resulting in creative innovation. One anthropologist has formulated hypotheses concerning processes involved in the reduction of stress and innovation, as follows.

MAZEWAY REFORMULATION

This contemporary mini-model is applied to a rather narrow range of change situations. The focus is on the individual and his or her mentalistic processes.

In the Grand Scale Model (Figure 1) it would fit at the "individual level" range. It can therefore be categorized as a "psychocultural process."

The Mazeway Reformulation model, created by anthropologist Anthony Wallace (1956), proves useful in analyzing revitalization movements that occur in situations where people have been placed under great stress while being required to change their behaviors and beliefs. The reformulation posits that each person has a mazeway which is his or her unique mental image or perception of physical objects in the environment. The mazeway includes nature, society, culture, personality, and body image as *seen by one person.* No two mazeways are identical but there must be some complementarity or general agreement in mazeways in order for communication to occur.

REVITALIZATION MOVEMENTS

Wallace uses the concept of mazeway in analyzing revitalization movements. When a group has to endure more stress than it has the ability to cope with, in times of disaster, or rapid change due to a dominant, oppressive group, a member of the group may undergo a sudden or radical mazeway resynthesis (sometimes through a dream or travel). He or she may become a prophet or leader, who teaches others who add new elements to their mazeways and are often converted. However, the followers do not usually have the complete resynthesis produced by the leader. A social movement (a revitalization or reactive movement) results and is aimed at creating a more satisfying culture. Movements vary in degree of success based on the amount of rationality and reality-based planning done by their leaders. The example of the innovator Wovoka, who originated the famous Ghost Dance, is an illustration of a nonreality based movement. Wovoka had claimed that the performance of a special ritual would cause whites to disappear and dead Indians to return.

Reactive or revitalization movements similar to the Ghost Dance occurred in many areas throughout the world when pressures from dominant groups became too great. In 1856 such a movement among the Xhosa of South Africa had tragic results for the people.

> The Xhosa first showed their opposition to Europeans and their culture by fighting. There were a series of "Kafir Wars." In 1856–1857 came the cattle-killing. Nongqawuse, a girl of 15 or 16, reported to her uncle (a diviner) visions of men who told her that people must consume their corn, cease to plant, and kill their cattle, and then, on a certain day, the ancestors would rise armed with guns and spears, and with the help of a whirlwind, Europeans would be swept into the sea. At the same time kraals would be full of cattle, and store-huts piled high with grain. Several other women and girls in different parts of the country reported similar visions. The people were also urged to destroy any material of sorcery they possessed. Many Xhosa, and a few Thembu, killed their cattle and refrained from planting. . . . Eventually vast numbers died from starvation, and others, weak and emaciated, entered the Colony in search of food and work. (Hunter 1936:159)

Melanesia was also the scene of reactive movements of an especially extreme type. One of the most spectacular and unrealistic was the Vailala madness which broke out in the Gulf of Papua after World War I.

This movement involved a kind of mass hysteria, in which numbers of natives were affected by giddiness and reeled about the villages. So infectious was it that almost the whole population of a village might be affected at one time. The leaders of the movement poured forth utterances in "djaman" ("german"), which were in fact a mixture of nonsense syllables and pidgin English. Sometimes these were incomprehensible, but sometimes the leaders gave intelligible utterance to prophecies and injunctions. The central theme of the former was that the ancestors would soon return to the gulf in a ship, bringing with them a cargo of good things. The leaders of the movement communed with them by means of flagpoles, down which messages were transmitted to the base where they were received by those who had ears to hear—an obvious adaptation of the idea of a wireless mast. Elaborate preparations were made to receive the ancestors, and offerings of food for them were placed in special houses under the control of the leaders. (Piddington 1957:739)

The prophets of the movement claimed that they were told by ancestors to have the people abandon the old ceremonies and burn the bullroarers and masks associated with them. This behavior is frequently associated with reactive movements of the more extreme type.

Another form of reactive movement involves a synthesis of patterns and elements from both the dominant and subordinate cultural systems. This type is represented by peyotism among the Menominee Indians of Wisconsin, a religion that is widespread among native Americans and often referred to as the Native American Church.

In the center of the tepee ground is a carefully laid fire of clean split staves, the ashes of which are swept at dawn into the form of a dove or mythical "Waterbird." . . . There is a half-moon altar of sand between the leader's place and the hearth, with a small pedestal for the 'master' Peyote, and an indented line drawn along the top of the half-moon's ridge to symbolize the difficult and narrow path the Peyote member must follow through life.

Christian symbols are apparent in the material structure and paraphernalia, as well as in the prayers and speeches. The tepee's poles represent Jesus Christ and the disciples. The staff is carved with crosses. The prayers and many of the songs are directed to Christ by name. The leader sometimes crosses his breast with his hand before lifting the blessed water to his lips in the sacred silver cup. The basic conception, premises, and procedures, however, are native North American, if not specifically Menominee.

The ultimate declared purpose of taking peyote is to acquire the power with which it has been invested by the Creator (kese•maneto•w). This power cannot be obtained by merely consuming peyote. It comes to one only when the person approaches it in a proper state of humility and after long preoccupation and concentration. If the person is 'filled with sin,' the medicine will only make him ill, but once the peyote power is acquired, it will enable him to do wondrous things and serves to protect him from evil, including sorcery. (G. Spindler 1955:83–85 and Spindler and Spindler 1971: chap. 3)

The Peyotists have combined, in a creative fashion, Indian and Christian elements such as the cross and the drum with the "master peyote." The Peyote

Cult is one of the more successful and realistic revitalization movements, which may be defined as *deliberate*, organized, conscious efforts by members of a society to construct a more satisfying culture (Wallace 1956:265). There are no spectacular miracles promised at a set time by peyote leaders. There is an escape from anxiety and tension offered to members of the group. The consuming of the peyote, which induces visions, while listening to the monotonous beat of the drum throughout the night, gives to the members a spirit of "oneness" with the powerful "master peyote" and each other, cleanses them of sin, and cures them of illness. It is not uncommon for a grown man to share his problems with the other members in a long speech, with tears flowing down his cheeks. Of greatest importance here is the fact that each member has the group behind him, sharing, supporting, understanding.

Wallace also applied the revitalization model to the contemporary scene, where it could include Yippies, Black Muslims, Young Americans for Freedom and many others, and successful revolutions such as those of the Russian Communists and the Peoples Republic of China.

SOCIOCULTURAL CHANGE AND PSYCHOLOGICAL ADAPTATION

A. Irving Hallowell introduced this model—relating psychological processes to changes in culture as people responded to the often abrupt changes in their existence wrought by the impact of Euro-American culture. In his study of the Northern Ojibwa near Lake Winnipeg, Hallowell isolated three groups representing different levels of acculturation. Using tests such as the Rorschach and extensive interviews, he found a continuity of the same basic psychological pattern through three stages of acculturation, suggesting a kind of persistence relatively unaffected over a long period of time by outside contact (Hallowell 1951:38).

G. and L. Spindler were heavily influenced by Hallowell in the initial phases of their study of the Menominee Indians of Wisconsin (G. Spindler 1955; L. Spindler 1962). Using a model similar to that used by Hallowell, their aim was to relate social, economic, and cultural change to the psychological adaptations of individuals. They isolated five acculturative groups that are the result, in the present, of all the coping strategies used by the Menominee in the past. In order to relate changes in social and cultural life to changes in the psychological patterning of individuals in each category, the Spindlers combined techniques borrowed from sociology and psychology.

Sociocultural indices, treated statistically, afforded data on subsistence, material culture, religious practices, etc. Data from Rorschach (inkblot) tests provided indices for assessing changes in psychological structure. The five categories are: the native-oriented, whose way of life exhibits identifiable continuities with the aboriginal past; the Peyote Cult, a stabilized form of reactive movement (discussed earlier), organized as a chapter of the Native American Church and representing a working synthesis of Christian and native patterns of belief and ritual; the ungrouped transitionals, who carry on some vestiges of the traditional culture but who are mainly poor "white" in their life way; and the acculturated personnel, subdivided into lower status and elite. The former are adapted to a laboring-class standard of behavior and achievement. The latter are adapted to an achievement-oriented middle or even upper-middle class standard. The life styles within these five sociocultural categories must be seen as coping strategies—as ways of getting along in a conflicted world. These coping strategies are changing as the world changes. They are described here as they existed in most full form through the 1950s and early sixties. Other forms of adaptation, intermingled with and in part derived from these, are emerging now but would require separate and prolonged discussion beyond the scope of this Basic Unit.

The psychological configuration of the native-oriented Menominee fits the cultural system of that group, and to the extent that system is a valid projection of the past, fits also the traditional Menominee culture. The key role expectations of this cultural system center upon restraint and control in interpersonal behavior, and dependence upon supernatural power rather than upon individual achievement. Competitive behavior, aggressive, self-gratifying achievement, boasting are all highly deviant behaviors. These behaviors are punished, and therefore controlled or eliminated by witchcraft. The key social control of this group is witchcraft, exercised not by deviant persons, but by respected and powerful elders (L. Spindler 1970), thus reinforcing the central values of the cultural system directly.

The psychological data show that the Menominee in the native-oriented group operate with deep internal controls over aggression. The people are inward oriented; they are not achievement oriented; they do not openly display emotions but are sensitive to the nuances of the interpersonal relations; they are fatalistic and exhibit quiet endurance under stress or deprivation. There is no marked evidence of anxiety or internal conflict, nor of free-flowing spontaneity.

The Peyotists are highly committed to the ideology and ritual of Peyotism stressing rumination about one's self, sins, and salvation, and attainment of power individually and through partaking of Peyote in an acceptant mood. There is significant relaxing of controls over emotions and overt expression of feelings, with public crying during testimonials and rituals and bids for collective expressions of sympathy, which are offered freely.

The ungrouped transitionals are characterized by very uneven adjustments to the vicissitudes of transformational culture change. Some are striving for an orderly way of life, toward goals recognizable in the surrounding non-Indian community; others are withdrawn and mostly just vegetate; others go on destructive rampages. Continuous drinking and disorder are a way of life for some. These Menominee transitionals are like human populations everywhere who have lost their way; for them neither the goals of the traditional nor the new culture are meaningful.

The acculturated, and particularly the elite, are different from the other

A traditional Menominee Dream Dance group.

Menominee groups. They utilize their emotional energy in the attainment of goals—personal success, material acquisition—approved of by middle-class persons in the surrounding communities. They are concerned about production and competition. They react to environmental pressures in a controlled but aggressive manner. They are also more anxious and tense than the native-oriented, but this anxiety is focused, rather than diffuse (as it is among the transitionals).

The acculturated Menominee have little social interaction with the members of the native-oriented group. Most of them do not speak their own language. The few who do rarely use it. Their homes and possessions are indistinguishable from those of the middle class in nearby towns.

The sociocultural and psychological data show that the native-oriented group and the elite acculturated are most unlike, socioculturally and psychologically. They also show that those people in-between adapt in a variety of ways. Some vegetate, others strike out in frustration, some attempt to combine elements from the conflicting ways of life, others try to move toward assimilation in the dominant society. A traditional Menominee would have the greatest difficulty in adjusting to the demands of American middle-class culture, since the requirements are so discongruent with his or her perceptions and beliefs about the world. As the Spindlers wrote:

> In United States culture people must be aggressive in interpersonal relationships and social interaction to obtain personal recognition or business or professional success. In traditional Menominee culture aggressive people are

A Menominee white collar worker.

suspected of being witches. In United States culture extroverted emotional expressiveness is valued as personal salesmanship. People should be friendly, evocative, lively. In Menominee culture emotions are rarely allowed to come to the surface. In United States culture the social interaction rate is fast, and matched by a torrent of words. In Menominee culture social interaction is slow and words are paced and few. In United States culture people are supposed to make decisions on the basis of rational and practical considerations. Among the traditional Menominee important decisions are made on the basis of dreams. (Spindler and Spindler 1971:9)

When the Spindlers used the same tests for the Blood Indians of Alberta, Canada, they were surprised to find that the Blood were not so divided among themselves. The most successful, progressive ranchers shared psychological features with the tradition-oriented people. The Spindlers hypothesized that this was true partly because there were so many convergencies between their values, behaviors, and cognitive organization and those of successful whites in the area that radical change was not required for the Blood to get along in a white dominated world. The aggressive, competitive, acquisitive way of life of the traditional Blood as buffalo hunters fit the modes of life and livelihood introduced to the Alberta plains by the Canadians. Cattle ranching, plus the outlets furnished by participation in rodeos, made it possible for the Blood to adapt to the new ways without fully abandoning the old and without a radical shift in psychological structuring.

BEHAVIORAL ANALYSES

Behavioral analyses are used by some anthropologists to analyze culture-change materials and by others in attempts to control behaviors by changing and shaping behavior patterns. Behavioral analyses depend heavily on social learning theory and upon works of psychologists such as A. Bandura and J. Rotter. The research by Ted and Nancy Graves, described below, is an example of the use of this type of analysis as a tool for dealing with research data and for hypotheses formulation. The Vicos Project is an example of its use as a technique for modifying behavior in a situation of controlled acculturation or modernization.

This latter type research would fall under the category of applied anthropology. Government change agents working in economic development programs in newly developing nations find behavioral analyses a useful means for controlling the direction of change. J. Kunkel (1970) has written a book about behavioral analyses and social change, focusing on economic growth. Following are a few of the basic premises of this approach:

> Behavior (R) is established and maintained or weakened by its consequences, usually called *contingent stimuli,* which may be either *reinforcing* (S^r) or *aversive* (S^a). More accurately, the presentation of reinforcing stimuli (loosely speaking, rewards) or the removal of aversive stimuli increases the probability that the behavior pattern will be repeated, whereas the presentation of an aversive stimulus (loosely speaking, punishment) or the removal of an S^r decreases the probability that the behavior pattern will be repeated in the future. The absence of contingencies (S^c) also decreases the probability that the activity will be repeated, and the extinction of behavior is the usual result. (Kunkel 1970:28)

According to the proponents of this type of analysis, the same learning principles operate in all cultures, races, and stages of the life cycle. The content of learning varies, however. What is rewarding in one culture may be aversive in another.

One of the best known programs of deliberate large-scale social change involving anthropologists is the Vicos Project, organized by the anthropologist Alan Holmberg. It is reported that it accomplished more in the space of five or six years than other programs have produced in decades. The Vicos hacienda in Peru approached the conditions of feudalism. Vicos peasants were characterized by hostility to the outside world, conservatism, and great poverty (Kunkel 1970:141). The project was designed to produce "higher standards of living, social respect, and a self-reliant and enlightened community which can eventually take responsibility for the direction of its own affairs as a functioning part of the nation" (Holmberg 1960a:82). Attention was directed toward education, nutrition and health, and community organization. For example, few children attended the school and no child could read or write well. Thus the major features of the Project's education program consisted of eliminating the aversive contingencies and attaching reinforcing stimuli to both the parents' sending their children and the children's attending classes. In order to do this, new teachers, interested in Indian children, were hired and the subjects they taught were relevant to the daily life of the village.

From the viewpoint of the behavioral analyst or the economic developer, the program was a success. "The modification of a large number of behavior patterns was accomplished by means of alterations in the relevant contingencies" (Kunkel 1970:149). On the other hand, the question is being asked today: could some of the necessary economic changes have been accomplished without the loss of identity experienced by the Vicoseños? John Collier and Anibal Buitron described a situation for the Otovalenos of Ecuador which was similar in general background to that of the Vicoseños, where the individuals of the community were able to modernize in the economic sphere and yet were able to maintain their Indian identities (1952).

When the proponents of behavioral analysis make statements such as the following,

> The behavioral component of any development program consists of three major parts: the shaping of "new" activities associated with industrialization, the maintenance of those "old" actions which are part of the process, and the extinction of incompatible behavior patterns. (Kunkel 1970:294)

the anthropologist may begin to worry about the "colonizing" influences of a technologically superior culture on a technologically inferior culture. Charles Erasmus, an anthropologist involved with community development, comments on the dangers inherent in the technique when applied by insufficiently trained change agents:

> Community Development educators, however, are seldom equipped with knowledge-intensive skill. I am reminded of those of my students (anthropology) who show an interest in the Peace Corps simply out of an irresistible urge to serve their fellow men in the backward areas. When I suggest they train themselves to meet the educational deficiencies of those areas in such knowledge-intensive subjects as medicine, plant pathology, engineering, and the like, they grimace and confess their dislike of math and science. When I ask them what sort of humanitarian endeavors they have in mind, they explain that they want to help people "progress" through education programs such as Community Development. And from what I have seen of Community Development personnel, I am convinced that just such knowledge-free individuals as these eventually find their way into that knowledge-free field. (Erasmus 1968:93–94)

In contrast, Theodore and Nancy Graves have used the theory and assumptions of behavioral analysis for analyzing the data from their research concerned with within-group differences in overt behaviors.

In the Tri-Ethnic Research Project—a team project in which Theodore Graves collaborated with psychologists—the explanatory model for deviant behavior in three ethnic groups (Anglos, Spanish Americans, Indians) drew from social learning theory as a framework for analyzing the psychological motivations of individuals in the sample for engaging in deviant behavior (mainly getting drunk). T. Graves (1967a) added the "acculturation" dimension as a variable in his theoretical scheme. Using measures of acculturation and of drinking behavior for Spanish American and Indian samples, Graves found a consistent pattern. Acculturating individuals were responding to the new pressures and opportunities in roughly the same way, *regardless of their ethnic affiliation.* The unacculturated groups differed sharply, however, in the general level of deviance and drinking they displayed. And Graves explained these gross behavior differences in terms of the contrastive control structures of the Indians and the Spanish Americans. For example, the tradition-oriented Spanish American had been subjected to strong controls through the family and church, controls that were lacking for the Indian sample.

Another use was made by Nancy and Theodore Graves of behavioral analyses, along with other related theories and techniques, in analyzing cultural-change materials from the Cook Islands. Their research dealt with the impact of modernization on Polynesian personality. It focused on Aitutaki Island, which is roughly midway in the process of modernization in the Cook Islands, with strong contrasts in degree of modernization and acculturation from one area to the next. There are more persons still involved in the traditional planting and fishing activities than in the neighboring Rarotonga Atoll, even though there are more opportunities for wage labor than are found in the northern atolls. The researchers, in investigating the psychological effects of wage labor and modernization on their sample, administered attitude tests and experimental procedures, developed in the field, to both adult and school-age children. One technique they developed, called the "coin game," was designed to elicit responses—choices—that could be categorized on a continuum of rivalry-generosity. The generosity was part of the traditional culture and the rivalry a result of the impact of Western culture. Students and adults made decisions that allowed the anthropologists to make correlations between the amount of exposure to Western influence and the respondents' place on the rivalry-generosity continuum. Many other factors, such as family type, household size, and age, were also used in the analysis.

One conclusion drawn by the Graves is that the Cook Islanders are taking on Western personality characteristics (that is, rivalrous attitudes) *not* as a deliberate adoption but *despite* themselves as a by-product of their efforts to become modern. And it was documented that Western schooling played a central role in this process.

Again Nancy Graves, in testing various hypotheses concerning changes in mother-child relationships among groups migrating to the city, contrasted to those remaining at home, used a behavioral analysis for developing hypotheses and interpreting data (N. Graves, n.d.). She called her model a "Parental Mediation Model," which was based on Rotter's social learning theory (1954). N. Graves found Rotter's concept of "internal control"—a *generalized expectancy* that reward is contingent on one's own behavior, rather than on that of external agents—especially useful. The groups compared were urban lower income Anglos—a potentially new reference group in the city for urban Spanish-American low-income mothers—the migrant group possibly assimilating Anglo traits, and rural Spanish Americans—a traditional group remaining behind in the area from which the urban Spanish had migrated. After using interview techniques and elaborate testing devices, N. Graves found that although Spanish in the city identified more highly with Anglo reference groups than did the traditional Spanish in the country, this shift in reference group was not affecting their child rearing in the way the theory had predicted. In contrast to expectations, urban Spanish mothers had lower expectations than did rural Spanish mothers of being able to control the course of child rearing and achieve the type of child they valued: the more contact a Spanish mother had with Anglos, and the more highly she identified with them, the lower were her scores on Mother Efficacy and Child Potential.

These studies and others show great promise for the use of behavioral analysis as a strategy for analyzing the coping techniques used by individuals in cross-national groups.

Following are examples of a different kind of model for inducing change as well as for studying it.

RAISING THE LEVEL OF CULTURAL AWARENESS

In contrast to the model of change applied in most behavior modification projects, the Brazilian Paulo Freire has developed a *conscientizacion* method of inducing change. The purpose of his work is to disseminate technical skills rapidly to illiterate and passive folk and at the same time awaken critical judgment and motivate the individual to active involvement in society. His method was developed in work with peasants in northeastern Brazil and then in Chile during the Christian Democrat regime. He starts with the anthropological concept of culture, underscoring the importance and value of the common man and popular and folk culture. He uses slides and wall poster drawings and paintings in group sessions to illustrate basic cultural processes, such as the sharing of culture by all humans, the relativity of culture, the transformation of culture through human effort, the creative nature of human intelligence, the culture of the slum as well as the countryside, and the influence of the environment on culture. He is not, however, primarily concerned with *illustration*, but with stimulating *participation*. The "culture of silence," rather than the "culture of poverty" is what is to be overcome. The people talk, express themselves, acquire and develop analytic skills in these group sessions. Another phase of the method involves the use of "generative words" chosen for their programmatic value. They are linguistic signs which command a common understanding in a region or area and which also present certain phonetic difficulties that must be mastered. These words likewise serve as generators for participant discussion and self-expression. As Freire says, "Culture, as an interiorized product which in turn conditions men's subsequent acts, must become the object of men's knowledge so that they can perceive its conditioning power" (Freire 1970:16). The relationship to praxis (practice or action) ". . . is involved in the concrete situations which are codified for critical analysis" (Freire 1970:17). (See also Freire 1973.)

Parallels to Freire's method and theory in the work of G. Spindler have been pointed out (Prieto 1975). Explicit parallels appear in Spindler's early work on "cultural therapy." He describes a fifth-grade teacher, one of many that he worked with as a member of a consultation service and research team in the 1950s, who was so immersed in his own Anglo middle-class culture that he did not interact effectively with non-Anglo or non-middle class children in his classroom (G. Spindler 1959:1963). Over a period of several months Spindler shared the data that he collected from the teacher's classroom and from him, including sociometric charts, expressed attitudes, interpersonal ratings, social class and ethnicity indices, and the interpretation of the teacher's autobiography, with the teacher.

> Over a period of several months I presented data to him and tried to guide him more or less gently to a broadened cultural perspective on himself, his students, and his teaching. At times, this being a mutual and cooperative relationship, he guided me, and in so doing contributed to my understanding of cultural transmission. We explored together his cultural background, his experience in the teacher-training institution, and the specific ways in which the dynamics resultant from this combination of cultural influences were expressed in his selective response to his students. . . . his perspective and understanding were broadened significantly, and he was able to interact more effectively with the cultural range represented by his students. He was able to do so because he had acquired a knowledge of his own cultural position, its influence upon him, the cultural diversity of his students and his selective relationships within this range. . . . he underwent a change in his cultural scope. (G. Spindler 1963:170)

Another parallel between the work of Freire and G. Spindler appears in the latter's "cultural sensitization" technique (G. Spindler 1974). The purpose of this technique is to sensitize students and teachers to probable cultural distortions in their interpretations of the behavior of people in other cultures. Respondents are asked to interpret slides showing scenes from other cultures. Their responses are then given back to them in a context of discussion that eventually leads to generalizations about the processes of distortion. Here also there is emphasis on self-discovery and development of cultural awareness.

The collaborative work of G. and L. Spindler using the Instrumental Activities Inventory model and technique, covered under the decision-making mini-model, is also related to Freire's strategy (G. and L. Spindler 1965; G. Spindler 1973, 1974). The conception of humankind as dynamic, choosing, developing, self-activated, rather than passive and mechanistically respondent, underlies the methods and theory of Freire and the Spindlers. The emphasis is on the people and *their* perceptions and understandings, not on "cultural invasions" (Freire 1970:33)—authoritative, normative, moralistic, hierarchical judgments stemming from authority. This authority may be a government official, an educator, or even an applied anthropologist.

DECISION-MAKING

Introduction

Studies of decision-making center on individuals interacting in a specific context, making choices of action. Most behavior involves individual decision-making, and the decision is usually made with alternatives in mind (see Bee 1974:chap. 8). The alternatives consist mainly of decisions between maintaining the old or accepting something new, and this is the beginning of the culture change process. This rather recent approach is best used when individuals in a sociocultural system are faced, sometimes rather suddenly, with a set of radically contrastive choices. Situations where individuals must make choices in behaviors and values related to the process of urbanization or modernization have rich data for the use of the decision-making model.

One method used for obtaining data with this model is to focus on individuals termed "entrepreneurs," a term borrowed from economists. These individuals tend to create more new alternatives than others; they are more willing to take risks in order to "maximize" gains. It is important to understand that one of the basic assumptions of those using this model and focusing on the entrepreneur is that human beings everywhere tend to choose the personal action that they feel will gain them the greatest benefit with the smallest expenditure of resources (Barth 1963). However, this does not carry the connotation that all human beings are self-oriented schemers. If the entrepreneur's decisions result in ways that increase benefits for the group and are communicated, accepted and "institutionalized," important cultural change has occurred.

This model is closely linked to the entire sociocultural system. The focus for analysis is at the social interaction level, where individuals are interacting and making mainly behavioral choices. However, the researchers find that the constraints placed upon persons while they are making choices are of utmost importance. The constraints may stem from the culture (special values, world view) or from the level of technology a sociocultural system has adopted. The relationships between the sociocultural system and its environment (ecology) furnish important kinds of constraints which determine in some measure whether an individual will choose the "new" behavior pattern or decide to adhere to the "old."

Following are examples of cases where the decision-making model was used.

Manus

In Margaret Mead's study of radical and rapid culture change among the Manus, she found that a study of the charismatic leader who was mainly responsible for the sweeping changes was most useful. As mentioned earlier, the Manus literally threw away their old culture and attempted to recreate a way of life modeled after the American way, as interpreted by them. The leader, Paliau, surrounded by a group of close associates, was able to make decisions that were then communicated to and accepted by the Manus. It was important for Paliau, and all innovative leaders, to have advisors to communicate information from the people and then to communicate the innovations and new decisions back to them.

Margaret Mead (1956:165) called Paliau "the man who met the hour"

and considered him to be an idealist and a genius. After a Cargo Cult Movement in the Admiralty Islands (of which Manus is a part) failed, and the
people had destroyed their goods while waiting for a new "Cargo," Paliau
appeared with a program for change that was accepted. Earlier, Paliau had
been sent by top administrators to Port Moresby, where he had been shown
infant welfare clinics and functioning cooperatives and had had explained to
him the new system of local councils, whereby natives could, with guidance,
manage their own affairs, and he learned quickly.

Paliau's program for action involved genuine ethical ideals. He wanted all
of the people in the Admiralties to become one people, forgetting their
tribal rivalries and hatreds and sharing their gardens and fishing rights with
each other. While Paliau and his advocates made decisions that created a
totally new way of life which would allow the people of Manus to cope in
the modern world, Mead attempted to document Paliau's decision-making and
that of his associates and to relate the decisions to the sociocultural context.
This meant that she attended many meetings to watch Paliau and his associates
as they listened to the people, talked informally with individuals, and made
important decisions. Paliau had to appeal to the mystical fanatics in his
following, make rational and effective plans that would keep the loyalty and
admiration of responsible and intelligent supporters, and work closely enough
with government officials to learn all he could about their methods. And Paliau
was a genius in that he was able to meet all these demands (Mead 1956:197).

In carefully documenting and analyzing the events in the rise of Paliau to
power—focusing on his key decisions and on his interaction with his cluster
of advisors and, in turn, the populace—Margaret Mead gained a special understanding of the role of the entrepreneur in sociocultural change.

Fur of Darfur

In contrast to studies of entrepreneurs, other anthropologists have focused
on decisions made by larger groups, with materials from a larger number of
individuals. Although the decisions have usually been made prior to the study,
the investigator still aims to understand what kinds of influences were responsible for the decision (including special sociocultural restraints) and
whether the same pressures for change continue to be operative.

An example of this approach would be the study of the Fur of the Darfur
province of Sudan made by Barth (1967). When some of the Fur farmers
became nomadic herders, the men and women chose to change radically the
patterning of their allocation of resources (time, food, cash). Originally, as
farmers, the husband and wife each cultivated their own separate millet fields
and each kept his or her separate cash account. The agreement was for the
man to provide the woman with some cash for consumer goods and for the
woman to cook and brew beer for the man. Aside from this, the husband and
wife had separate ways of spending their time and money. When these Fur
families became nomadic herders, the husband and wife began to pool their

cash resources, forming a joint cooperative unit, rather than keeping their former separate units. It was agreed that the wife would farm and cook while the husband would herd. In this situation, the advantages of jointness were great. Each could specialize and share greater returns. The Fur nomads could have borrowed some of these new patterns from Arab herders, but Barth makes a convincing argument that this was not the case here. After careful detailed documentation concerning what happened, Barth claimed that the changes were the result of rational decision-making—choosing from many alternatives those that would "gain them the greatest benefit with the smallest expenditure of resources" (Barth 1963, 1967).

Schönhausen

Another analysis focusing on change as it occurs in a group was made of a small, urbanizing rural German village by George Spindler in 1968. He was able to document and analyze on-going adaptive processes—decision-making as it occurred among a group of elementary school children as they adapted to the constraints of their traditional culture and to the alternative choices of the outside, urbanizing world (G. Spindler 1974). Greater Germany has been urbanizing for many decades, but there has been a cultural lag in the change from rural to urban models in many small villages.

In the elementary school in Schönhausen, a small village in the Rems Valley of southern Germany, students learned about the history and ecology of their immediate area in great detail during each day in a class called the *Heimatskunde.* Here they were taught how the land (predominantly used for growing grapes), animals, plants, and weather were all functionally interrelated. They learned to appreciate the meaning of free space, good earth, and clean air from teachers who were themselves mainly village and tradition oriented. George Spindler wanted to find out what kinds of choices these children would make when offered alternatives related to the surrounding society (G. Spindler 1974). Many of the children were acquainted with the urban models through TV viewing or relatives who had taken jobs in nearby urban areas. G. Spindler used a picture test termed the IAI (Instrumental Activities Inventory) that he and the author first developed for use with the Blood Indians (Spindler and Spindler 1965). Line drawings were made of 37 activities that represented both rural and urban traditions. Care was taken to represent the activities with meticulous accuracy. Students were asked to give their preferences and their rationale for these preferences. (Choices included activities such as farmer versus machine worker, a grape-grower versus white-collar office work, farmer versus draftsmen, modern versus traditional home, and so on.) The test was designed to elicit responses related to a person's perception of realistic social alternatives—of life styles and the instrumental means to them. The researcher was able to gain insight into the mental (cognitive) organization of the children, which stood behind their decision-making.

Before making their choices between line drawings of specific activities or

Instrumental choices—(left) *Weingärtner and* (right) *white collar worker*— *from the Schönhausen IAI Series.*

material symbols of urban versus rural life styles, such as a modern home versus a Bauernhaus, students were asked to write short essays stating agreement or disagreement with statements supportive of city life as against village life and of being a Weingärtner (wine grape grower) as against being a factory worker.

In the essay responses the children in the sample as a whole showed an idealistic bias toward life in the small village. They supported their choices with values such as more fresh air, less traffic, quietness, nearness to nature, friendliness, etc. The same bias operated in the essay responses in favor of the life of the Weingärtner. The supporting values here included: self-determination and independence, being near nature, breathing fresh air, being owner of one's land. Girls and older children, however, expressed a more urban orientation than did boys and younger children.

The majority of the children in their essay response expressed generalized, idealized value orientations, traditional in nature. The essay question did not require finite judgments and decisions. However, when specific practical choices were required of the children in the form of paired contrastive activities, or life styles, the children tended, with some exceptions, to choose in an urbanized direction. For example, when they are asked to decide whether they preferred a traditional (Fachwerk) house or a very modern single-family dwelling, their decision was to choose the modern dwelling more often. Girls again were more urban oriented in their type of choice than were the boys. Using this kind of decision-making model in this context allowed the researcher to probe at once to find the reasons—the rationale—for the decisions that were present in the students' minds. In the case of this example, it consisted of pragmatic answers such as "convenience, luxuries, practicality, a better life, more comfortable, warmer, easier to keep up, more valuable." The children were thinking, implicitly at least, of what would give them "the greatest benefit." Using this kind of analysis where concrete decisions related to folk or urban orientation were required, George Spindler was able to conclude that the idealized kind of identity provided by the school was not a barrier for the students in maintaining a reality-based perception and understanding of the practical aspects of the urbanizing sociocultural systems surrounding them. "The analysis (of the decision-making process) permitted us to see how the children managed to maintain cognitive control in a changing milieu" (G. Spindler 1973:131).

CONCLUDING REMARKS

There is, as stated in the introduction to this section, little to hold the various approaches subsumed by the Psychocultural Mini-Model together except a focus upon the individual as innovator, decision-maker, entrepreneur, adapter to change, revitalizer, reformulator, synthesizer, behavior and self-consciousness-raising member of a group in change. But this focus is of great importance for it calls attention to processes that are left out of analyses, as useful as they may be, at the systems level. Without this emphasis on the individual level of adaptive behavior one's understanding of sociocultural adaptation is one-sided and abstract.

PART III

Change and Persistence
in Special Areas

Part III departs from the style of presentation used in Part II. The purpose of this section is not to systematize the various approaches to the study of culture change, urbanization, and modernization and to relate case materials to these, as in Part II. The purpose of Part III is to explore the results of research concerning special and very dynamic changes taking place in the modern scene in core areas. Changes in women's roles, seen cross-culturally in situations where rapid change is taking place, are the first special topic. The second is change and persistence in cultural values in the contemporary United States. The third is youth cults, such as the Hare Krsna and Hippies. The fourth deals with minority groups in the United States.

Although the materials presented in this section cannot be fit into special niches and models as were those in Part II, the understandings gained from the study of Parts I and II should be useful aids for appreciating the significance, in anthropologically relevant terms, of the following discussions.

7

Women's Adaptations

INTRODUCTION

What is the fate of women as cultures throughout the world are becoming urbanized or modernized? In the past, data collected from women have been sparse and generalizations have consequently been hazardous. One popular generalization that has been made, yet without advancing our understanding of process, is that in all human cultural systems males are dominant and women have inferior status. This generalization is simple to arrive at from ethnographic reporting, where it has been customary to evaluate female roles in terms of male roles. Rarely has the focus been on the complementary nature of sex roles or on the differences in male and female world views, and women's adaptations to sociocultural change have been little studied.

When women's adaptations are studied separately, new generalizations become apparent. In our fieldwork in four cultures and from research materials available from others, it would seem, for example, that women are more oriented than men toward the new life style of the modern world. The gadgets and apparent affluence of the urban world are especially appealing. In many cases change will mean a loss of prestige and status for the women, but they are willing to take their chances.

There are exceptions, of course. In interviewing Isthmus Zapotec women in Oaxaca, Mexico, Beverly Chiñas asked wives who were successful in processing goods and selling them in the marketplace what they would do if they won a sum of money in the national lottery. To her surprise, only two of forty-seven wives stated that they would expand their processing-vending activities. All others stated that they would discontinue their selling activities and simply stay at home and care for their families. It is true that family roles are most important to Zapotec women. However, their processing and vending activities in the marketplace are a major contribution to the household and afford them status and a special, complementary type of relationship with their husbands. As B. Chiñas wrote: "Isthmus Zapotec society in fact is a blend of roles which leads to a fine balance of equality between the sexes" (1973:93). While searching for the reason for this unexpected response by the women, Dr. Chiñas found that it was due to the cherished mental image women held of the

Zapotec women in the marketplace (courtesy of Beverly Chiñas).

"lady" as represented by a small but powerful mestizo elite living in urban centers! The elite lady would never carry heavy burdens or sell in the market-place and would, in fact, seldom be seen in public.

More in line with the general trend were the Blood Indian, Cree Indian, and German peasant women who were asked to make choices between activities representing modern versus traditional life styles, using the IAI technique. The choices were presented in line drawings, different for each group, of significant activities. When the choices were presented to the Blood women of Alberta, Canada, relating to what they would like their husbands or sons to do, the highest ranked choices were mechanic, artist, doctor, white-collar office worker and barber. Male choices, in contrast, were ranch work, farming, haying, and rodeo. The female choices were not realistically related to activities on the reservation. The women were looking for something different in the "outside" world (G. and L. Spindler 1965).

A similar trend was found among Cree girls at Mistassini Post in Quebec. Again, top ranking choices were the white-collar worker and auto mechanic rather than male choices of hunter and beaver trapper.

Again, in the peasant village of Schönhausen, Germany, older girls were urban oriented and chose white-collar work or factory work rather than the work of the traditional grape cultivator in their village, in contrast to the boys, who were more tradition oriented in their choices.

These are examples of what women believe they want. It is important to have case materials to show us what is *actually happening* to women as they are faced with the new demands placed upon them by the modernizing world. Following are examples of several cases of women adapting to the pressures of the modern world.

BLOOD INDIAN WOMEN OF ALBERTA, CANADA

When the Blood Indians were forced to adapt to the white power structure and reservation life, women fared badly. There was some continuity for the men in owning horses, handling cattle, or gaining honors in rodeos. On the other hand, women lost most of their traditional subsistence and household-encampment functions of the semi-nomadic Blood Indian way of life. They also lost important ceremonial roles in the Sun Dance, due to white missionary pressures. A few women were able to gain an education on white terms and get jobs as secretaries, in teaching, or nursing. However, most women were isolated in small houses out on the prairies with little community life, while the men, for the most part, herded cattle, cut hay, or participated in rodeos. (See Chap. 6 for psychocultural adjustment.) Today the new mobile home factory employs some women but the majority of the workers are males.

Blood Indian culture was male oriented. However, there existed a special female model. They were daughters of wealthy parents who owned many horses. These daughters were encouraged to be assertive, to handle property, and to be aggressive in interpersonal relations, with men as well as women. They were

"Manly-hearted woman" at a Blood Indian Sun Dance encampment.

called "manly-hearted women," and greatly admired by all. This assertive image persists on the contemporary scene, making it far easier for a Blood Indian woman to play an important role in the new society. When the opportunities occur for Blood Indian women, as they are beginning to now, they already have a model for taking advantage of them.

MENOMINEE INDIAN WOMEN OF WISCONSIN

Menominee women, like those discussed above, also lost ground during the first periods of adapting to the conditions created by white dominance and reservation life. The lumbering industry on the reservation provided jobs for several hundred males but few for females. Women who were seers and sorceresses in the old culture lost their power roles except among the very small native-oriented group.

However, due to a unique set of events, a group of women, in 1974, gained control of most of the leadership positions in the newly created reservation. The Menominee were terminated (all federal control and support withdrawn) in 1961, but after a long struggle, restored to reservation status in 1974. A well-educated, articulate activist woman was a prime mover for the restoration of the Menominee to reservation status. After being elected chair person of the Restoration Committee, she appointed other women to key power positions. A "Warriors Society" of young males formed to unseat what they termed the "dictatorship of women."

Having done extensive fieldwork with the Menominee, could an anthropologist have predicted the rise of women to power? The traditional Menominee culture was also male oriented in that the public activities were centered mainly on the male. However, the Menominee had a strong ethic of equality and respect for the individual, which applied to women as well as to men. Women were free to choose the kinds of roles they wished to play. If a woman chose to, she could fish, hunt, dance like a man, compete in foot-races and build houses, while grandparents cared for the children (see Spindler and Spindler 1971). Thus we might posit that the flexibility and equality of the traditional situation provided a cultural system conducive to these particular developments—provided what might be termed a "conducive base." The Menominee people themselves supported the leader as she rose to power. The trouble began when she was perceived (by the dissident groups) as having stopped acting like a "Menominee" with egalitarianism and respect for all groups and individuals. At this point, the "Warriors Society," many of whom had helped put the women into power positions, was formed as a protest group.

An anthropologist understanding the traditional culture could at least see the antecedents for the female rise to power in the flexibility in role-playing, tolerance of deviancy, equality, and respect for women. Thus when the socio-political conditions called for it—the particular sequence of events related to federal termination and consequent restoration—a compatible conducive base

Menominee women in the dance troupe.

A Menominee family ready for a trip to Chicago.

in the traditional culture existed for what was to ensue. Of course the traditional culture had ceased to function in full form before these women were born, but they grew up in its shadow and learned about sex roles from mothers and grandmothers who were relatively traditional in their orientation.

ADAPTING GERMAN PEASANT WOMEN

German peasant women adapting to the modern scene represent a case drawn from western culture that parallels many processes in our own country. The area of the Remstal, where fieldwork was done by George Spindler in southern Germany, is urbanizing rapidly. A small number of people in the village of Burgbach, however, are still engaged in agriculture and growing wine grapes (see G. Spindler 1973). Without a woman in the traditional *Bauernhaus* (the great structure sheltering family and livestock) there was no possibility of adapting to the demands of the environment. After rising at 5 A.M. to feed the pigs and chickens and milk the cows, every minute of her day and evening was filled with household jobs and child care plus many trips up the hill to the vineyard to hoe or prune or spray the vines. There are no operations in the field or vineyard that women do not do, including spraying, pruning, cultivating, running all forms of equipment and spreading manure, and they care for the household as well. There is a strong tendency toward egalitarianism in the family and a high degree of complementarity in the male-female sex roles within the working traditional household. Again it is the male who takes the visible public roles (in the town council, deacon of the church), but the wife plays very important informal roles (i.e., completely organizing all church social functions) that are crucial to the functioning of the formal structure of the society. Although it is not obvious, the woman's influence in decision-making is great.

What happens to the peasant wife as the forces of modernization and urbanization close in upon her? The male usually takes a part-time factory job and continues to work after hours on the land during the first phases of adaptation, but more of the work has to be done by the wife. The wife's work is increased to the point where the couple finally gives up their dependence on viniculture as a means of subsistence. The young couple eventually leaves the land to become urbanites or suburbanites. As in the other cases discussed, the woman again loses her meaningful roles. She doesn't have to work as hard or as long, but she is no longer essential to the household, excepting as a child-care center, sexual partner, and housekeeper. She is socially isolated in her apartment or single family house, in a noncommunity of other uprooted people. She is no longer working closely with her husband on tasks that, although demanding, carried with them many rewards. In her new situation as an urbanite her influence on anything but relatively petty decisions about the household is reduced. She is separate and unequal. Women under these conditions become bored and restless, as their potential as contributing members of the system is impaired.

KAKTOVIK ESKIMOS OF NORTH ALASKA

As discussed earlier in the section on acculturation, the Kaktovik Eskimos experienced positive kinds of changes as they adapted to the technologically superior U.S. culture. New norms seemed to be successfully substituted for old and a high intensity of communication among the Eskimos was retained. The traditional Eskimo leaders (male) were respected and admired by the whites.

At the social and cultural level, the Kaktovik were making a successful adjustment to rapid change, but a different situation existed at the psychological level. When N. Chance obtained elaborate psychological data from the group, he found symptoms of emotional difficulty, and the women tended to have many more than the men. Chance (1966:96–97) attributes this in part to the greater stress placed on most of the women as a result of their loss of many traditional roles without adequate replacement. Both males and females experienced emotional difficulty from conflict which arose when an individual was committed to change his or her identity without an accompanying knowledge of the appropriate roles to play.

Chance was impressed with the fact the community could make such a successful adjustment to rapid change at the social and cultural levels when a significant segment of its population showed symptoms of maladjustment at the individual level. He found that many of the symptoms—related to feelings of inadequacy and tension—did not actually severely impair individuals in carrying out their daily tasks. An explanation for the successful smooth functioning of the sociocultural system is that Eskimo society is male dominated. "Most of the family and community decision-makers are men and as long as these individuals are free from major psychological difficulties, they can serve as a powerful force in maintaining community integration" (Chance 1965: 387). Thus the personality maladjustments experienced by the majority of Eskimo women are camouflaged by the fact that they are a part of an extremely male-dominated society, both before and after the influence of the whiteman.

CONCLUDING REMARKS

We have seen from the foregoing case materials that the adaptation to the modern world has robbed women of significant roles, separated them further from the public domain, and even from their mates, and reduced their overall significance and influence. They have responded to this deprivation in a variety of ways, as described. It is significant that the IAI data collected by the Spindlers from the Blood Indians, Mistassini Cree, and in Germany indicate that women perceive their situation accurately and react to it by choosing instrumental alternatives available in the world outside their communities. The Menominee case seems quite unique and due in part to chance factors that provided exactly the right time and place for the female rise to power. It was important, however, to understand role-playing in each traditional culture, as it may furnish a conducive base for the particular way in which women will adapt to change.

We now turn to an examination of culture change and the adaptations of individuals and groups in our complex, dynamic, conflict-ridden United States of America. Our country represents a rather new field for anthropologists and appropriate models to guide inquiry are just being worked out.

8

Coping in Contemporary U.S.A.

American Values: Change and Persistence

BACKGROUND

What is most surprising in reviewing the wealth of literature on Americans and American values is the striking consensus of opinion—with the same descriptive terms used over and over—among authors from the 1700s to the present. In one of the earliest essays written about Americans (1782), Hector St. John de Crèvecoeur attempted to describe what made "Americans" out of Europeans. Crèvecoeur noted that some of the key factors leading to this transformation into "Americans" were an equality based on plenty for all and a tolerance of differences based on ample space. The rejection of the past and the pursuit of new values is a prominent theme in early America. Crèvecoeur, noting the self-conscious sense of mission (commented on by many later observers), states: "We are the most perfect society now existing in the world" (in McGiffert 1970:42). This "superior" way of life was based on the values of equality and freedom. And this freedom to pursue self-interest in a hospitable environment seemed to lead naturally to productive enterprise (Nay 1974:25). The reference to equality as a central value is found in all writings about American values from 1700 to the present.

Authors began to mention more and more the emphasis on material success, with equal opportunity for it. And as early as 1840, de Toqueville noted the role of religion in America. Referring to America, he remarked: "We find them seeking with nearly equal zeal for material wealth and moral good—for well-being and freedom on earth, and salvation in heaven" (in R. Heffner 1956:48). This theme led to the well-known writings of Max Weber on the *Protestant Ethic and the Spirit of Capitalism* (1930), in which he views the spirit of capitalism as an outgrowth of the Protestant belief system. And many contemporary social scientists are in agreement with this interpretation.

As mentioned, there was and is a remarkable consensus among novelists, political scientists, anthropologists, and other social scientists about what is "American"—what the core American values were and are.

TRADITIONAL TO EMERGENT VALUES

In the 1940s and 1950s it became clear to many social scientists that a major shift was taking place that could be described as a movement from "traditional" to "emergent" (G. Spindler 1955a:149). The two sets of values are listed in Table 1 (see opposite page) with explanatory statements.

No one would claim that individuals were making complete shifts, but many persons, youth in particular and teachers trained in liberal institutions—showed a predominantly "emergent" profile of values.

VALUES PROJECTIVE TECHNIQUE

In an attempt to secure concrete data on what is actually happening to American values, George Spindler collected materials from Stanford students over a period of 22 years (1952–1974). The sample included graduate and undergraduate students and ranged in age from 19 years to 57 years. Students represented were from a broad range of the middle class. The value projective technique used to elicit data was later specifically applied to minority groups. The technique was an open-ended sentence technique containing 24 items arranged around values about which there was consensus in the anthropological and sociological literature plus a request that the respondent describe in one paragraph his or her conception of the "ideal American boy." Students are asked to fill in the sentence with what "first comes to mind." The responses are ready-made statements of belief and may be regarded as influences on behavior.

Examples of the open-ended statements were: "Intellectuals should _____." Responses for this would fall into one of three value categories: (1) negative ("drop dead," "keep it under cover," "be more humble," or "get with it," "be more involved," more "reality-oriented"); (2) neutral ("share knowledge," "study," "make use of their minds"); (3) positive ("be admired," "be influential," "govern"). For the sentence "The future is _____," the three categories of responses are: (1) pessimistic ("uncertain," "lost," "frightening"); (2) noncommittal ("before us," "to come," "tomorrow"); (3) optimistic ("wide open," "challenging," "our for the making"). Responses to the sentence "Nudity is _____" ranged from "indecent" to "wonderful."

In analyzing and comparing the results over the period of 22 years, questions were asked such as whether there is any stable core of values and what changes or reformulations of them have occurred. Studies by others, using the same and different techniques on other samples in the United States, including a massive American College Entrance (A.C.E.) survey in 1974, support the generalizations drawn from the Stanford (University) sample (Spindler 1977).

TABLE 1

Traditional Values	Emergent Values
Puritan morality: Respectability, thrift, self-denial, sexual constraint: a puritan is someone who can have anything he wants, as long as he doesn't enjoy it!	*Sociability:* One should like people and get along well with them. Suspicion of solitary activities is characteristic.
Work-success ethic: Successful people worked hard to become so. Anyone can get to the top if he tried hard enough. So people who are not successful are lazy, or stupid, or both. People must work desperately and continuously to convince themselves of their worth.	*Relativistic moral attitude:* Absolute in right and wrong are questionable. Morality is what the group thinks is right. Shame, rather than guilt-oriented personality is appropriate.
Individualism: The individual is sacred, and always more important than the group. In one extreme form the value sanctions egocentricity, expediency, and disregard for other people's rights. In its healthier form the value sanctions independence and originality.	*Consideration for others:* Everything one does should be done with regard for others and their feelings. The individual has a built in radar that alerts him to others' feelings. Tolerance for the other person's point of view and behaviors is regarded as desirable, so long as the harmony of the group is not disrupted.
Achievement orientation: Success is a constant goal. There is no resting on past glories. If one makes $9000 this year he must make $10,000 next year. Coupled with the work-success ethic, this value keeps people moving, and tense.	
Future-time orientation: The future, not the past, or even the present, is most important. There is a "pot of gold at the end of the rainbow." Time is valuable, and cannot be wasted. Present needs must be denied for satisfactions to be granted in the future.	*Hedonistic, present-time orientation:* No one can tell what the future will hold, therefore one should enjoy the present—but within the limits of the well-rounded, balanced personality and group.
	Conformity to the group: Implied in the other emergent values. Everything is relative to the group. Group harmony is the ultimate goal. Leadership consists of group-machinery lubrication.

The Constant Values

The responses revealed that there *is* a profile of core values that have remained fairly constant (G. Spindler 1977). And virtually every serious analyst of the American scene has included some or all of these values in interpretations. As one analyst, J. Adelson, writing on the "Generation Gap," maintains, "An overwhelming majority of the young—as many as 80 percent—tend to be traditionalist in values" (in McGiffert 1970:380). With his long-term study, G. Spindler was able to not only identify the constant values over the years but to tell when they declined or increased in frequency of mention over the years.

Following are some of the constant values. "All men are born equal" say 50 percent of the respondents in 1974. Seventy-five percent responded this way in 1952. The value of honesty in the general sense appears to be a strong constant but has declined somewhat in the last decade. Honesty as a personal trait has gained strength, however. The value of effort, work, and of having clear goals in an open system has retained surprising strength. Ambition, however, in the traditional sense, is no longer a declared ideal value—there is little agreement that everyone should want to achieve. Time is still valuable but not considered quite as "all important."

An analysis of responses describing the "ideal American" shows that the value of being sociable and personable still holds good but has been modified by a consideration for others and sensitivity to their needs.

These constant values are what bind the generations together. There is growing divergence and much reinterpretation, yet there is a considerable degree of continuity and an indication that the rate of change has been less rapid over the past five years.

Changing Values

Aside from these constant values described above, there are other values that have undergone shifts and changes. They include:

The *future* is regarded pessimistically by an increasing number of respondents. *Nudity* is accepted or valued positively by an increasingly larger proportion of respondents. (Attitudes toward nudity appear to be associated with other values diagnostic of a relativistic versus absolute moral position.) *Success* in the traditional, individualistic, material sense has almost disappeared for the Anglo sample. Success is being defined as a state of competence and personal satisfaction—of happiness and harmony and of self-knowledge. Achievement for its own sake has low or negative value. Success is also related to "contributing to society" and "helping others." The *individual* today, rather than being "all important," is "important in relation to society." And the emphasis on self-knowledge gives individualism a new twist. In contrast to earlier responses, *artists* are today regarded positively. The majority of respondents are more critical of *intellectuals*, saying that they should "face reality" and "get out of the ivory tower."

From these materials we can trace the shift from values emphasizing egocentric achievement, success by the individual, and absolute morality, to a more humanistic, tolerant, relativistic position. The most extensive change occurred between 1961 and 1968.

The collection of responses to the values technique resumed again in 1977. Another significant change occurred. Beginning in 1978 more responses of a traditional nature began to appear. By 1981 the value profiles of Stanford students resembled, in some ways, those of the 1950s. The value of hard work, success, the individual, came back full force, and this is still true in 1984. However, the greater tolerance for deviation and the concern for the relationship of the individual to society that had emerged during the sixties, are retained. It appears that values shift in a cyclic fashion but that there is not a full return to the framework of the past. New points of view are picked up over the years and retained, despite the cycling toward traditional values.

Most social scientists engaged in researching American values agree as to what values are predominant at particular periods and agree on a set of "core values." However, there exists little data for tracing long-term changes in values. The model described here of the "traditional and emergent" values seems useful and conforms to the actual shifts in values supported by data. Much of the strain and "paradox" of American values can be traced to the pulls and pushes between the "traditional" and the "emergent" patterns. It is difficult to be sociable, friendly, sensitive to the opinions of others, and responsive to group norms, and at the same time egocentrically individualistic, and driven by the need for achievement.

MINORITY GROUP VALUES

The value projective test was given to a minority group sample to see if their position was similar to that of the Anglos. The groups included Blacks, Chicanos, Native, and Asian Americans. The sample was from Stanford students, presumably more achievement oriented than the national average. However, it was claimed that these individuals would be likely to serve as influential models for others. Results revealed that the minority groups do not express any radical deviations from the pattern expressed by the Anglo sample of 1974, except that they tend to support the core values more strongly. They are less pessimistic, more goal oriented, more work and success oriented, more concerned with mobility. On the "emergent" side of the ledger, they are even more interested in helping others, particularly the disadvantaged, than the Anglos, and they are not as concerned with self-knowledge as are the Anglos. These patterns also found support in the responses of a sample of Chicano junior high school children (Warth 1972). The Chicano students place about the same emphasis on honesty, the value of time, and equality as do the Anglos. They more

frequently support the more traditional values of effort and hard work, believed necessary for success, the belief in the openness of the system, and the
value of the individual.

A sample of another minority group—Jewish students who were members
of Hillel and religiously conservative—also supported the core "American
recipe." They support the work-success-achievement ethic, give materialistic
answers to "I wish I had," value the individual in the old-fashioned sense,
and are relatively optimistic about the future. They are strongly family
oriented and conservative in the area of sexual behavior (DuBois 1972).

One might ask why groups who have often had less reward from the
system would support more or less traditional values. G. Spindler hypothesizes
a need on the part of these individuals to *believe* in these values, as they
are the best chance they have. If it were true that honesty is the best policy,
one can succeed if only he or she tries hard enough, that the system is open,
individuals are important, and all men are born equal—minority groups would
have no very serious problems. However, the fact that the system has *not*
been these things for them does not mean that these things are not valued
(G. Spindler 1977).

CONCLUDING REMARKS

It would seem from these data and the interpretations above (including materials from U.S. lower class and minority groups) that there is a
relatively stable and shared core of American values. They have not remained
static, however. The responses in G. Spindler's sample indicate that some
values that were once a part of the central configuration have eroded or been
reformulated; other values have moved from a peripheral status to a central
position; and minorities generally support the core "American recipe."

Some contemporary writers, in contrast to the interpretation made here
from data over an extended period of time (22 years), interpret the mixture
of "traditional" and "emergent" as representing a state of confusion (Inlow
1972:182). Others suggest that there is no such thing as compromise: "We
are either strong enough to lever the train onto a new track or it stays on the
old one or it is derailed" (Slater 1970:103). These views would seem to dis-
count the fact that American culture and the individuals representing it have
sustained dichotomous value systems and mixed values for at least two hundred years, and their patterned core of values still shows great vitality.

American Youth Cults

BACKGROUND

As one influential writer C. A. Reich (1971:front cover) commented on the modern scene:

> There is a revolution coming. It will not be like revolutions of the past. It will originate with the individual and with culture, and it will change the political structure only as its final act. It will not require violence to succeed, and it cannot be successfully resisted by violence. This is the revolution of the new generation.

However much one may question the ultimate validity of Reich's statement, he is correct in assigning motives for change to modern youth as they have become disillusioned with and alienated from the values and goals of adults. Many youth feel that adults have been separated from nature, have no relationships to their own work and have become insensitive to others. As various interpreters have observed, "It is the middle class young who are conducting this politics of consciousness . . ." (Roszak 1969:51). And this nonviolent kind of revolution was expressed by students (mostly middle class) in the 1960s and early 1970s in the shift in values already noted. Many of the shifts in values, such as consideration and concern for others, the questioning of the validity of success and achievement as traditionally defined and a search for self-knowledge, are expressed in their radical form in communes, hippie ghettos, and, with various twists, in the proliferating religious sects. It is impossible to tell among which group the change in values first occurred and in which direction diffusion took place. It would seem logical to assume that there was a large-scale cultural ground-swell (as reflected in changes from "traditional" to "emergent" values since 1955) which took expression in exaggerated forms in various youth cults. Materials from minority groups and non-middle-class groups would indicate that the same general shift in values is represented more or less among all American youth.

In this picture of social change, many American youth are playing the important roles of challenger and innovator. They face the same personal problems in adjusting to what they perceive as an incompatible system as did

119

many American Indian and African peoples when they were temporarily overwhelmed by the impact of European culture and colonialism. Traditional patterns in American and European cultures are breaking down. Standard solutions to problems no longer work for many of the young. They view the older system as threatening both physically, due to fear of destruction of the environment by pollution or a nuclear holocaust, and psychologically, due to fear of the uncontrolled power exercised over them in an age of machines.

Some of the shared, common problems of the disillusioned youth groups on the contemporary scene are intense awareness of loneliness and confused identities. Particularly in the urban complex, people are anonymous and separated from each other. And the fear of separation and insignificance, according to Freud (1936) and Fromm (1941) arouses great anxiety. Modern youth are in a stage of life that lacks any clear definition—neither "psychological adolescents nor sociological adults" (Daner 1976:9). Coupled with the need to choose between traditional or emergent value sets, many are experiencing acute identity crises. And the new cult membership is comprised mainly of alienated lonely youth searching for an identity.

THE PROLIFERATION OF CULTS

One of the most common techniques used in adjusting to the conflict situation and feelings of "loneliness" is represented by the appearance of a seemingly limitless number of cults. These cults represent a way used by youth for coping while seeking for a personal identity or a release from hostilities bred from frustration, or while simply searching for a "different" American dream. As one author describes this proliferation of cults:

> The techno-societies, far from being drab and homogenized, are honeycombed with . . . colorful groupings—theosophists and flying-saucer fans, skin divers and sky divers, homosexuals, computerniks, vegetarians, body builders, and Black Muslims.
> . . . The same destandardizing forces that make for great individual choice with respect to products and cultural wares, are also destandardizing our social structures. This is why, seemingly overnight, new sub-cults like the Hippies, burst into being. We are, in fact, living through a "sub-cult explosion." (Toffler 1970:285)

During the late 1960s these cults, and mainly the original "hippie" cult, grew into what has been termed the new "counter-culture" by some (Roszak 1969). These cults can be thought of as potential sources of creative cultural innovation.

The term *cult* is used here for most of the new groupings rather than sub-culture because the turnover rate is extremely rapid. For example, many LSD advocates in specialized drug cults are, after a few years, calling "acid a bad scene" and underground newspapers warn followers against getting too in-volved with "tripsters" (Toffler 1970:296). The original Hippie Haight-

Ashbury subcult in San Francisco, known as the "flower children," ended after a brief period because it became too large and had to diversify. Many Hippies later formed tribes and lived in communes; some lived near Indian tribes or in simulated "Indian" style; others established specialized nonviolent subgroups, using various models offered by established groups such as the Hutterites and Amish. Some groups dedicated to violence developed as the original Hippie movement waned. Their ideology, focusing on affronting behaviors, converged in many respects with that of the Hell's Angels, a motorcycle subcult originating in southern California. The earlier street gangs that had engaged in warfare declined in the early 1960s. (See Keiser 1969 for a study of a Chicago gang.) The aggressive passions, however, given stimulus from the oppressive conditions of ghetto life, are represented by new subcults emerging in the ghetto, cults directed at the social system itself rather than at rivalry between street gangs.

Religions of variegated types in the form of cults have answered a need for many seeking a meaning to life and something to identify with. As Davidson (1971:40) describes these special cults:

> The Three H (Happy, Healthy, Holy) Organization, founded by Yogi Bhajan, and all schools of yoga, have had wild bursts of growth, as have groups dedicated to Zen Krishna Consciousness, Jewish Mysticism, Scientology, Abilatism, Gurdjieff, light radiation, macrobiotics, Jesus Freaks, Sufism, Buddhism, Taoism, Naturalism, and Astral Projection.

Much of the ideology of the Hippies is shared by these religious groups, but each religious subcult tends to be specialized. A striking difference between many of the religious cults and the Hippie cult, however, is that religion does not necessarily require withdrawal from the world or rejection of straight society, and many members of the religious cults remain a part of the traditional culture. The Jesus Movement includes subcults of this type. Although the adherents to the movement are critical of the traditional modes of worship, many attempt to work through the existing structure of the Church. They are met with antagonism for the most part. The movement includes a great variety of young people with a range of hair styles and dress. But they are all seeking the same goal—individual salvation and a personal relationship with God.

The resurgence of fundamentalism in the United States during the 1980's, evidenced by Creationism, support for school prayer, and Bible study groups among college students, reminds us that fundamentalism is a basic aspect of American culture, from pre-revolutionary times to the present. And a personal relationship with God furnishes some security in an increasingly threatening world environment.

While the majority of the religious subcults are dedicated to the ideals of a better understanding of the self and the creation of a "better world," some are dedicated to "Satan" and Evil. These subcults, which center in southern California, practice various forms of Black Magic or enact the "Black Masses," according to descriptions recovered from early writings of the Church (see *Esquire*, March 1970). But the life span of most of these subcults is even shorter than that of others.

For a fuller understanding of cults and cult movements, it is important to examine particular case studies. Two anthropologists were accepted by cult groups and were able to gather extensive firsthand materials for publication. One cult was a Hippie ghetto and the other the Society for Krsna Consciousness (ISKCON). Materials from these two groups will be discussed below.

THE HIPPIE GHETTO

What is a "Hippie?" The answer is not very clear if one tries to dissect the strange conglomeration of Christian mysticism, Vedic teachings, revolutionary tracts, Madison Avenue pop psychology, American Indian religions, hedonism, and the particularly American virtues of Horatio Alger, such as individualism, independence, and frontier courage (Partridge 1973:9–10).

The sharing of the sacrament (marihuana) is a prerequisite for communication in the particular group studied by Partridge. The communication takes the form of a "rap" session and occurs frequently for the purpose of establishing rapport. Members claim the session is for open and honest communication with one another. Since newspapers and media from the "straight" society are to be mistrusted, the emphasis is upon personal experiences. The rap session includes tales relating "groovy" (in this case implicitly or explicitly "confronting") behavior toward straight society, the dangers of living in straight society, or projected alternatives to living in straight society.

Females sometimes find themselves uninvolved with the important instrumental roles of the group. The associational groups in the Hippie ghetto are often male oriented, with females appended on as such alliances shift. The males handle the drug traffic and the females don't fit the needs of a tight associational network existing for finding jobs or buyers for drugs (Partridge 1973:33).

Some interpreters of the modern scene (Roszak 1968) regard the Hippie cult as a counterculture. On the other hand, Partridge, with his first-hand knowledge of the subcult, described the movement as a "part and product of American society" (Partridge 1973:xii). Hippie ideology—with emphasis on the quest for self-knowledge, self-discovery, and spiritual growth—converges with the cultural tradition of American adolescence.

Anthony Wallace (1969:121–122) traces core Hippie values to the cultural values of Western Civilization and Judeo-Christian mythology. The Hippie movement may indeed represent the lost spirit of the Crusaders. The emphasis in Western mythology is on the individual, not the society, which is considered immoral. It is the self that must be examined and altered to achieve happiness in Western mythology. And it is the fervent seeking for self-expression and identity that furnishes a common link between many grouped and ungrouped youth of the present.

The Hippie ghetto described by Partridge does not exist today. The Hippie movement has largely come and gone from the American scene. Nevertheless, its lasting effect is apparent in the freedoms expressed in personal style, marriage and family patterns of living, and in the search to "know," or "find" oneself that persists into the eighties.

THE INTERNATIONAL SOCIETY FOR KRSNA CONSCIOUSNESS (ISKCON)

At many youth scenes or antiwar demonstrations the yellow-robed men and women can be seen begging and chanting mantra. The chosen mission of ISKCON members is to bring the Hindu cult of Krsna worship to modern western society. According to Francis Daner, an anthropologist who spent two years observing members and was accepted in the cult as a neutral friend, the accepted goal of the members is to "change the polluted atmosphere until pure love of God (Krsna) dominates modern society" (Daner 1976). Each member strives to cleanse his or her soul and to overcome a false identity with a temporary body in order to obtain release from the endless wheel of birth and rebirth. The final state to be achieved is spiritual eternal life to be spent in "loving service" (bhakti) of the supreme Lord. A prime instruction is that one must revive his dormant love for Krsna, and, in the present age, the recommended method is by constantly chanting the holy names of Krsna.

The ex-members of the middle-class sociocultural system have blatantly rejected their parents' orientation toward the world, and the mystic orientation of the Buddhist and Hindu traditions focus on spiritual matters as opposed to the materialism, rationalism, and acceptance of science espoused by their parents. In seeking to destroy many of the underlying assumptions of the technocratic society, the ISKCON movement could be thought of as a revitalization movement, as discussed in the Mazeway Mini-Model. Again, as was true for the Hippies and other youth cults, the devotees gave their reasons for joining as a need for identity. They constantly repeated to Francine Daner, "I did not know who I was." And the completely organized and subservient attitude of the life of a devotee offered a special kind of identity.

In July 1966, ISKCON was formally inaugurated, with Bhaktivedanta Swami Prabhupada from India as spiritual master. He is worshipped as a pure devotee of the Lord, the latest descendant in a long line extending back to Krsna's appearance on earth 5000 years ago. The Guru travels from temple to temple and carries on a voluminous correspondence (via a secretary), with few devotees actually seeing him. He furnishes taped monologues to which devotees listen each night as they sip bowls of warm milk. For most followers he is the real father *and* mother.

In 1968 Prabhupada made a new translation of the Bhagavad-gita (the Song of God), the original dating back to 2–5 B.C. and considered the most important of all Hindu scriptures. What is interesting is that the leader of the new cult introduced a new element in his translation of the old scriptures—the love of God for man and of man for God. The most salient feature of the scriptures is the importance of the devotional activities, revolving around the forms and images of God and consisting of seeing, touching, worshipping, praising, cleaning, decorating, and making offerings (Daner 1976:24).

The devotees of Krsna are organized into an elaborate network of temples

Krsnas chanting on Boston Common (courtesy of Marjorie Daner).

(asramas) located throughout urban United States and in other modern cities around the world. Daner focused on the Boston temple but visited many others. Entrance into a temple provides a crucial self-degradation ritual whereby many disoriented individuals find new identities as devotees. The individual is reeducated in the temple and socialized into the terminology and strategies necessary to life in the temple—apart from the dominant society.

A new devotee is assigned to one or more devotees who show him how to behave, including how to work if he or she doesn't have a skill, and explain temple rules and regulations. There are four rules which must be observed by all devotees. They are: (1) no gambling or engaging in conversation unrelated to the teachings of Krsna or the performing of a duty; (2) no intoxicants of any kind, (3) no illicit sex, and (4) no eating of meat, fish, or eggs.

Life in the temple consists of a strictly organized daily round beginning at 3:30 A.M. with the chanting of Hare Krsna, followed by special ceremonies, cooking, performing of specified jobs, attending religious classes until 10:00 P.M. Temple life is communal, with no privacy. Most devotees aid in raising money by begging or selling religious books. The real financial aid, however, comes from the Spiritual Sky Incense Company, which has been very successful.

The position of the ISKCON regarding marriage has undergone changes since the first year. At first marriage was regarded (as in India) as an important institution and devotees were encouraged to marry. After a great deal of trouble arising between married couples, Prabhupada forbade married couples to live together and cohabitate in the temple. At present, there is a trend away from marriage. Women are relegated to inferior positions in line with the Vedic tradition, which is a major cause for marital friction. Women are under the care of their godbrothers (ISKCON males) until they marry and are discouraged from doing anything on their own. A married woman should ask her husband's permission to do anything beyond her prescribed duties. Ideally, she is her husband's submissive servant. The cult has about one third as many women as men members.

The esoteric qualities of ISKCON belief and behavior would lead one to assume that in every respect members represent a departure from American values. In looking beyond the "un-American" values of obeisance to authority and a rigid adherence to ritual and rule, the devotees emphasize certain old-line American values such as hard work, asceticism, salvation through service (Calvinism), and self-knowledge. Both the Hippies and the devotees of Krsna have isolated themselves from mainstream U.S. culture because they found it too incompatible, but in doing so they both sometimes appear to rediscover and reassert, in a creative fashion, the "original" American principles.

U.S. Minority Groups

INTRODUCTION

As said earlier, it is surprising to find that most minorities generally support core American traditional values, especially those related to mobility, work and success, since the system is, more often than not, unrewarding for these groups. If the system worked as it was ideally meant to work, and as it does work for some individuals from minority groups, there would be few problems. Some minorities, due to special cultural traditions, have found American and Western culture relatively easy to accommodate to. Japanese minorities, for example, were able to adapt to the U.S. values and way of life as successfully as they were able to adapt to Westernization in Japan and for the same reasons. In many respects the Chinese could be included in this group, as there are many convergences and compatible aspects between Chinese and American cultures. Likewise Blood Indian males, and some Eskimo males in particular, found adjusting to Western culture relatively easy. In the case of the Menominee, success in terms of mainstream middle-class American culture, for a person maintaining traditional Menominee values, is more difficult. The traditional world view and personality were incompatible with Western culture.

The case materials discussed below deal mainly with large minorities who have had to overcome obstacles in an environment structured by mainstream American culture and power relations—Blacks, Chicanos, and American Indians (Native Americans). There is a sizeable number of individuals from these groups who have chosen to identify themselves as middle-class Americans. They have become successful in these terms in spite of great odds. They often become targets of criticism for those of their own people whose way of life they have rejected in favor of "making it" on the middle-class scene. The materials in this section will not be directed at this process but will focus on those who have maintained their identity as minorities.

Case materials will include groups which live within the law and other groups (comprised mainly of youth) who are marginal criminal groups and strongly anti-establishment in orientation.

URBAN BLACK FAMILIES

When social scientists study Black culture or Black family life they tend to either interpret their data as indicating a continuing tradition or as an adaptation of middle class norms to conditions of poverty. It would seem that the "culture of poverty" cannot account for the richness and variety in the Black cultural tradition. "The strength of Black people stems from a social organization that has been created in the face of adversity, and not merely in adjustment to it" (Aschenbrenner 1975:7). Anthropologist Joyce Aschenbrenner worked intimately with Black families in Chicago, collecting lengthy life histories and observing crises events, ceremonials, and daily encounters to enable her to present a rich picture of the social reality of the urban Black family. Her sample represents a range in socioeconomic station, the majority however being lower middle class. She focuses on the Black family as an institution. Rather than using middle class white norms and using the nuclear (husband-wife-children) family model, she recognizes the importance of the Black extended kin group (father, mother, children, aunts, cousins, uncles, nieces, nephews, grandparents, and, to a lesser extent, "in-laws"). Extended family relationships are basic to the functioning of the urban Black sociocultural system.

In societies with extended families, other relationships, such as father-son, mother-daughter, brother-sister, may be more important in terms of social and economic support than that of husband and wife, and that is true in the case of the urban Black family. The Black family is more frequently oriented toward the mother's side, with a mother-daughter tie especially important. The mother often has complete domestic authority and is the main support for the children—often with no husband. This has been termed a "matrifocal" family. Aschenbrenner views the extended family here as "adaptive" and adaptable. There is a shortage of males and more often than not a shortage of jobs for them. As Aschenbrenner (1975:139) explains:

> For a Black man, complete commitment to one household carries with it the risk of loss of pride if he loses his job or is unable to handle emergencies; further, the high fertility rate together with the higher death rate among young men means there are more children per able-bodied man to support than in the white population. A solution to this problem that may be considered adaptive is the relative independence of men from a particular household, while they may be attached to a number of households in a variety of roles contributing financial and emotional support.

While this type of part-family without a permanent male puts a strain on the women, it gives support to the continuance of the extended family. The women are supported by the larger family group, while exercising domestic authority, given the freedom to raise their children and conduct their relationships with males as they see fit.

The male role is far more complex than would be seen if measured in terms of the American middle-class family norm. The Black male plays many more roles than the father or husband role. Some males do focus on the roles of husband and father, but they are in the minority. Most men have or play other roles. Some men may be family leaders (the uncle role), others are sources of rivalry or support (brother roles) and other younger males are a focus of pride *or* concern (the son or nephew roles). And some men may never play any of the adult family roles.

When Black families moved from rural areas in the South to urban settings, the extended family was extremely important for survival. Many later migrants had relatives to initiate them into the new set of roles that were required. The family became the "focus of childrearing; they are an economic boon to working parents and are the agents of socializing the young" (Aschenbrenner 1975:3). When the sons and daughters marry, they usually leave home but often remain in the parents' neighborhood and form a closely knit group—a localized family group. In this group the sense of obligation is extremely strong. If a person chooses to move or travel, there is always a part of his family that will take care of him or her in the new environment. Aschenbrenner points out that there are many families where the household group consists of husband, wife, and children, especially in economically middle-range groups. However, most families, except those groups who choose to identify with whites, function in the context of wide kinship relations.

Whereas the husband-wife role is de-emphasized in the urban Black family, it does not mean that the male-female love relationship is less intensive or satisfying. Black men and women agree on the supreme importance of a love relationship between a man and a woman and of the necessity of caring for and bringing up properly any offspring resulting from their union. Romantic love and sex have made poverty and ghetto life far more bearable. "Black Americans have glorified romantic and erotic love to its highest expression, and have utilized the binding and healing qualities of sex to great advantage" (Aschenbrenner 1975:29). In their love relationships, however, there is a desire to work out a compact between lovers, allowing for individual freedom and self-awareness, understandable values given the history of Black Americans.

Many social scientists have studied Black culture and have agreed, to a surprising degree, upon what some of the shared values and life styles consist. Many authors refer to a special "style" (sometimes referring to speech patterns, dress, importance of verbal expression) and "soul" (depth of emotion, appreciation of special "soul" music with deep feeling) (see Cole 1970). Following are some of the characteristics agreed upon by social scientists:

1. *A high value placed on children.*

Children were wanted and loved. In families where parents work, children are allowed to take care of themselves at an early age. They are treated as potential adults. According to Aschenbrenner, they develop a profound understanding of social situations and a strong social identity at a comparatively early age, since they have an intimate knowledge of a wide range of social relationships and experience, and of a complexity of attitudes and values not found in the small middle-class family. The Black mother does not have the same kind of intense psychological involvement with her individual children as is found in the middle-class white families, though she values children deeply. They are made to feel independent.

Parents in ghetto areas worry about their children and try to protect them from the gangs by surrounding them with a wide circle of family and friends. Some parents are so concerned that they attempt to limit their children's contacts with peers and socialize with them themselves, which usually makes the children rebellious and confused.

2. *Emphasis on strict discipline and respect for elders.*

There is an unusually great emphasis placed upon teaching children to respect elders, and children learn well.

3. *Approval of strong, protective mothers* is another feature of Black culture.

No one contests the mother's authority. Being a mother is a highly valued role in Black communities. It is difficult for members of the middle class to understand the role relationship between a Black woman and her grown daughter. In the absence of a husband, mother and daughter were made strongly interdependent by children born to either. Mothers made little attempt to establish contact with the father of their daughter's child or with his family, and they did not encourage their daughters to marry (Aschenbrenner 1975:71). In losing her daughter a mother's support and domestic authority would be threatened.

4. *Strength of family bonds* was described by all social scientists who studied Black families throughout the United States. Some students were able to trace the importance of these bonds to early accounts of slaves in the South.

5. *The ideal* of an "independent spirit" is agreed on by social scientists. This spirit is fostered in children and guarded by adults.

Most contemporary social scientists agree that Blacks have a special culture which is the medium through which most, but not all, Blacks communicate and with which they identify as a group. The Black family, reflecting the basic values of Black culture, has been maintained through space and time by means of conscious and ritualized practices such as funerals, reunions, visiting, and the like. It has persisted since the American slavery period and studies of Caribbean families report a similar type of kinship group. Other authors present evidence for the existence of a strong kinship group among Black slaves combined with other African cultural patterns (Rawick 1972). Herskovits (1941) working in Africa and United States found convergent family practices and attitudes toward legal marriage and divorce which would further support the claim that the Black family and Black culture have a long tradition.

AN URBAN BLACK DELINQUENT GROUP (THE VICE LORDS)

In contrast to the picture we have of Black families living mostly as law-abiding people, the Black youth and all other youth belonging to street gangs of the ghetto are usually "delinquent" and engage in criminal activities. Due to the extreme poverty of the ghetto plus the stigma of ethnicity, the Black youth have found the reward system of the American mainline culture out of reach. They, as other ghetto youth, have created special alternative subcultures, based on outgroup violence, in which they can gain status with which they can identify. Lincoln Keiser was accepted by members of the Vice Lords, a Black street group, and allowed to interview them and observe their behaviors. This was a special privilege under the circumstances, when many of these activities had to be concealed from the police.

The Vice Lord Nation is a large federation of street-corner groups in Chicago's Black ghettos. It can be termed a subculture as it has an elaborate structure, social organization and sets of commonly held values. The Vice Lords are divided into branches, with a special set of leaders, which, in turn, are divided into sections, each with its own officers and leaders. Branches are essentially residence areas from which other gangs are excluded. Members of one's own gang, but a different branch, are welcome, but only to "visit." Sections within a branch are closely associated, due to obligations. Sections must cooperate to see that alien gangs do not penetrate areas of their allies. As Keiser (1969:27) writes: "Sections have the responsibility of protecting particular parts of Vice Lord City from enemy attack."

The organization of the group is predicated on violence and aggression perpetrated on outgroups. The significance of membership in the gang is dependent upon the activity of raiding or "gangbanging." An individual's prestige is largely determined by the way he conducts himself in intergang fights and the relations among gangs themselves are a function of the aggression. Aggressive acts are carefully patterned. A gangbang involves different rules if it occurs accidentally, if it is planned, or if it occurs as a result of fights between an individual Vice Lord and a member of an alien club. The complexity of the rules is indicated by the decisions made after a Vice Lord is beaten up by an enemy club. The form of retaliation depends upon the individual's personal reputation and his alliance with a particular subsection and the Nation. Another form of aggression is called "wolf packing" which is carried on by small cliques and does not contribute to the solidarity of the group, as does gangbanging. Wolfpacking is a form of strong-armed robbery. It is done to enhance a person's reputation and to make money. However, more often than not, a group of boys will attack someone to release some of their pentup aggressions. As one member said: "Wolfpacking—like for instance me and some other fellows go out and knock you down 'cause we feel like it. That's what it is. I might take your money, but I really want to kick some ass anyway, so I decide to knock the first thing in my way down" (Keiser 1969). It can be an old man, white or black, and result in his death or crippling, but he is an enemy and an "outsider." Only close friends wolfpack together, as it is important that they be able to trust each other.

Some of the same values and rights and duties are found among gang members as were noted for the Black families. The idea of mutual help was extremely important to all members. Help might take the form of material things or of aid in fighting. In regard to material things, however, Vice Lords played verbal games with each other, giving money or material only when a "brother" was in real need.

Keiser summed up the beliefs and values of Vice Lord culture as consisting of four ideological sets: heart ideology, game ideology, soul ideology, and brotherhood ideology. Heart is related to gang behavior and means bravery of a special type, being willing to follow any suggestions regardless of personal risk. Game ideology is also important to a Vice Lord. It relates to the ability to manipulate others, or, as Vice Lords say, "whupping the game." Individuals who are thought to be good at whupping are said to have a "heavy game," while those judged to be poor at this activity are said to have a "lightweight game."

The values of soul and brotherhood ideology are of a different order. They are not specifically related to patterned aggression and are shared in the wider context of the extended family. "Soul" is listed as a shared Black value. One who acts in a hip manner has soul, as does someone who puts real effort into what he is doing. It also refers to the stripping away of superficiality. Soul is often judged in the context of music and dancing, when intense feeling and involvement are expressed. The brotherhood ideology, when a member says, "Man, we're just like brothers" is also a part of the extended family tradition. Thus it can be seen that, although the group is anti-establishment and anti-outgroup, it still retains some of the basic features of the extended family in which the individuals were socialized.

As a postscript of importance, as it relates to the changing scene, it must be added that the Vice Lords as a group underwent a rather complete metamorphosis several years after Keiser had worked with them. The club became legally incorporated and received a government grant to undertake self-help projects. They started a youth restaurant, began an employment service and opened a recreation center named "House of Lords." In becoming strongly involved with Black pride and Black consciousness programs, they were able to cooperate with whites and realize special rewards while operating on the terms of the "straight" world.

It is important to note once again that a large and increasing number of Blacks are acquiring middle-class American economic status and cultural patterns, living in suburbs and small cities or towns, and represent significant deviations from the patterns described in this section. Given the positive features of the Black adaptation as described, there is both gain and loss for individual Blacks in this trend.

MEXICAN-AMERICANS (CHICANOS)

The term "Chicano" is preferred by most youth today of Mexican-American heritage. Older, more traditional individuals, and some elite groups still refer to themselves as Mexican-Americans, Latins, or Spanish-Americans. When referring to groups of mixed age and status the term "Mexican-American" or "Latin" will be used since it is used in many studies.

Problems have been somewhat less intense for most Latins than for Blacks making their way in a society dominated by Anglo mainstream culture. The culture of the Latin, derived in part from the Spanish, is respected by Anglos. And a lighter skin color has also an advantage, due to deep built-in prejudices—racism—carried by whites.

Latins have a strong sense of pride in their heritage and are usually unwilling to sacrifice their special identity. "The Mexican-American thinks of himself as both a citizen of the United States and a member of *La Raza* (The Race). The term refers to all Latin-Americans who are united by cultural and spiritual bonds derived from God" (Madsen 1973:17). And the spiritual aspect is often more tenacious than the cultural. As one Mexican-American expressed it, "We are bound together by the common destiny of our souls" (Madsen 1973:17). A college student expressed his dilemma in adapting to Anglo culture and maintaining his sense of Mexican-American identity. He said:

> My ancestors came from one of the most civilized nations in the world. I'm not going to forget what they taught me. I'm proud of being an American but I won't become a gringo . . . the Anglos are denying me the right to be myself. They want me to be like them. I want the chance to be a Mexican-American and to be proud of that Mexican bit. The Anglos offer us equality but whatever happened to freedom? (Madsen 1973:16).

In his study of a town on the Mexican border in Texas, William Madsen found that the Mexican-Americans who attempted to give up their identity were scorned by others and called *Inglesados*. He also found that the elite Latins in the town lived apart and associated freely only with their perceived equals. These elite are descendants of the Spanish land grant families and believe in the old European tradition—that wealth in itself is meaningless unless it is accompanied by an honorable family tree and the refinements of a "cultured life." They look down on other Mexican-Americans as peasants, tradesmen, and upstarts. Thus, in the changing scene, they adapt and keep their identity and status quo by using their special boundary-maintaining devices.

As discussed in the section on values, it was found that Chicano students, representing a wide range in economic and cultural backgrounds, had adopted many American core values. They, more frequently than the Anglos, supported the linkage between success and effort, the belief in the openness of the system, and the value of the individual. And this despite the fact that most had had language problems, experienced culture conflict when they entered school, and suffered because of racism.

Madsen found that the processes of change had produced three acculturative groups among the Mexican-Americans in a Texas county border town. The base line of the culture change process in this community was the traditional folk culture, derived from Mexico and modified by its Texas setting. Although it has been strongly influenced by United States technology and economic factors, the core values of Mexican folk culture are retained. The Mexican-American folk community consists mainly of manual laborers.

The second acculturative group includes people who are caught in the value conflict between the two cultures. They are individuals who were born in traditional families but recognized the conflict between the two sets of values they had learned—those learned from the parents and those learned in school and from the Anglos. These individuals often get along by compartmentalizing their lives, a common tactic used by persons in this kind of situation. On some occasions they live by their parents' values and on other occasions by the values of the Anglos. Some individuals in this group are experiencing severe anxiety over their identity crisis.

Another—the third acculturative group includes those Mexican-Americans who embraced Anglo American values and have acquired status in the English-speaking world. They are relatively successful in economic terms. The three acculturative levels are correlated with the social class structure and are related to a time element, as the three levels usually represent a three-generational process (Madsen 1973:3–4).

In attempting to interpret or understand change and the conflict of cultures inherent in this situation, an analyst, teacher or individual must have some understanding of the core values of their traditional cultures. This understanding on the part of teachers, for example, could reduce the problems encountered by Mexican-American children coming from the more traditional groups.

What are some of the focal values of traditional Mexican-American culture, derived from Mexico, and how do they relate to the adaptation process? A strong belief in fatalism characterizes Mexican and Mexican-American folk culture. The belief that every occurrence is predestined sometimes produces an attitude of resignation, often dulling a person's motivation to succeed. Related to this attitude is a lack of future orientation. Planning ahead is considered presumptuous. Indeed, planning ahead is risky. This attitude can be an impediment to change however justified it might be in the old situation.

As in the case of the urban Black family, most important is the individual's familial role, and the family (an extended family) is the most valued institution in Mexican-American society. The value placed upon family and extended family relationships furnishes support for persons suffering from the effects of culture conflict. The importance of the family persists throughout all of the three acculturative and socioeconomic levels. It is when the emotional and economic constraints become too strong—as when, for example, a son is not allowed to go away to school—that the family becomes an impediment to change.

An important assumption in the traditional folk culture is that the man is stronger, more reliable, and more intelligent than the female. And the concept of *machismo* or manliness is related to this assumption. It is said that one of the common anxieties found in male Latin society is the fear of failure in roles calling for manly behavior. A man must defend his family's honor at all times and remain independent and without obligation to outsiders. Being manly also involves being able to drink without becoming drunk and demonstrating sexual prowess, according to Madsen. This marked male/female dichotomy and an open double standard of sex morality is somewhat incongruent with upper middle-class Anglo values. And wives of upper middle-class and upper-class Mexican-Americans exert more influence in public decision-making than did traditional women. As changes begin to occur in this direction, some males are deeply disturbed by the demands of their wives. There are wives in the upper middle class, however, who prefer to use subtle means for gaining their ends. As one woman remarked, "When I need something from my husband, I don't demand it. I encourage him to think of giving it to me by himself" (Madsen 1973). However, Erich Fromm and Michael Maccoby, in their study of social character in a Mexican village, found that as men accept the new ethic of material progress, they reject the machismo pattern "for an image of manliness based on skill and profit rather than aggression" (Fromm and Maccoby 1970:178).

In the traditional culture, competing with one another for desired ends and trying too hard to succeed is considered dangerous behavior. People believe that there is only a limited amount of desired goods and resources, and one must not try to get more than his or her share. To evoke another's envy is a fearful thing and can result in retaliation through an act of witchcraft. If a person tries to gain more material or social success than his friends, he becomes the subject of ridicule and gossip. One man said:

> My people cannot stand to see another rise above them. When I rented my own little store, my best friends became jealous. When I painted my house, my neighbors thought I was trying to shame them. . . . Everyone tries to pull the one above him down to his own level. If you try to get ahead, you make enemies. If you don't get ahead you are criticized for laziness or stupidity. My people are hard to live with (Madsen 1973: 24).

This is an excellent example of the double-bind people in transition find themselves in when they are subject to the demands of two cultures at the same time. In spite of many problems, however, the Mexican-American, unlike the Black, is functioning without the historical experience of slavery and the consequent hatreds towards whites, plus the fact that the part of his or her culture derived from the Spaniards is shared by Anglos as "Western culture."

CHICANO PRISONERS

Chicano prisoners at San Quentin (comprising 18 percent of the inhabitants) joined with other Chicano prisoners in California to create a special subculture—the "Baby Mafia" or "Family"—that enables them to survive with honor as prisoners. Chicano prisoners in particular fared badly, as many could not understand English. They were intimidated and unjustly punished some times because they could not verbally defend themselves.

R. Theodore Davidson, an anthropologist, was able to gain the confidence of

Chicano prisoners at San Quentin and to present in his case study (1974) the prisoners' subculture as the prisoners themselves experience and know it.

The subculture created was first called "Baby Mafia" and later changed to "Family." Only Chicano convicts were allowed membership. Most Chicanos were "convicts," defined as prisoners who never cooperated with the staff. "Inmates," in contrast, cooperated with the prison establishment, often to the extent of "snitching" on convicts.

The founding members of Family realized that the typical Chicano prisoner is at a disadvantage. He is undereducated and either unskilled or poorly prepared to make a decent living. He is often treated with contempt by authorities, which creates a non-*macho* situation. Thus the primary "Family" goal is to preserve the right of Chicano prisoners to live as human beings in a *macho* manner (Davidson 1974:82). A strict code of Family ethics is adhered to by all members. If another prisoner should cheat or threaten Family in some way it is an affront to Family's pride and means certain death to the individual. As Davidson (1974:82) wrote:

> Family members take great pride in their daily dealings with each other and with other prisoners. They feel that their morality and ideals are above reproach, especially when compared with the immorality or lack of ethics of some staff members and most inmates. Members are fair and trustworthy. If a member says he will do something there is no questioning by others; for it is done. Group decisions are carefully considered and adjudged moral. Family goes to great effort to be sure that its actions are right; if mistakes are made, they are honest ones. . . . Family actions accord with the highest ideals of *machismo*; they are honest and moral when viewed from within the prisoner culture.

Davidson is able to give a detailed account of Family organization—leadership, the power structure, and major activities. The two main types of activity are protective (related to members) and economic. Family has a Chicano Fund to help needy members or dependents on the outside. They also support Chicano causes and contribute to a Chicano education fund.

Family members are very secretive about their group, and inmates and most convicts know very little about the organization. A few trustworthy convicts act as "go-betweens" for Family. Family controls the economy of all prisoners, the prices of goods, and the complicated market exchange system. It is impossible for the small number of guards to keep all areas of the prison under surveillance, thus Family is able to engage in elaborate illegal economic activities. The narcotics trade is the most lucrative and is made possible through guards (bulls) who act as "runners." About 10 percent of the guards who run do get caught, but one guard netted around $100,000 in one year before quitting his job, according to Davidson.

Family was successful in protecting Chicano prisoners. For the prisoner it seemed as a family substitute. It supported the traditional values of *machismo*, family loyalty, honor, and respect for the individual. Davidson did his work at San Quentin at the request of prison administrators who wanted to see if an anthropologist could determine what subcultural factors were responsible

for Mexican-American prisoners being excessively violent and unusually re-
luctant to participate in rehabilitation activities. The study did point out the
salient factors related to the violence (importance of *machismo*, honor, etc.)
and the smooth functioning of the Family geared to "protect" its members.
Protection meant violence, but it was patterned and predictable violence and
"ethical," as related to the Chicano Family code, however it seemed from outside.

AMERICAN INDIANS (NATIVE AMERICANS)

Introduction

American Indian youth prefer to be called "Native Americans," but the
term "American Indian" will be used when it refers to specific cultures and
to the literature where that term is employed.

The traditional cultures of all American Indians were, of course, non-
Western. Views of the world and of nature were divergent. The future in
most traditional Indian cultures was not important; even time itself may have
had little significance. This meant that a profound reformulation of belief
systems at the cultural level, and of mentalistic processes at the psychological
level, has been required as American Indians have adapted to Western culture
from a traditional cultural baseline.

Each American Indian culture is unique and distinctive, with its own
language and system of beliefs. We also find a great variety of coping strategies
adopted by individuals from various tribes. For reasons often related to the
type of traditional culture, some groups are able to cope with Western culture
with less cost than others. Some of these variations among American Indian
groups have been dealt with in previous sections of the book. In analyzing
cultural factors, we saw that the Navajo were open to change and welcomed
the veterans who returned with new ideas. As was pointed out, the Navajo
system had always been adaptive, with patterns of social relations that permitted areas of freedom for the expression of individuality. It is erroneous to
assume, however, that the Navajo are readily embracing the tenets of mainstream American culture. In spite of their positive attitude toward change,
the Navajo have rigorously rejected the American middle-class value system.
These values, expressed in the Protestant ethic, are in direct conflict with
Navajo values. The conservative Navajo are mainly interested in the here and
now rather than in the future. The Navajo enjoy the religious experience, and
their rituals furnish a vehicle for expression of pleasurable emotions. Thus it
is difficult for a Navajo to accept the austere Christian attitudes of reverence
and repression of pleasurable feelings in the religious situation. To a Navajo,
man is the greatest thing in the universal scheme. Thus, the idea that he is
conceived in sin and must sacrifice and do penance is incomprehensible
(Reichard 1949). And by tenaciously clinging to some of their basic values,
Navajo have been able to retain their identity.

The Hopi, living in the same environment, had historically resisted change and rejected their returning veterans who could not conform to traditional ways. Their system is tightly organized, with emphasis on the group and cooperation.

It must be added that in recent years, many of the Pueblos—the Hopi being one group—have abandoned their subsistence farming economy and have adopted the Western credit system. Working for wages in nearby towns is common. But in spite of outward materialistic and economic changes, the Pueblo remain a communal people with their traditional religion and ceremonial life remaining intact. They, like the Navajo, are still able to retain their Indian identity.

Due to cultural and psychological convergences, the Blood Indian male could function in whiteman culture and retain his Indian identity. It was also found that Blood Indian women became isolated and lost important cultural roles while adapting to the contemporary scene. We saw that the perceptual structure (mentalistic patterning) of both male and female Menominee Indians in the traditional culture would be a severe block to their adaptation to the whiteman's world. Thus the "successful" (in middle-class American terms) Menominee are people who have changed drastically both culturally and psychologically. Modern Menominee women on the contemporary scene are playing vital roles in the reservation leadership. This was due to events which allowed them to assume the most important power roles on the reservation.

Other coping strategies noted earlier in the book included some where people gave their lives attempting to keep their traditional religious beliefs. Wovoka was cited as a leader of an ill-fated revivalistic movement. The Peyote Cult was one of the more successful movements. Menominee peyotism was used as an example of a unique coping strategy, combining Indian and Christian elements in a creative fashion.

Basin Groups

Keeping an Indian identity has been a crucial problem for all groups faced with coping with the dominant American culture. The Pueblos and Navajo were relatively successful in doing so, but some groups fared very badly and were essentially annihilated physically or culturally by the whiteman with his superior technology. The Basin groups, inhabiting the semi-arid area between the Rocky Mountains and the range further west, are an example. Living at a basic subsistence level with meager material equipment and available food in the desert-like areas was precarious in the old culture. But when Indians such as the Ute moved to the whiteman's towns, hoping to find food and lacking any skills, they segregated into small groups and became apathetic. The people in the small towns in the area believed that the Indians were incompletely evolved and biologically incapable of successful participation in American culture, partly because of their marginal subsistence level and partly because of their lack of adaptation to town life. These beliefs placed insurmountable barriers in the path of the Indian (Stewart 1952).

On the other hand, some Basin groups, such as the Washo Indians of California and Nevada, made a unique kind of temporary adjustment to the impact of another culture. Unlike the Paiute raiders, the Washo had no escape. They were surrounded by ranchers and trading posts. The invading whiteman provided opportunities for the Washo who wished to take advantage, and the constant scarcity of food for the Basin groups made them ready to seize any advantage available. The farmers of Western Nevada needed the Indians to harvest crops and help around the farm. A symbiotic relationship developed between individual Washo families and individual farmers. James Downs describes this relationship:

> ... few white ranchers would let Indians starve if he knew them. Individual families and bunches began to develop close relationships with individual farmers. In the spring, the Indians drifted into the mountains to fish and hunt, but as the summer wore on, they came back into the valleys to gather what wild food was still available and to work in the harvests, hold a "gumsaba," pick pine nuts, and then set up a winter camp near a ranch or farm. If their food ran short, they could depend on the farmer to contribute a few sacks of potatoes or flour or even a side of beef for their survival. During this period many Washo began to adopt the last names of their rancher benefactors. Because Indian girls often bore the children of early ranchers, the names were often deserved. These Indian-white relationships were the basis on which many Indian families recognized their kinship to a white family. The whites, more inhibited about the sexual adventures of their ancestors, are less willing to openly recognize the relationship. But nonetheless, there is a curious unspoken recognition even today between Indian and white descendants of the same pioneer forefathers. (Downs 1966:87)

This adaptation lasted only as long as the family-run pioneering ranches were in operation. And the Washo later found themselves in the same predicament as the Ute.

Comanche

Some people in transition among the Comanche Indians also fared badly and reacted to the confusion and tension inherent in the transitional status by developing what the Comanche refer to as "ghost sickness," a paralysis of voluntary muscles believed to be inflicted by a ghost. E. Jones, who studied this phenomenon among the Comanche, found that the victims were individuals who had *failed to adapt* to white society, and, finding cultural marginality unendurable, wished to reintegrate with the traditional group. Jones believes that the sickness is comparable to a hysterical conversion (Jones 1972:85–86). This is an efficient and effective disorder for the victim, as he becomes visibly "Indian" and can only be cured by a native doctor. By becoming the patient of the native doctor, he indicates his faith in the ancient Comanche curing ritual and, when cured, will have his faith substantiated. In this condition, the individual is pitied by other Comanche who, in ideal Comanche form, show him generosity and kindness. And, usually, the victim has found a way out of his intolerable emotional state (Jones 1972). The transitional state, where they were caught between two cultures, was unendurable for these people.

Menominee

There are some who find this in-between situation advantageous and feel quite comfortable in it. One Menominee woman, for example, was born of Catholic parents but chose to identify with her great-grandmother, who had a widespread reputation as a curing doctor and a witch. The woman herself soon became known as a "witch." Her longing for power was a chief motivating force in her life, and she is proud of her reputation. She says: "I can cure anyone of sickness. When she (great-grandmother) died, she said, 'Here's a seed, eat it and dream of medicine I know.' When someone's sick, I know what's wrong. Then I go out and pick it. She said I would know what she knowed" (L. Spindler 1962:80).

Many people on and off the reservation came to her for cures. With outsiders she would sometimes use a crystal ball for looking into the future and could sometimes charge large fees. With her Indian identity, she functioned relatively well in the white world.

Seminole Indians

"Keeping their identity at all cost" is creating some serious problems for a group of Florida Seminole Indians studied by Merwyn Garbarino (1972). Intent on keeping their identity as "Mikasuki," a small, isolated Seminole or "Creek" Indian community, the Indians did not consider themselves part of any larger group in the general society. They realized they were American citizens, but they felt themselves set apart from all other ethnic groups and, to some extent, other Creek Indians. The traditional culture valued individualism and keeping out of others' affairs. Today, in traditional fashion, they refuse to take any community responsibility or to even interfere with the activities of their teenagers. This means, for example, danger to public health because of lack of garbage disposal or properly constructed latrines for the community. It also means that unsophisticated teenagers sniff glue without parental constraint. This Seminole group has been able to maintain its identity and to live apart. Very few have ever been in a whiteman's home and when they view the outside world through TV, they see no correspondence to their own lives (Garbarino 1972).

Blackfeet Indians

One Indian group made such a unique adjustment to the dominant white culture, enabling those who wished to retain their Indian identity to do so, that the observer anthropologist believes it could serve as a model for others.

Malcolm McFee found this special type of adjustment to modernization among the Blackfoot Indians of Montana. After 230 years of adaptation and adjustment to change, a bicultural community has evolved, held together by special bonds. The white-oriented group is organized around basic values such as work, self-dependence, individuality, acquisitiveness, and work toward future goals. The major goal of the Indian-oriented group is to retain its ethnic identity. It maintains traditional definitions of the good person, and particularly the value placed upon generosity. This value operates against the achievement necessary for full economic integration with the dominant society (McFee 1972:120).

McFee (1972:121) describes the bicultural community, with two distinct groups sharing a common reservation social structure:

> The past events have not resulted in tribal disorganization, but in a reorganization that accommodates the simultaneous persistence of many traditional social and cultural characteristics from both interacting societies. A large part of the tribe has adopted the culture of the dominant society and aspires to assimilate. A smaller number, for reasons already mentioned, retains more from the Blackfeet past and resists further change. The reservation social structure has changed to accommodate these contrasting points of view. The structure of a nonreservation community tends to be unilinear, with one general set of values, and one status hierarchy. But the physical and social boundaries of the reservation and the tribe incorporate two societies, and make possible a linear structure that offers a choice of alternative limitations and possibilities for adaptation. An individual, consciously or otherwise, can choose, and possibly choose again, which pattern he wishes to follow. His choice, and his acceptance and class assignment, depend upon what he brings to the situation in the way of aspirations, experiences, and capabilities.

McFee believes that the Blackfoot example of cultural pluralism could serve as a model for American society as a whole. It was possible to become a "successful" Indian economically, while retaining a "Blackfoot" identity.

As more Indians are demanding and gaining the right to make their own decisions and are replacing whites in power and leadership roles in Indian communities, problems of coping are diminishing. Maintaining an Indian identity is of prime importance. "Red Power" groups of Native Americans were created primarily by Indians to assert their separate identity and receive equal treatment and opportunity. The youth in particular are ready to join a common "Indian" cause, while at the same time maintaining their own Indian identity.

And now many thousands of Native Americans live in cities. They are often the least conspicuous minority group in the city and live and work like most Americans. Nevertheless, most retain contact with other Indians through organizations like the Association of Confederated Tribes, the United Brotherhood, and many others, and through a network of social and kin relationships extending, usually, back to the reservation community. Some retain active membership in traditional religious groupings or peyotism. In a truly pluralistic society this kind of adaptation will become more possible.

PART IV

Overviews

It is customary to end books with conclusions. This book does not end with conclusions but with overviews of methodology and perspectives on the future. We have not arrived at a,b,c,d kinds of conclusions, as one might as the result of a laboratory experiment. We have, hopefully, acquired some understandings of how human groups adapt to change. The understandings are in the case materials and discussions and have been stated. The Highlights section at the end of this unit summarizes the most important ones as an aid to study and review. The Overviews following serve a different purpose. The first one explores briefly the overall strategy of the analysis of sociocultural change in this Basic Unit and its implications for change theory. The second samples the ways in which an anthropological view of sociocultural process, as gained from studying this unit, can influence one's perception of something as all-encompassing and significant as the future.

Comments on Models

The purpose of the first two sections of this book was to furnish a way of thinking about and a way of ordering the ideas, processes, and models that comprise the important and complex field of sociocultural change. Models were used as a means of categorization, since a model is, as stated in the introduction, a statement of working relationships between processes within a problem area.

The grand model of a sociocultural system and its interrelated parts was the author's attempt to diagram in broad terms the various kinds of stimuli, both from within and without the system, that cause cultural change. It seems relatively obvious that sociocultural systems change through processes of borrowing from other systems and reintegrating or resynthesizing the new elements. It also seems clear that another very important source of culture change is the individual and his or her creative acts of innovation, most of which, like genetic mutations, do not survive. The ones that do survive, that are accepted and become a part of the sociocultural system, are a continuing source of change. The role of the environment represented in Figure 1, however, is often misunderstood or ignored. It must always be taken into account. Contemporary anthropologists are again recognizing the importance of some of the tenets of neo-evolutionary theories. Sociocultural systems evolve as they are adapting to their environment, and natural selection, as in biological evolution, plays an important role in determining what will survive. In a limited sense, then, the Grand Scale Model is related to a neo-evolutionary model. The discrepancy between the two, however, is that the model presented in this book emphasizes the individual—individual behavior, individual mentalistic processes, individuals innovating and making decisions.

Mini-models were used as an aid in categorizing the vast array of processes, problems, and interests in the field of contemporary culture change. They represent special emphases and limited relationships between processes in the field of action that was delimited by the grand model of a sociocultural system furnished in Figure 1. The mini-models are interrelated, as are the processes of sociocultural change, and these interrelationships are crucial to an understanding of the dynamics of change. As each mini-model was introduced an attempt was made to relate it briefly to other mini-models and to its placement (level of analysis, relationship to environment, or relationship to other systems) in the grand scale model. Mini-models varied in the degree of complexity of inter-relationships with other models and the relationship to the sociocultural system represented in Figure 1.

For example, it was pointed out that the Acculturation Mini-Model related to systems in contact was functionally related to all of the mini-models except the Ecological and Innovation Mini-Models. The analyses included in the Acculturation Mini-Model are mainly related to the social and cultural levels of the sociocultural system represented in Figure 1. On the other hand, the Ecological Mini-Model is only indirectly related to other mini-models. It acts as a limiting and causative factor for behaviors such as innovating, making decisions, and the invention of personal coping strategies for survival. Analyses by anthropologists who use this model are mainly done at the social or cultural level, in terms of the grand model for sociocultural change.

An attempt was made to bring the mini-models up to date. Some have antecedents extending far back in the history of the field (the Acculturation, Diffusion, and Modernization Mini-Models in particular) and others are of relatively recent origin (the Ecological, Decision-Making, and Behavioral Analysis Mini-Models). All, however, have some very contemporary foci and the discussion was largely confined to these foci.

In keeping with the contemporary focus of the mini-models, extensive case study materials were selected as relevant mainly to contemporary changes. The reason for including the case materials was to acquaint the student with the varieties of coping strategies used by individuals and groups in reacting to internal and external stimuli. It was hoped that reading about actual socio-cultural change in process would enable the student to understand better the abstract concepts and theories about sociocultural change.

The third part of the book—Change and Persistence in Special Areas—focuses on change crucial to an understanding of the great transformation rather suddenly affecting most sociocultural systems today. Focal areas of con-flict and change were selected for discussion—women's roles, and, related to the American scene, changing core American values, youth cults, and the identity conflicts and problems of ethnic and Third-World peoples. The justification for turning attention to special change processes in the United States is that from most readers' point of view this is where the most relevant action is taking place, and also because anthropologists are reorienting much of their current research to complex societies in general and the United States in particular.

The scheme used for the first sections of the book to present culture change materials related to all problem areas was not applied explicitly in the presenta-tion of data in Part III. The shift was from a focus on concepts and research strategies to one on content. The materials presented were derived from analyses using the mini-models in the first sections, but the data in Part III are sometimes in summary form and are the result of many pieces of research, using many mini-models. To untangle these relationships to the mini-models would take us well beyond the purpose of this section.

Most anthropologists viewing the present status of the field of sociocultural change would agree that it is not yet possible to build a comprehensive model of sociocultural change that reveals precise interconnections of ecological, economic, ideational, psychological and social factors (Keesing 1976:224). Some suggestions by contemporary anthropologists for building this comprehensive model would lead us to combine an expansion of neo-Marxist theory with systems theory.

The question might be raised as to whether or not we need a grand scale model for sociocultural change. The mini-models presented here, and others, refined sufficiently, might serve by themselves to make these complex materials more manageable. Perhaps combinations of special models such as the Decision-Making Mini-Model and some aspects of the adaptionist specific evolution model might introduce order to the complex kinds of data produced in the study of contemporary sociocultural systems and their continuing adaptations.

Each mini-model, however, includes quite a range of processes in order to provide a framework within which the researcher and analyst can work. The problem is to be able to see relationships between the models. Otherwise we may end up calling the same processes of change by different names and not understanding the interconnections. This is particularly problematic in dealing with new areas of research such as modernization and urbanization. Acculturation, diffusion, innovation, psychocultural adaptation, ecological processes are all involved. So far there has been little systematic ordering and analysis of these processes and their interrelationships in modernization and urbanization studies. This unit has taken some steps in this direction.

Looking into the Future

This book has dealt with what has been and is now happening around the world as humankind struggles to adapt to the changing conditions of life on our planet. The future remains, as it always has, a challenge. Our understanding of probable events and their consequences will remain uncertain and tentative, no matter what knowledge we have or what intellectual discipline we have acquired. Nevertheless, our understandings have been shaped by the concepts and case materials we have encountered in this Basic Unit, including our understanding of the future.

The variety of case materials presented in this book, drawn from peoples throughout the world adapting to change shows us that the human potential for adaptation is almost limitless. The results of this potential in action are unpredictable in any formal or specific sense. Some human communities virtually transform their way of life overnight, as did the Manus. Others resist, sometimes at bitter cost, being assimilated or reduced to a common standard, as have the Hutterites, Gypsies, and only a little less dramatically, the people of Almonaster, Spain. Others create unanticipated solutions to conflict and alienation as have the Peyotists, Children of Krsna, and the Hippies. The varieties of strategies individuals and groups use to avoid being swept up by the forces of change seem entirely unpredictable, from a common-sense point of view. And yet, using the tools and concepts of anthropology we can classify them, isolate and describe basic processes, and identify, to some extent, the conditions that bring them about.

This still does not enable us to make highly specific predictions about the shape of the future, but it does enable us to ask the right questions and sketch out alternative answers. Recently the editors of the *National Geographic* invited five "famed thinkers to discuss possible outlines of the future" (July 1976:68). Would our views as anthropologically informed thinkers differ from theirs? The five guests included a publisher, an author, an attorney, a biochemist, and the inimitable Buckminster Fuller. All are exceptional people, with wide experience, expertize in certain areas, and maturity. But none had any anthropological training, insofar as we know. All were asked to comment on the future. Their comments attended to technological developments, the habitation

146

of outer space, future concepts of land ownership, the restoration of the land, income redistribution, communication, and urbanization.

Buckminster Fuller commented, "In times past, with 90 percent of humanity living on farms, the human race was inherently remote. Every nation looked out for its own welfare. But now we are in absolute critical proximity. A completely new world has come about" (1976:73).

Edmund N. Bacon, noted city planner who helped spark the rebirth of Philadelphia, said: "In the future we have to perceive ourselves as urban people. The mere acceptance of the notion that we are an urban civilization will be an important revolution in thought, because we still cling to the nostalgic idea that we are primarily rural" (1976:74).

Isaac Asimov, author of 172 books ranging from science fiction to a guide to science, described a ". . . global village, tied together electronically, with every citizen able to communicate instantly with every other" (1976:73).

The concerns to which these commentators addressed themselves are similar to those we have encountered on the pages of this Basic Unit. Their comments, quite understandably, lack anthropological specificity, and at times imply a lack of background knowledge that our journey through ideas and cases could supply.

What do the commentators mean by "urban people" and "critical proximity"? What are their models? What is the urbanization process we must pass through to become urban people? As we saw, urbanization is not a linear or simple process. It occurs in a variety of ways, depending upon many factors— geographical, ethnic, historical, and so on. And the "rational" city model, as we have come to understand it, has not been able to deal with the life and death problems of overpopulation, pollution, and depletion of critical resources.

In general, the commentators seem to be talking to and about modern industrial nations, or perhaps just the Western nations. There does not seem to be a model of cultural differences and of the enormously different rates and kinds of development in different parts of the globe. Buckminster Fuller, for example, might be surprised to learn that one half to two thirds of the world population today may be considered peasant and that much of this population may well be arrested in a post-peasant stage, subsisting on individual family labors and cultivation. When he refers to the "human race" is he including small tribal groups, peasant villages, the ethnically distinctive minorities within large-scale societies? Probably only a student of peasantry such as Fred Gamst would comment that when and if urban civilization again collapses, the post-peasantries will still be around to constitute the supportive sector of the new post-industrial civilization (1974:71).

A student of anthropology, knowing something of cultural differences and responses might be critical of Asimov's concept of instant communication everywhere in our "global village." Not everyone wants to communicate, instantly or not, with everyone else. The traditional Menominee would have been horrified by the idea. It implies a violation of privacy and autonomy that would be intolerable to them. True, there are not enough traditional Menominee about to make this a serious problem in itself, but the point is valid that intercultural and ethnic differences may have more to do with communication than electronic know-how does.

It is difficult to understand from the vantage point of the urban-oriented Western sophisticate that urbanization is not a one-way street and that urbanization and industrialization are not necessarily concomitant. Some people, like the Qemant, industrialize without urbanizing. And we know that urbanization occurred long before industrialization in Africa, the Middle East, and elsewhere. Further, we understand from our studies that the old and the new exist side by side in many urban settings. People stubbornly recreate their pasts in new contexts. All "rational" environments are humanized by irrational beliefs, identities, and social relationships. If people don't want to become urban on urban planner terms, they will create their own definitions of urban and of the good life within the new environment. We encountered, in this Basic Unit, many cases where this was occurring in one way or another.

It is imperative, from the anthropological point of view, to specify the intended range of one's statements, taking into account cultural diversity both within and between the world's populations. It is particularly important not to let a kind of generalized model of "twentieth century Western urban industrial sociocultural system" dominate one's imagery and thinking.

The student of anthropology should also have broadened insights into his or her own culture. "American," for example, should mean something very complicated. The many strands of conflicting values, rural-urban differences, the variety of ethnic groups, the "core" culture and its influence, the current coping movements, and the colorful and dynamic results in sects and life styles, the changing statuses and roles of men and women in relationship to each other and to the community make generalization hazardous. We proceed with caution to analyze our society. It defies sweeping characterization. And yet we make progress by organizing our observations and thoughts about our diversity and its many-faceted movement.

And what of the future? It is not possible to make definitive statements, particularly as anthropologists. We can be sure, however, that the future world population will be diversified. While old cultural and ethnic differences are disappearing, new ones are emerging. Traditional identities are fading, but new, quite unexpected ones are proliferating. No matter that they may be created virtually overnight and often as a base for power politics, they are a part of a new diversity.

We may also be sure that the people in our coming New World will creatively combine the past and present in unexpected ways, just as the Hippie movement, so patently counter-cultural on the surface, should in some ways represent a uniquely American approach to problems of alienation in a too-affluent and grievously threatened society. We must know our present basic assumptions, values, and beliefs in order to acquire any intimation of what our future will be like, and the same applies to every other people of the earth.

The future may well see a world that is inhabited by substantially fewer people, most living in an essentially peasant mode, if we do not move rapidly enough from a petroleum based technology to new forms of power. But even if the new technologoy does rescue us in time, an electronic "instant communication" future does not ensure homogeneity, for contact and communication beget message resistance, withdrawal, and attempts to define identities (so one knows whom one is talking to) as well as common understandings.

More likely than world cultural standardization in any complete sense is a surface commonality and likeness in material goods, technology, and survival values (such as positive value placed on environmental preservation) but diversity in habits, values, and beliefs in all sorts of private and semi-private sectors. One of our problems will be what kinds and how much diversity can be tolerated in view of our common need for survival and reasonable global management (presuming that we survive the transfer from petroleum to other power sources). The present period of intense proliferation of cults and deviant life styles is unlikely to result soon in a stabilized, standardized world society. The future, in many ways, will probably be an extension of the present, with minimum effective constraints and reorientations to make it possible to survive, and some new technology that most of us will accept as a part of our environment but not something that we understand or control.

The long range effects of this technological revolution, and particularly the so-called micro-electronic revolution, are the subject of a great deal of speculation. The astrophysicist Robert Jastrow predicts that computers will, indeed, "take over" and that our life form as we know it, based on the oxygen cycle, will become obsolete as silicon based computer-like entities become dominant. While we need not immediately contemplate this particular transformation of life as we know it, there is little doubt that the effects of the microelectronic revolution will be enormous.

Some social scientists are engaged in "Futures" research which attempts to delineate the shape of things to come. Robert Textor, a Stanford University Anthropologist, has developed a method for developing the "art of anticipation" or "conditional forecasting" of futures during rapid technological change. His work helps raise consciousness about the nature of the microelectronic revolution that we are already well into, and the need to assert human and humane influence over it. His method includes collecting specific scenarios with respect to alternative futures for certain societies from political leaders, critics, policy makers, and planners. The scenarios are subjected to systematic analysis using well worked out models. The futures research done by him and Stanford Students at Stanford in Austria is reported in his book, *Austria 2005*, 1983, listed in the Selected Recent References.

Microelectronic developments can cause serious unemployment problems, and our work ethic will be challenged when the twenty hour week is the norm. The use of computers in the workplace and in the home is already causing a realignment of values, relationships, concepts of productivity, definitions of work, sex roles, and leisure time. A systematic anticipation of these influences upon our lives can prove to be very useful.

PART V

Study Aids

Questions to help guide review of this Basic Unit and a summary of the highlights of the entire book are included below to help master the content of this very complex field. Some people will find it useful to read both the questions and the highlights before starting to read the book, then work out answers to the questions, using the highlights as a further guide to the text.

Questions to Help Guide Review

Part I

1. What does the term "culture" mean as used in this book?
2. What is meant by the term "cultural compulsives"?
3. What does the term "sociocultural system" include?
4. Into what three aspects or levels is the sociocultural system divided for analytic purposes?
5. How is cultural diffusion related to acculturation?
6. In what ways is the sociocultural model for change related to functionalism?
7. What is the relationship between the mini-models and the grand model for change?
8. Why is the study of persistence important to the study of change?

Part II

Diffusion Mini-Model

1. What are the differences between reinterpretation and syncretism? Give some examples from the contemporary United States.
2. What kinds of change dynamics does the case of substituting steel axes for stone axes among the Yir Yiront illustrate?
3. What is unusual about the cultural borrowing from the American Indian?

Innovation Mini-Model

1. How is the Innovation Mini-Model interrelated with the Diffusion and Acculturation Mini-Models?
2. Describe an innovative recombination of ideas that you have had.
3. At what point does an innovative pattern generate change?
4. How is the concept "cultural focus" related to innovation?
5. How is "world view" related to the spread of innovations?

Ecological Mini-Model

1. How does the case of the Tanala illustrate the importance of the role played by the social environment in ecological adaptation?
2. How do the decisions of the Yungay illustrate the observation that scientific realities and sociocultural realities are often different and in conflict with each other?

153

Acculturation Mini-Model

1. How does the use of the Acculturation Mini-Model by contemporary anthropologists differ from the use by earlier researchers (that is, compare 1936 and 1954 uses with contemporary concepts)?
2. What does the term "emulative model" refer to?
3. How, through contact with Americans, was the Palauan sense of identity revived?
4. How would you define "boundary-maintaining" devices?
5. How can it be made easier for peoples to cope when they are being "forced" to adapt to a technologically superior culture?
6. What does the term "compartmentalization" refer to?

Modernization-Urbanization Mini-Model

1. What are the important features of a "city"?
2. Who are peasants and how widespread is peasantry?
3. What countries furnish the models for modernizing?
4. What is "network analysis"?
5. What is meant by the term "lagging emulation" introduced in the case study of the Greek village?
6. How do the modernization processes in Orašac, the Serbian village, differ from those in other communist countries?
7. Contrast the modernizing processes in the two Spanish villages. How has Almonaster been able to curtail out-migration?
8. What are some of the strategies used by the following groups to resist change: Toba Batak, Qemant, Zinacantecos, and Burgbachers?
9. Why was modernization relatively simple for the Japanese?
10. What positive features do some authors (Redfield and Toffler) describe for the modernization process?

Psychocultural Mini-Models

1. How do studies using Psychocultural Mini-Models differ in focus from those using other models?
2. What is a mazeway? How is it related to revitalization movements?
3. Why is peyotism a reactive movement?
4. How were social, economic, and cultural changes paralleled by changes in psychological adaptation for the Menominee?
5. In what different ways are behavioral analyses utilized by anthropologists and others?
6. What does "raising the level of cultural awareness" mean?
7. What kinds of constraints does a member of a sociolcultural system experience when he or she is making a choice?
8. What is a basic assumption made by those focusing on the "entrepreneur" as an important agent for change?

Part III

1. What appears to happen to women's roles during the earlier phases of modernization?
2. Do women appear to be more or less conservative in their attitudes toward change than men? Why?
3. Explain the reasons, in each case presented, for the attitude toward change.

4. What are the most important features of the traditional-emergent values shift?
5. What American cultural values have remained constant for the Stanford sample over the 22 year period?
6. Which values appeared to have changed substantially during this period?
7. What core values did minority students appear to support?
8. What are some of the probable reasons for the disillusionment of many modern youth with American culture?
9. What do the Hippies and the children of Krsna have in common? How are they different? What are their relationships to mainstream society?
10. Why is it misleading to interpret the urban Black family as described by Aschenbrenner from the viewpoint of the white middle-class family? How are male and female roles different in the Black family type described? How are children treated?
11. What functions do violence and aggression fill for the Vice Lords with respect to group cohesion and organization?
12. What are the ideological sets in Vice Lord culture?
13. What are the major features of the traditional Mexican folk culture? How, given these features, does it conflict with Anglo culture?
14. What are the major levels of acculturation posited by Madsen? Can you see ways to relate the conflicts mentioned above to the processes described?
15. Why did Chicano prisoners at San Quentin create the "Family"? What functions does the Family have for convicts? How does it work?
16. What are some major differences in the ways in which the American Indian groups mentioned adapted to the impact of the dominant Anglo culture? How do you explain these differences?

Highlights for Review

The strategy used in analyzing sociocultural change in this Basic Unit, including the relationship between the grand scale model and the mini-models was discussed under "Comments on Models." In the section following, the main points of the case materials and discussions related to the mini-models, and the special areas included under Part III, are summarized as an aid to review.

Materials included in the *Innovation Mini-Model* illustrate how innovations, although spread through diffusion, represent the special products of a unique and creative recombination of previously existing ideas into new ideas. While innovation is commonplace and all normal individuals have innovative ideas, until a new idea or thing is accepted by a large number of individuals in a social group, it is not an innovation. A variety of case materials showed how real individuals innovated new *things* (i.e., the invention of a detachable outrigger) or ideas (i.e., Wovoka's new religious movement). In posing the question why some innovations are accepted and some rejected, the importance of understanding the "cultural compulsives" and "world view" of a people was pointed out.

The *Diffusion Mini-Model*, referring to cultural borrowing, included case materials that made us aware of the enormous amount of the cultural paraphernalia of United States that has been borrowed (perhaps around 90 percent). Concerning most areas of a culture—included in customs, habits, language, or modes of thought—the borrowing has been from the most prestigeful (usually Western) to the less technologically developed culture. Thus it comes as somewhat of a shock to Americans when they learn of the extensive influence the first Americans—the American Indians—have had on their culture.

The diffusion mini-model also included materials relating to how people select certain special items and then, in unique and creative ways, syncretize and reinterpret them to "fit." And, in the classic case of the Yir Yiront, we saw how disruptive borrowing could be.

The *Ecological Mini-Model* includes materials relating to individuals coping with environmental demands. The "environment," as mentioned, consists not only of the natural environment (flora, fauna, rainfall) but of the way it is interpreted by groups of people in terms of their belief systems. Some groups conceive of individuals as being able to manipulate and change their environment while others believe that humans should simply live in and make adjustments *to* their environment. The Chinese were forced to accommodate to the environment of the Tibetans. The Tanala culture underwent sweeping changes while adapting to new environmental demands. The Maori, on the other hand, were able to preserve the "core" of their old culture in the totally new environment of modern New Zealand. In adapting to the environment resulting from a disastrous earthquake in Peru, the inhabitants of Yungay adjusted to the first phases of the new situation with new adaptive patterns. However, after a short period of time had elapsed, we saw that the leaders were willing to place greater value on the maintenance of their former ecological adjustment than upon the possible physical dangers inherent in the new situation. These kinds of findings should make us aware of how important it is for the anthropologist focusing on humans relating to their environment to be aware of the fact that *scientific realities* and *sociocultural realities* are different and often in direct conflict with each other.

In the discussion of the *Acculturation Mini-Model*, it was stressed that most modern anthropologists focus on the modification and reciprocal relationships that occur when individuals from two or more different sociocultural systems come into prolonged contact. When reactions of individuals to new stimuli from another culture are accepted by their group, culture change is occurring. The reactions of individuals, which may later become "group" reactions, are variegated. Case materials represented a sample of the many kinds of reactions to the different situations in which people come in contact with one another.

It was noted that when a more powerful group decides to introduce change in a less politically or technologically powerful group, reactions of the receptor group vary. We saw that when the change is "forced," as illustrated by the Tiwi, it takes a different form than when it is introduced with the support of the people, as in the case of the Swazi. And when the United States technological model is regarded as a superior and "emulative" model, the dynamics of change take on a special form, illustrated by the cases of the peoples of Palau and Manus. We found also that some groups in contact with other cultures resort to extreme strategies in order to resist change. Some, as the Hutterites and Gypsies were successful in controlling the stimuli from outside through the use of elaborate boundary-maintaining devices.

The case materials enabled us to see what happened when new ideas and things were introduced—sometimes they were *incorporated* into the receiving group or were, by the process of *replacement*, merely substituted for the old idea or item. Other methods, discussed in the "Diffusion Mini-Model" were used when accepting new elements into the system, such as *syncretism* and *fusion*.

The Acculturation Model has had some strong critics, but still serves a useful function in aiding the student in analyzing interrelationships between complex phenomena.

Under the *Modernization-Urbanization Mini-Model*, introductory comments were made concerning the *city*. Peoples have been urbanizing for over four thousand years, and although the early cities lie in ruins, the basic model for the city still survives. The "new" city, wherever it is found, is heterogeneous in origin, built upon worldwide interests and based upon "rationality" and efficiency, with varieties of associations serving special interests. The urban model is often presented as one of depersonalized human relationships, with emphasis on progress and efficiency. In reality, however, the situation is modified by people who are continuously creating a human environment wherever they are. The case materials presented were aimed at giving you some insight concerning the variations in strategies peoples use as they become urbanized or modernized. Most populations today undergoing urbanization and modernization are of peasant origin and between one-half to two-thirds of the world population may still be considered peasants. The focus is therefore largely on modernizing peasant communities. A description was given of the personalized world of the peasant, of peasantry, and of the disadvantaged position of the peasant. Colonizing was discussed as a part of modernization and as a method for spreading the culture of the conquerors and exploiting the resources of those colonized.

There are, it was pointed out, contemporary societies of tribal origin that are beginning modernization and industrialization that have never experienced the agrarian peasant level. Modernization, we found, meant an increasing scale of social relationships and development of bureaucracies for all persons and an introduction of standardized machine products to replace traditional arts and crafts for most. Although all peoples in small communities are influenced by the city, which is a "model," industrialization and modernization do not require all persons involved in the process to live within the city. With modern communication systems, the *influence* of the city can be readily diffused to the countryside.

Many contemporary groups, it was pointed out, are pursuing alternate routes to becoming modernized. Some groups have been able to maintain their ethnic identities during the process. These are groups that did not wish to become "Westernized." Some modernizing groups focus on the material achievements of the West and others adopt social values, such as emphasis on individualistic achievement and a "rational" social order. It is not surprising then to find "dual societies" evolving where a modernized sector might exist side by side with a traditional one. Individuals in a developing country sometimes become modernized in political attitudes and remain traditional in agricultural attitudes. The United States serves as a model for many developing countries, but Russia serves as a model for many small new nations, since it represents a rapid development. As Gamst (1974:71) noted, due to lack of sufficient resources, related to pollution and overpopulation, large parts of the peasantries of many countries will be arrested in a postpeasant stage, with a focus on individual family labors and cultivation.

In studying the modernization-urbanization process anthropologists have used sociological survey techniques and concepts along with their anthropological strategies to great advantage. "Network analysis" in particular has proven useful for exploring the relationships among individuals in a village and between individuals there and people in the nearby city. When a village begins to modernize, it is important to understand the kinds of networks, usually ties of kinship and friendship that are being established with the urban dwellers. Network analysis, we found, includes analysis of first and second order contacts and the many-stranded role relationships of the small community, in contrast to the single-stranded role relationships typical of city dwellers.

Although modernization and urbanization processes are generalizeable and rather predictable, each society adds a special, unique twist in the manner of adapting to new stimuli. A variety of factors play important roles in influencing or limiting modes of adaptation, however. In Swiss villages such as Kippel (Friedl 1974) the mountain environment is extremely limiting. Chance factors, such as the development of mines that required only intermittent labor, influenced the course of modernization in a village in Serbia. In some instances, regardless of the pressures to do otherwise, a group of people will objectively assess the social and emotional costs involved in modernizing and will self-consciously decide to slow down the process, as was seen in the case of the inhabitants of Almonaster, Spain.

The variety of case studies presented should help to rectify some of the misconceptions about the regularity of change. Although many social scientists emphasize the negative aspects of modernization and urbanization, some view it as a creative, positive development. As Redfield (1953b) explained, the kinds of people found in the city—such as the administrative elite, the literate jurist, the artist, the musician—are different from the peasant. They can spend time reflecting and looking inwards with a self-consciousness allowing for creativity. And a contemporary author Alvin Toffler (1970:187) feels that the technological revolution will "radiate new opportunities for personal growth, adventure and delight."

The treatment of the Modernization-Urbanization Mini-Model was extensive due to the global relevance and importance of the problems involved in this area of culture change. It comprises one of the most important concerns of the contemporary anthropologist.

Some anthropologists work within the framework of *Psychocultural Mini-Models*. These models deal with the third level of analysis represented in Figure 1, with focus on the individual and his or her psychological processes. The majority of studies of culture change are made at the "systems" level or at the observable social interaction level, omitting the individual. However, working at this level, when the sociocultural system begins to disintegrate and individuation takes place, the anthropologist is unable to explain how individuals adapt during periods of change. An individual's cognitive processes—the way he or she views, sorts, and synthesizes things and events believed to exist in the world—are of first order importance to an understanding of how a person adapts to new stimuli in a changing situation.

Innovation, which was dealt with as a special model, is treated by some anthropologists as mentalistic, as part of the psychocultural process (Barnett

1953). Innovation can in this context be viewed as a recombination of previously existing ideas into a new idea or mental configuration. And changes in ideas are basic and crucial to the study of culture change.

One author, Anthony Wallace (1956), focused on the concept of *mazeway* to relate mentalistic processes to innovation and to the problem of stress reduction during change.

"Mazeway," as was explained, is one person's mental image of nature, society, culture, personality, and body image (Wallace 1956:266). A person's mazeway, under stress conditions related to culture change, can undergo a radical resynthesis. We saw how an individual undergoing this kind of resynthesis can become a prophet, or a leader, creating a new revitalization movement, often recruiting members and teaching them the "new way."

Some forms of revitalization or reactive movements, however, are not the result of a sudden radical mazeway resynthesis. The Peyote Cult, for example, is a synthesis of ideas and patterns from both the dominant and subordinate systems that developed over time. It too is a response to the conflicts inherent in the meeting of incompatible systems and to economic deprivation resulting from the dominant-subordinate relationships. Peyote behavior and ideology serve to reduce stress.

Some anthropologists focus on what happens to an individual's perceptions of himself or herself and the world when the entire sociocultural system undergoes change. This focus was represented by the case materials from the Menominee Indians of Wisconsin.

The use of a behavioral model was discussed as a research tool (Theodore and Nancy Graves) and as a means for manipulating change (Vicos Project). And the problem of the ethics involved in the planned alteration and extinction of a group's behavior was considered.

The behavioral method of the Brazilian social scientist, Paolo Freire, contrasted to the other models used in behavioral modification projects. Freire attempted, through his *conscientizacion* method, to stimulate individuals in a culture to actively participate and interact in their social settings. His aim was to help individuals to become conscious of their own cultures and to become more articulate about their needs and self interests.

Parallels to Freire's method were made to the work of G. Spindler, in which teachers were made aware of the cultures of their non-Anglo or non-middle-class students. Also related to Freire's concepts and methods is the "cultural sensitization" technique and the Instrumental Activities Inventory Model. The former is aimed at sensitizing students and teachers to cultural distortions in interpreting behaviors of people in other cultures. The latter, the Instrumental Activities Inventory Model is based on the assumption, as is Freire's model, that humans are self-activated beings, able to make conscious choices.

The Decision-Making Mini-Model, although used by a small minority of anthropologists, has been growing in popularity. It is particularly useful in studying development and change in newly modernizing nations. The focus is on the behaviors of interacting individuals as they are actually responding to new stimuli, or very shortly thereafter. The model is also termed an "event-analysis" approach, as specific events are being analyzed. An example of this special model was the study of the Fur of Dafur by Barth. He observes changes by statistically measuring new ways that individuals begin to divide their time and resources. M. Mead's study of Paliau, who was responsible for making decisions that resulted in sweeping changes for the people of Manus (1956), was used to illustrate the Decision-Making Mini-Model. Many studies such as this focus upon the activities of the "entrepreneur," a term borrowed from the economists. The term refers to individuals who are controlled less than most people by the constraints of their culture, and Paliau was such a person.

T. Graves and Van Arsdale used this model to advantage in the analysis of why some migrants decided to remain in the city while others returned home. Other researchers using the decision-making model combine it with the mentalistic psychocultural model and are thus able to get at an individual's own perception of the situation. To the extent this is so, this is an *emic* (inside view) in contrast to an *etic* approach which depends upon the anthropologist's perception of the situation. The case materials illustrating this type of decision-making approach were drawn from a study using a modified emic approach, of school children in an urbanizing German village. The choices students made when they were presented with instrumental alternatives related to the greater urbanized area around them, furnished the data for analysis. This approach enabled the researcher to see how the children managed cognitive control in a changing milieu.

The special areas in Part III included the adaptations of women to culture change; change in contemporary U.S.A., including a discussion of American values; the coping strategies of youth cults; and change and minority groups.

We saw that at one level, when women were asked to make choices between the old and the new, many women in cultures such as the Zapotec, Blood Indian, Cree Indian, and peasant German preferred the new life style of the modern world. The women believed they wanted the gadgets and affluence of the urban world, but could not foresee the kind of price they would have to pay for them. The Kaktovik Eskimo women, the Blood Indian women, the Menominee Indian women, and the German peasant women, it was pointed out, were all robbed of significant traditional roles with few rewarding new roles to replace them, at least during the early phases of change, with a consequent reduction in the women's influence and prestige.

In the section on American values, the consensus over a long period of time among authors writing about American culture was pointed out. There have been shifts in values, such as "traditional" to "emergent," but a profile of core American values appears to have remained constant. Minority groups (Blacks, Chicanos, and Native and Asian Americans) also appear to support the core values. This core exhibits great vitality today in spite of the fact that American culture has sustained dichotomous values for at least two hundred years.

The proliferating cults, movements, and communes among American youth reflect in dramatic form the apparent shift in values. They also reflect the search for identity. Although the cults are often called "counter-cultures," many of their values can be traced to cultural values of Western civilization. Hippies, for example, placed emphasis on the individual who must find himself in a crusadelike venture. And the children of Krsna, apparently wholly deviant, emphasize the old American values of hard work, aestheticism, salvation through service, and self-knowledge. Many youth, while rejecting mainstream U.S. culture, appear to be rediscovering, in a creative fashion, the "original" American values.

The section on U.S. minorities focuses on those who have maintained their identity as minorities (Blacks, Chicanos, and Native Americans).

Case materials dealing with the Black family made it clear that the term "culture of poverty" cannot account for the richness in the Black cultural tradition. The Black family has a core of shared values and a life style of its own. It has very special ways for coping with the pressures of the city. And it has been maintained through space and time by means of conscious and ritualized practices.

In contrast to the Black family, which lives within the law, a Black street gang engaged in criminal activities was described. The Vice Lords, as it was called, could be termed a subculture. It has an elaborate structure, a social organization, and commonly held values. The spirit of group solidarity and mutual help assisted the members in coping with and rejecting the establishment.

Another minority group, the Mexican-Americans or Chicanos, it was noted, have a strong sense of pride in their heritage and special identity as members of La Raza (The Race). As in mainstream America, there are class differences recognized among them and means for keeping the status quo. A discussion of core traditional Mexican-American values was presented, since it is crucial to an understanding of the problems faced by this group in its coping with mainstream U.S. culture. Contrastive case materials were included of Chicano prisoners in San Quentin, who created a special subculture called "Baby Mafia" or "Family" in an effort to cope efficiently with the establishment personnel. As was pointed out, they were so well organized and presented such a united front that they were able to realize all their goals and furnish emotional and economic security for their fellow members.

American Indians, or Native Americans, stem from non-Western cultures with views of the world that are sharply divergent from those of the West. They have special problems in coping with this divergence and, at the same time, keeping their identity as Native Americans. Since each American Indian tribe has a distinct culture, and the social and economic situations vary widely, we find a great variety of coping strategies used by Native Americans when adjusting to the impact of white U.S. culture. We saw that some groups like the Blood Indians and the Navajo found coping easier than other groups, such as the Basin tribes. The Blackfoot Indians of Montana furnish a unique example of cultural pluralism. They have succeeded in maintaining their "Indian" identity by forming a bicultural community which held the Indian-oriented and the white-oriented groups together by special bonds. And the researcher, M. McFee, proposes that this example of cultural pluralism could serve as a model for American society as a whole.

The student involved in the study of contemporary sociocultural change soon realizes how rapidly it is occurring today. Today's changes are of such temporary duration that by the time they have been studied they are history. The "Hippie movement," for example, so important a few years ago, can be analyzed now in terms of its impact on mainstream American culture. It was only from the elaborate materials, furnishing a record of how individuals cope with change, such as those recorded here, that we are able to compare and contrast and do limited predicting. With these studies of individuals innovating and experimenting in their attempts to cope with the modern world, we can almost pinpoint what some of the formulae were that led to the successful adoption of some innovations and the rejection of others.

There are many areas on the contemporary scene where there is a special need for more data than we have. We need, for example, to know more about what is happening today to women and to Third World peoples, as both move toward equality. We need more data on decision-making, conscious coping strategies, networks, and specific events.

It has been particularly difficult to sort and organize data into neat schemes or models, since anthropologists are so eclectic in their use of methods, techniques, and theory. The anthropologist rarely uses a single model for the study of change but draws from several in the same study. And anthropologists do not respect a model as such and often change and recombine the models to fit their changing needs. Flexibility is the hallmark of the anthropologist. As the dimensions of change—the social, the cultural, the individual, and the environmental—are closely interrelated, it follows that the models themselves (or mini-models) can be viewed as interrelated patterns of concepts and ideas, related to the sociocultural system itself.

Selected Recent References

Selections most suitable for beginners in anthropology are marked with an asterisk.

Abbot, Susan and John van Willigen, eds. 1980, Predicting Sociocultural Change. Athens: University of Georgia Press. Seven articles examine predictions based on fieldwork in Brazil, Guatemala, Kenya, the Southwestern U.S., West Ireland, and Minnesota.

Bodley, John H. 1982, Victims of Progress. Menlo Park: Benjamin/Cummings. Details the consequences and implications of state-tribal confrontation, when states are increasingly concerned with exploitation of resources and tribes stand in the way.

Butterworth, Douglas, and John K. Chance, 1981. Latin American Urbanization. New York: Cambridge University Press. Examines factors shaping social life in both rural and urban areas, including a final chapter on the Mexican-United States experience.

*Chagnon, Napoleon, 1983, Yanomamo: The Fierce People. 3rd Ed. Attention to change and the challenge to Yanomamo continuity created by new roads, settlement, and destruction of the tropical forest is included in this edition.

*Chance, Norman, 1984, China's Urban Villagers: Life in a Beijing Commune. New York: Holt, Rinehart and Winston. Chance, who lived in a commune in the P.R.C., analyzes changes in family relations, the political economy, and problems in development, in the context of an ethnography of the commune, Half Moon Village.

*Chu, Goodwin C., and Francis L.K. Hsu, 1979. Moving a Mountain. Honolulu: University Press of Hawaii. Seventeen papers on culture change in China grouped under communication systems, popular culture, and value changes.

Dauber, Roslyn and Melinda L. Cain, eds. 1981, Women and Technological Change in Developing Countries. AAAS Selected Symposium 53. Boulder: Westview Press. Both of the above volumes analyze the ways in which the interests and capabilities of women are often overlooked in development plans and implementations.

D'Onofrio, Pamela M., M. Flores and Sheila M. Pfafflin, eds. 1982, Scientific-Technological Change and the Role of Women in Development. Boulder: Westview Press.

*Esman, Marjorie, 1985, Henderson: A Cajun Community. New York: Holt, Rinehart and Winston. The forces for continuity and change are analyzed for this Louisiana Cajun community. Tourism is seen as both a factor in change and a factor in persistence of culture.

Gunn, Chase A., 1979, Tourism Planning. New York: Crane Reissak. An interdisciplinary description of tourism and a planned change model. Weak in attention to empirical studies on tourism by anthropologists.

*Harris, Marvin, 1981, America Now: The Anthropology of a Changing Culture. N.Y.: Simon and Schuster. Explains technological breakdown and change as related to areas of American life such as women's liberation, gay liberation, rising crime rates, religious movements, and so forth, using a material-determinist framework.

*Hatch, Elvin, 1979, Biography of a Small Town. New York: Columbia University Press. Changes in Starkey, an agricultural service town in mid-California, since World War II, are described, showing how a loss of commitment to small town life has occurred—a process replicated in small towns across the land.

*Kuper, Hilda, 1985, The Swazi. 2nd Ed. New York: Holt, Rinehart and Winston. Dr. Kuper has added four chapters on events in Swaziland since independence. As Sobuza II's biographer, she had an insider's view.

*Lee, Richard B. 1984. The Dobe!Kung. New York: Holt, Rinehart and Winston. Lee provides a well-rounded and captivating description of traditional !Kung life, then analyzes changes taking place now. With such a pleasing traditional culture why should the !Kung want manufactured clothes, radios, jobs, money, and the assorted ills of "civilization"?

Leung, C.L. and Norton Ginsburg, eds. 1980. China: Urbanization and National Development. Research Paper 196. University of Chicago. Eight empirical studies on urbanization in the P.R.C.

Lowe, John W.G. and Elizabeth D. Lowe, 1982, "Cultural Pattern and Process: A Study of Stylistic Change in Women's Dress." American Anthropologist. 84:3: 521-544. The basic question to which the dress data relate is how and why do cultures change? Alfred Kroeber's idea of cultural configuration is converted to a less ambiguous mathematical formulation.

Merelman, Robert, 1984, Making Something of Ourselves. Berkeley: University of California Press. Merelman analyzes American culture as "unbounded," a condition brought about by recent change. Uses structural anthropology, though he is a political scientist.

Nann, Richard, ed., 1982, Uprooting and Surviving: Adaptation and Resettlement of Migrant Families and Children. Hingham, MA: D. Reidel Publishers. The nature and effects of uprooting and resettlement among South East Asian refugees in the U.S., immigrants in North America, and Europe, Asia, mobility in West Africa, foreign workers in Europe, and youths returning home after study abroad.

Netting, Robert C., 1981, Balancing on an Alp: Ecological Change and Continuity in a Swiss Mountain Community. New York: Cambridge University Press. The author analyzes continuity and change in population, social structure, and technology, in Törbel in the Swiss canton of Valais.

Padilla, Amado M. ed., 1980, Acculturation Theory: Models and Some New Findings. Boulder, Col.: Westview Press. Research on Hispanics, with attention to the multidimensional processes of acculturation, and attempts to build models of these processes using statistics. One anthropologist and six psychologists do the building.

Smith, Michael French, 1982, "Bloody Time and Bloody Scarcity: Capitalism, Authority, and the Transformation of Temporal Experience in a Papua New Guinea Village." American Ethnologist. 9.3:503-518. An intriguing analysis of the development of perceptions that time is scarce as a part of the process of incorporation into a capitalist political economy.

*Spindler, George and Louise Spindler, 1983, "Anthropologists View American Culture," In the Annual Review of Anthropology, 12:49-78. 161 references to writings by anthropologists on American culture are included, many of them concerned with both long and short range changes.

*Spindler, Louise and George Spindler, 1979, "Changing Women in Men's Worlds." In Ann McElroy and Carolyn Matthiasson, Sex Roles in Changing

Cultures. Occasional Papers in Anthropology. 1:35-49. Department of Anthropology, State University of New York at Buffalo, New York. Analyzes changes in sex roles as rapid culture change takes place among the Menominee, Mistassini Cree, Blood Indians, and in rural German villages. See also other papers in this volume on various aspects of sex roles in culture change and modernization in 14 different cultures.

*Spiro, Melford E. 1979, Gender and Culture: Kibbutz Women Revisited. Durham, N.C.: Duke University Press. Describes the shift of modern Kibbutz women back to femininity and domesticity.

Strathern, Andrew, 1982, The Division of Labor and Processes of Social Change in Papua New Guinea. American Ethnologist. 9.2:307-319. Coffee and cash cropping bring conflicts in male/female relationships in the western highlands of Papua New Guinea. See other articles in this special issue on economic and ecological problems in cultural change.

Textor, Robert, 1983, Austria 2005. Projected Sociocultural Effects of the Microelectronic Revolution. Vienna, Austria: Verlag ORAC Pietsch. An attempt to elicit and analyze scenarios for the future offered by leaders, critics, and citizens, applied to Austria but applicable elsewhere.

*Toffler, Alvin, 1980, The Third Wave. N.Y.: Bantam Books. Toffler discusses a "prosumers" society, with the two sexes working together in electronic, computerized family industry and a technology that enables destandardization.

Turnbull, Colin M., 1983, The Mbuti Pygmies: Change and Adaptation. New York: Holt, Rinehart and Winston. Describes traditional life in the Ituri forest, then analyzes changes that took place during the late phases of colonialism, then independence.

Wallace, Anthony F.C., 1982, The Social Context of Innovation: Bureaucrats, Families, and Heroes in the Early Industrial Revolution as foreseen in Bacon's New Atlantic. Princeton: Princeton University Press. A historical view of the social context of technological revolution in England during the 17th Century. See also Wallace's (1980) Rockdale: The Growth of an American Village in the Early Industrial Revolution. New York: Knopf, for a related analysis of the American scene.

Whitten, Norman E., ed., 1981, Cultural Transformation and Ethnicity in Modern Ecuador. Urbana: University of Illinois Press. This is a general treatment on ethnicity with case studies of cultural transformation in a rapidly changing country.

*Yinger, J. Milton, 1982, Countercultures: Promise and Peril of a World Turned Upside Down. Riverside, N.J.: Free Press. Countercultures in confrontation with established norms.

Bibliography

Acheson, J. M., 1972, "Limited Good or Limited Goods?" *American Anthropologist* 74:1152–1169.

Adair, J., and E. Vogt, 1949, "Navaho and Zuni Veterans: A Study of Contrasting Modes of Culture Change." *American Anthropologist* 51:547–561.

Aguilera, F., n. d., Changes in Economic Strategy: Secularization of Peasants or Normal Community Process? Unpublished ms.

Aschenbrenner, J., 1975, *Life Lines: Black Families in Chicago.* New York: Holt, Rinehart and Winston.

Barnes, J. A., 1972, *Social Networks.* Reading, Mass.: Addison-Wesley Publishing Company, Inc.

Barnett, H. G., 1942, "Applied Anthropology in 1860." *Applied Anthropology* 1:19–32.

———, 1942a, "Invention and Culture Change." *American Anthropologist* 44:14–30.

———, 1953, *Innovation: The Basis of Cultural Change.* New York: McGraw-Hill, Inc.

———, 1960, *Being a Palauan.* New York: Holt, Rinehart, and Winston.

Barrett, R. A., 1974, *Benabarre: The Modernization of a Spanish Village.* New York: Holt, Rinehart, and Winston.

Barth, F., ed., 1963, *The Role of the Entrepreneur in Social Change in Northern Norway.* Bergen: Scandinavian University Books.

———, 1966, "Models of Social Organization." London: Royal Anthropological Institution, Occasional Paper No. 23.

———, 1967, "On the Study of Social Change." *American Anthropologist* 69:661–669.

Beals, A. R., 1962, *Gopalpur: A South Indian Village.* New York: Holt, Rinehart and Winston.

Bee, R. L., 1965, "Peyotism in North American Indian Groups." *Transactions of the Kansas Academy of Science* 68 (1):13–61.

———, 1974, *Patterns and Processes.* New York: The Free Press.

Benedict, R., 1934, *Patterns of Culture.* Boston: Houghton Mifflin Company.

Bennett, J. W., 1973, *The New Ethnicity: Perspectives from Ethnology.* Proceedings of the American Ethnological Society. St. Paul: West Publishing Company.

Berndt, R. M., 1957, *Social and Cultural Change in Aboriginal Australia.* Proceedings of the Third Pan Indian Ocean Science Congress, Section E., Tananarive.

Boissevain, J. F., 1969, *Hal-Farrug: A Village in Malta.* New York: Holt, Rinehart and Winston.

167

Bruner, E., 1961, "Urbanization and Ethnic Identity in North Sumatra." *American Anthropologist* 63:508–521.

———, 1974, *The Expression of Ethnicity in Indonesia.* Association of Social Anthropologists Monograph no. 12. London: Tavistock Publications.

Calverton, V. F., 1931, "Modern Anthropology and the Theory of Cultural Compulsives." In V. Calverton, ed., *The Making of Modern Man.* Westport, Conn.: Greenwood Publishing Company.

Chance, N. A., 1965, "Acculturation, Self-identification, and Personality Adjustment." *American Anthropologist* 67:372–393.

———, 1966, *The Eskimo of North Alaska.* New York: Holt, Rinehart and Winston.

Chiñas, B. L., 1973, *The Isthmus Zapotecs: Women's Roles in Cultural Context.* New York: Holt, Rinehart and Winston.

Cole, J., 1970, "Black Culture: Negro, Black and Nigger." *The Black Scholar* 1 (8):40–43.

Collier, J., and A. Buitron, 1952, *The Awakening Valley.* Chicago: University of Chicago Press.

Daner, F., 1976, *The American Children of Krsna: A Study of the Hare Krsna Movement.* New York: Holt, Rinehart and Winston.

Davidson, R. T., 1974, *Chicano Prisoners: The Key to San Quentin.* New York: Holt, Rinehart and Winston.

Davidson, S., 1971, "The Rush for Instant Salvation." *Harper's Magazine* July, pp. 46–54.

Diamond, N., 1969, *K'un Shen: A Taiwan Village.* New York: Holt, Rinehart and Winston.

Diaz, M. N., 1967, "Introduction: Economic Relations in Peasant Society." In M. J. Potter, M. N. Diaz, and G. M. Foster, eds., *Peasant Society: A Reader.* Boston: Little, Brown and Company.

Downs, J. F., 1966, *The Two Worlds of the Washo: An Indian Tribe of California and Nevada.* New York: Holt, Rinehart and Winston.

Driver, H. E., 1961, *Indians of North America.* Chicago: University of Chicago Press.

Dubois, L., 1972, "A Jewish Subculture at Stanford University." Unpublished ms., Stanford University.

Edgerton, R. B., 1974, "Pastoral-Farming Comparisons." In R. A. LeVine, ed., *Culture and Personality.* Chicago: Aldine Publishing Company.

Ekvall, R. B., 1968, *Fields on the Hoof: Nexus of Tibetan Nomadic Pastoralism.* New York: Holt, Rinehart and Winston.

Elkin, A. P., 1951, "Reaction and Interaction: A Food Gathering People and European Settlement in Australia." *American Anthropologist* 53:164–186.

Erasmus, C. J., 1968, "Community Development and the Encogido Syndrome." *Human Organization* 27:65–75, 91–94.

Esquire, March, 1970. "California Evil," C. Karpel et al. 73:99–123.

Foster, G. M., 1965, "Peasant Society and the Image of Limited Good." *American Anthropologist* 67:293–315.

Freire, P., 1970, "Cultural Action for Freedom." *Harvard Educational Review and Center for the Study of Development and Social Change.* Monograph Series No. 1.

———, 1973, *Education for Critical Consciousness.* New York: The Seabury Press, Inc.

Freud, S., 1936, *The Problem of Anxiety.* New York: W. W. Norton and Company, Inc.

Friedl, E., 1959, "The Role of Kinship in the Transmission of National Culture to Rural Villages in Mainland Greece." *American Anthropologist* 61:30–38.

————, 1962, *Vasilika, a Village in Modern Greece*. New York: Holt, Rinehart and Winston.

————, 1964, "Lagging Emulation in Post-peasant Society. *American Anthropologist* 66:564:586.

Friedl, J., 1974, *Kippel: A Changing Village in the Alps*. New York: Holt, Rinehart and Winston.

Fromm, E., 1941, *Escape from Freedom*. New York: Farrar and Rinehart, Inc.

Fromm, E., and M. Maccoby, 1970, "A Sociopsychoanalytic Study." In *Social Character in a Mexican Village*. Englewood Cliffs, N.J.: Prentice-Hall, Inc.

Gamst, F. C., 1969, *The Qemant: A Pagan-Hebraic Peasantry of Ethiopia*. New York: Holt, Rinehart and Winston.

————, 1974, *Peasants in Complex Society*. New York: Holt, Rinehart and Winston.

Garbarino, M. C., 1972, *Big Cypress: A Changing Seminole Community*. New York: Holt, Rinehart and Winston.

Goodenough, W. H., 1961, "Comment on Cultural Evaluation." *Daedalus* 90: 521–528.

Graves, N. B., n.d., *City, Country and Child Rearing: Cross-national Observations of Mother-child Interaction*. Westport, Conn.: Redgrave Publishing Company (in press).

————, and T. D. Graves, 1975, "The Impact of Modernization on Polynesian Personality." *South Pacific Research Institute Inc.*, Report No. 7, August.

Graves, T. D., 1967, "Acculturation, Access, and Alcohol in a Tri-ethnic Community." *American Anthropologist* 69:306–321.

————, and N. B. Graves, n.d., "Psychological Anthropology." In *The Making of Psychological Anthropology*.

Grinnell, G. B., 1923, *The Cheyenne Indians*, Vol. 1. New Haven, Conn.: Yale University Press.

Hallowell, A. I., 1951, "The Use of Projective Techniques in the Study of the Sociopsychological Aspects of Acculturation." *Journal of Projective Techniques* 15:27–44.

————, 1957, "The Impact of the American Indian on American Culture." *American Anthropologist* 59:201–217.

————, 1963, "The Ojibwa World View and Disease." In I. Galston, ed., *The Image of Man in Medicine and Anthropology*. New York: International Universities Press.

Halpern, J. M., and B. K. Halpern, 1972, *A Serbian Village in Historical Perspective*. New York: Holt, Rinehart and Winston.

Hart, C. W. M., and A. R. Pilling, 1960, *The Tiwi of North Australia*. New York: Holt, Rinehart and Winston.

Haviland, W. A., 1974, *Anthropology*. New York: Holt, Rinehart and Winston.

Heffner, R. D., ed., 1956, de Tocqueville, A., *Democracy in America*. New York: New American Library of World Literature, Inc.

Herskovits, M. J., 1941, *The Myth of the Negro Past*. Boston: The Beacon Press.

————, 1950, *Man and His Works*. New York: Alfred A. Knopf, Inc.

Hoebel, E. A., 1949, *Man in the Primitive World*. New York: McGraw-Hill, Inc.

————, 1972, *Anthropology: The Study of Man*, fourth ed. New York: McGraw-Hill, Inc.

Holmberg, A. R., 1960, "Changing Community Attitudes and Values in Peru: A Case Study in Guided Change." In R. N. Adams, et. al., eds., *Social Change in Latin America Today: Its Relationship for United States Policy*. New York: Harper Bros.

Hoselitz, B., 1960, *Sociological Aspects of Economic Growth*. New York: The Free Press.

Hostetler, J. A., and G. E. Huntington, 1967, *The Hutterites in North America.* New York: Holt, Rinehart and Winston.

Hunter, M., 1936, *Reaction to Conquest.* London: International Institute of African Languages and Cultures. Oxford: Oxford University Press.

Inlow, G., 1972, *Values in Transition.* New York: John Wiley and Sons, Inc.

Jones, D. E., 1972, *Sanapia: Comanche Medicine Woman.* New York: Holt, Rinehart and Winston.

Jones, H. M., 1952, "Prose and Pictures: James Fenimore Cooper." *Tulane Studies in English,* 3:126–137.

Kearney, M., 1972, *The Winds of Ixtepeji: World View and Society in a Zapotec Town.* New York: Holt, Rinehart and Winston.

Keesing, R. M., 1976, *Cultural Anthropology: A Contemporary Perspective.* New York: Holt, Rinehart and Winston.

Keiser, R. L., 1969, *Vice Lords: Warriors of the Streets.* New York: Holt, Rinehart and Winston.

Kluckhohn, C., 1949, "The Philosophy of the Navaho Indians." In F. S. C. Northrop, ed., *Ideological Differences and World Orders.* New Haven, Conn.: Published for the Viking Fund by Yale University Press.

Kroeber, A. L., 1944, *Configurations of Culture Growth.* Berkeley: University of California Press.

Kuper, H., 1963, *The Swazi: A South African Kingdom.* New York: Holt, Rinehart and Winston.

Leighton, D., and C. Kluckhohn, 1947, *Children of the People.* Cambridge, Mass.: Harvard University Press.

Linton, R., 1936, *The Study of Man, an Introduction.* New York: Appleton-Century-Crofts, Inc.

———, 1939, "The Tanala of Madagascar." In Abram Kardiner, ed., *The Individual and His Society.* New York: Columbia University Press.

Mabogunje, A. L., 1967, "The Morphology of Ibadan." In P. C. Lloyd; A. L. Mabogunje; and B. Awe, eds., *The City of Ibadan.* Cambridge: Cambridge University Press.

Madsen, W., 1973, *The Mexican-Americans of South Texas,* 2d ed. New York: Holt, Rinehart and Winston.

Malinowski, B., 1945, *The Dynamics of Culture Change.* New Haven, Conn.: Yale University Press.

Mandelbaum, D. G., 1941, "Culture Change among the Nilgiri Tribes." *American Anthropologist* 43:19–26.

McFee, M., 1972, *Modern Blackfeet: Montanans on a Reservation.* New York: Holt, Rinehart and Winston.

McGiffert, M., ed., 1970, *The Character of Americans.* Hollywood, Ill.: The Dorsey Press.

Mead, M., 1956, *New Lives for Old.* New York: William Morrow and Company, Inc.

Middleton, J., 1965, *The Lugbara of Uganda.* New York: Holt, Rinehart and Winston.

Nay, B., 1974, *American Values.* Unpublished ms., Stanford University.

Niederer, A., 1956, *Gemeinwerk im Wallis.* Schriften der Schweizerischen Gesellschaft für Volkskunde, Band 37, Basel: Buchdruckerei G. Krebs.

———, 1969, "Überlieferung im Wandel: Zur Wirksamkeit älterer Grundverhaltensmuster bei der Industrialisierung eines Berg-Gebietes." *Alpea Orientales* 5:289–294. Slovenska Akademija in Umetnosti.

Norbeck, E., 1976, *Changing Japan.* Rev. ed. New York: Holt, Rinehart and Winston.

Oliver-Smith, A. R., 1973, *Yungay Norte: Disaster and Social Change in the*

Peruvian Highlands. Unpublished Ph.D. dissertation, Dept. of Anthropology, Indiana University.

Partridge, W. L., 1973, *The Hippie Ghetto: The Natural History of a Subculture.* New York: Holt, Rinehart and Winston.

Pelto, P. J., 1973, *The Snowmobile Revolution: Technology and Social Change in the Arctic.* Menlo Park, Calif.: Cummings Publishing Company.

Perry W. J., 1923, *Children of the Sun.* London: Metheun & Co., Ltd.

Piddington, R., 1957, *An Introduction to Social Anthropology,* vol. II. London: Oliver and Boyd, Ltd.

Prieto, A. G., 1975, "American Education—The Image in the Mirror." *Reviews in Anthropology* 2 (2):286–290.

Quintana, B. B., and L. G. Floyd, 1972, *Que Gitano! Gypsies of Southern Spain.* New York: Holt, Rinehart and Winston.

Radcliffe-Brown, A. R., 1952, *Structure and Function in Primitive Society.* New York: The Free Press.

Rawick, G. P., 1972, *The American Slave: A Composite Autobiography.* Vol. I. Westport, Conn.: Greenwood Publishing Company.

Redfield, R., et al., 1936, "Memorandum for the Study of Acculturation." *American Anthropologist* 38 (1):149–152.

———, 1947, "The Folk Society. *American Journal of Sociology* 52:293–308.

———, 1953a, "The Natural History of the Folk Society. *Social Forces* 31: 224–228.

———, 1953b, *The Primitive World and Its Transformation.* Ithaca, N.Y.: Cornell University Press.

Reich, C. A., 1971, *The Greening of America.* New York: Bantam Books.

Reichard, G. A., 1949, "The Navaho and Christianity." *American Anthropologist* 51:66–71.

Ribeiro, D., 1962, "The Social Integration of Indigenous Populations in Brazil." *International Labour Review* 85, no. 4, 325–346.

Rideman, P., 1950, *Account of Our Religion, Doctrine and Faith.* Bungay, England: Hodder and Stoughton, Ltd.

Rogers, E. M., 1962, *Diffusion of Innovations.* New York: The Free Press.

Rohner, R. P., ed., 1969, *The Ethnography of Franz Boas.* Chicago: University of Chicago Press.

Roszak, T., 1969, *The Making of a Counter Culture.* New York: Anchor Books.

Rotter, J. B., 1954, *Social Learning and Clinical Psychology.* Englewood Cliffs, N.J.: Prentice-Hall, Inc.

Ryan, B. F., 1969, *Social and Cultural Change.* New York: The Ronald Press Company.

Schmidt, W., 1939, *The Culture Historical Method of Ethnology.* New York: Fortuny's Publishers, Inc.

Schusky, E. L., 1975, *The Study of Cultural Anthropology.* New York: Holt, Rinehart and Winston.

Service, E. R., 1971, *Cultural Evolutionism: Theory in Practice.* New York: Holt, Rinehart and Winston.

Sharp, L., 1952, "Steel Axes for Stone Age Australians." In E. H. Spicer, ed., *Exploring Human Problems in Technological Change: A Casebook.* New York: Russell Sage Foundation.

Siegal, B. J., 1962, "Some Recent Developments in Studies of Social and Cultural Change." In *The Annals of the American Academy of Political and Social Sciences* 185:157–174.

Skilton, C. S., 1939, "American Indian Music." In *International Cyclopedia of Music and Musicians.* New York: Dodd, Mead and Company, Inc.

Slater, P., 1970, *The Pursuit of Loneliness.* Boston: The Beacon Press.

Social Science Research Council, 1954, "Acculturation: An Exploratory Formulation. Social Science Research Council Summer Seminar in Acculturation, 1953. *American Anthropologist* 56:973–1002.

Spicer, E. H., ed. 1961, *Perspectives in American Indian Culture Change.* Chicago: University of Chicago Press.

———, 1962, *Cycles of Conquest.* Tucson: University of Arizona Press.

Spindler, G. D., 1955a, "Education in a Transforming American Culture." *The Harvard Educational Review* 25:145–156.

———, 1955b, *Sociocultural and Psychological Processes in Menomini Acculturation.* University of California Publications in Culture and Society, Vol. V. Berkeley.: University of California Press.

———, 1958, "New Trends and Applications in Anthropology." In Roy A. Price, ed., *New Viewpoints in the Social Sciences.* Washington, D.C.: Twenty-Eighth Yearbook of the National Council for the Social Studies, 115–143.

———, 1959, *The Transmission of American Culture.* Cambridge, Mass.: Harvard University Press. (The Third Burton Lecture, 1957.)

———, 1961, "Peasants with Tractors." Paper presented at the Southwestern Anthropological Association meetings, University of California, Santa Barbara, Calif., March 31, 1961.

———, ed., 1963, *Education and Culture: Anthropological Approaches.* New York: Holt, Rinehart and Winston.

———, 1974, "Cultural Sensitization." In G. Spindler, ed., *Education and Cultural Process: Toward An Anthropology Of Education.* New York: Holt, Rinehart and Winston.

———, 1974, "Schooling in Schönhausen: A Study of Cultural Transmission and Instrumental Adaptation in an Urbanizing German Village." In G. Spindler, ed., *Education and Cultural Process: Toward an Anthropology of Education.* New York: Holt, Rinehart and Winston.

———, 1977, "Change and Continuity in American Core Cultural Values: An Anthropological Perspective." In Gordon DiRenzo, ed., *Social Change and Social Character.* Westport, Conn.: Greenwood Press.

———, and L. S. Spindler, 1963, "Psychology in Anthropology: Applications to Culture Change." In Sigmund Koch, ed., *Psychology: A Study of a Science.* Vol. 6. New York: McGraw-Hill Book Company, Inc.

———, 1965, "Instrumental Activities Inventory: A Technique for the Study of the Psychology of Acculturation. *Southwestern Journal of Anthropology* 21:1–23.

———, 1971, *Dreamers Without Power: The Menomini Indians.* New York: Holt, Rinehart and Winston.

———, and Student Collaborators, 1973, *Burgbach: Urbanization and Identity in a German Village.* New York: Holt, Rinehart and Winston.

Spindler, L. S., 1962, "Menomini Women and Culture Change." *American Anthropologist,* Memoir 91, 64 (1:2).

———, 1970, "Menomini Witchcraft." In D. Walker, ed., *Systems of North American Witchcraft and Sorcery. Anthropological Monographs* no. 1, University of Idaho.

SSRC (*see* Social Science Research Council above)

Stewart, O. C., 1952, "Southern Ute Adjustment to Modern Living." *International Congress of Americanists Proceedings* 29:80–87.

Toffler, A., 1970. *Future Shock.* New York: Bantam Books.

Tonkinson, R., 1974, *The Jigalong Mob: Aboriginal Victors of the Desert Crusade.* Menlo Park, Calif.: Cummings Publishing Company.

Underhill, R. M., 1953, *Red Man's America*. Chicago: University of Chicago Press.

Vogt, E. Z., 1970, *The Zinacantecos of Mexico: A Modern Maya Way of Life*. New York: Holt, Rinehart and Winston.

Wallace, A. F. C., 1956, "Revitalization Movements." *American Anthropologist* 58:264–281.

———, 1969, "The Trip." In *Psychedelic Drugs*. New York: Greene & Stratton.

Warth, P., 1972, *A Study of Values in a Mexican American Junior High Sample*. Unpublished ms., Stanford University.

Weber, M., 1930, *The Protestant Ethic and the Spirit of Capitalism*. Translated by Talcott Parsons. New York: Charles Scribner's Sons.

Wolf, E. R., 1965, "Aspects of Group Relations in a Complex Society: Mexico." In D. B. Heath, and R. N. Adams, eds., *Contemporary Cultures and Societies of Latin America*. New York: Random House. Pp. 85–101.

———, 1966, *Peasants*. Englewood Cliffs, N.J.: Prentice-Hall Inc.

———, 1969, *Peasant Wars of the Twentieth Century*. New York: Harper and Row.

Index

NAME INDEX

Acheson, J., 57
Adair, J., 45–46
Adelson, J., 116
Aguilera, F., 61, 69, 72
Aschenbrenner, J., 127–129
Asimov, I., 147

Bacon, E. N., 147
Bandura, A., 93
Barnes, J. A., 60
Barnett, H. G., 20, 34–35, 86, 159–160
Barrett, R. A., 69–71
Barth, F., 98, 99–100, 161
Beals, A. R., 61–63
Bee, R. L., 18, 98
Benedict, R., 46–47
Bennett, J. W., 33
Berndt, R. M., 48
Boas, F., 17
Boissevain, J. F., 82–83
Bruner, E., 73–74
Buitron, A., 94

Calverton, V. F., 3
Chance, N. A., 36–37, 111
Chiñas, B. L., 105–106
Cole, J., 128
Collier, J., 94
Crèvecoeur, de, H., 113

Daner, F., 120, 123–124
Davidson, R. T., 121, 134–136
Diamond, N., 81–82
Diaz, M. N., 57
Downs, J. F., 138
Driver, H. E., 18, 23
DuBois, L., 117

Edgerton, R. B., 25
Ekvall, R. B., 26
Elkin, A. P., 48
Erasmus, C. J., 94

Floyd, L. G., 40–42
Foster, G. M., 56, 57
Freud, S., 120
Freire, P., 96–97, 160
Friedl, E., 63–64, 159

Friedl, J., 61, 65–67
Fromm, E., 120, 134
Fuller, B., 146, 147

Gamst, F. C., 54, 57, 60, 74–75, 147, 158
Garbarino, M. C., 139
Goldschmidt, W., 25
Goodenough, W. H., 4
Graves, N. B., 93, 94–96, 160
Graves, T. D., 93, 94–95, 160, 161
Grinnel, G. B., 14
Gsell, Fr., 49

Hallowell, A. I., 23, 85, 89
Halpern, B. K., 61, 67–69
Halpern, J. M., 61, 67–69
Hart, C. W. M., 38, 49
Haviland, W. A., 55
Heffner, R. D., 113
Herskovits, M. J., 13, 19, 20, 31, 129
Hoebel, E. A., 14, 20
Holmberg, A. R., 93
Hostetler, J. A., 42–44
Hunter, M., 87
Huntington, G. E., 42–44

Inlow, G., 118

Jones, H. M., 23

Kearney, M., 57
Keesing, R. M., 145
Keiser, R. L., 121, 130–131
Kluckhohn, C., 46
Kral, H., 43
Kroeber, A. L., 18
Kunkel, J., 93, 94
Kuper, H., 21, 50

Leighton, D., 46
Linton, R., 14–15, 18–19, 27, 31

Mabogunje, A. L., 59
Maccoby, M., 134
Madsen, W., 38, 132–134
Malinowski, B., 8
Mandelbaum, D. G., 39
McDowell, E., 23

McFee, M., 140, 163
McGiffert, M., 113, 116
Mead, M., 35–36, 98–99, 161
Middleton, J., 51

Nay, B., 113
Niederer, A., 66
Norbeck, E., 78–81

Oliver-Smith, A. R., 28

Paliau, 98–99, 161
Partridge, W. L., 122
Pelto, P. J., 29–30
Perry, W. J., 17
Piddington, R., 88
Pilling, A. R., 38, 49
Prabhupada, B. S., 123
Prieto, A. G., 96

Quintana, B. B., 40–42

Radcliffe-Brown, A. R., 8
Rawick, G. P., 129
Redfield, R., 31, 53, 56, 73, 83, 84, 159
Reich, C. A., 84, 119
Reichard, G. A., 136
Ribeiro, D., 49
Rideman, P., 42
Rogers, E. M., 16, 18, 57

Rohner, R. P., 18
Roszak, T., 119, 120, 122
Rotter, J. B., 93, 95
Ryan, B. F., 55, 59

Schmidt, W., 17
Sharp, L., 22
Skilton, C. S., 23
Slater, P., 118
Sobhuza, 50
Spindler, G. D., 32, 33, 76–78, 88, 89–92,
    96–97, 100–102, 106, 108, 110, 111,
    114–116, 118, 160
Spindler, L. S., 32, 33, 88, 89–92, 97, 100–
    101, 106, 108, 111, 139
Stewart, O. C., 137

Toffler, A., 84, 120, 159
Tonkinson, R., 47–48
Toqueville, de, A., 113

Underhill, R. M., 15

Vogt, E., 45–46, 75

Wallace, A. F. C., 87, 89, 122, 160
Warth, P., 117
Weber, M., 113
Wolf, E. R., 57, 58

SUBJECT INDEX

Acculturation, 7–8; definition, 31; early
    models of, 31–32; emulation, 33–37;
    forced, 48–49; forced vs. voluntary, 31;
    Menomenee Indians, 90–91; mini-model,
    31–51, background of, 31–33; voluntary,
    50–51
Adaptation, 8–9
African cult groups, 19–20
Almonaster la Real (Spain), 72
American core values, 161; change and per-
    sistence of, 113–118; and minority
    groups, 126
American historical model, 18
American Indians, Basin groups, 137–138;
    bicultural community, 140; Blackfeet,
    139–140; Cheyenne, 20; Comanche, 138–
    139; Menominee, 88–89, 89–92, 139;
    women, 107–110; as minority groups,
    136–140; Navajo, 45–47; and reciprocal
    borrowing, 23; Seminole, 139; traditional
    values and change, 136–137; Washo,
    138; Zuni, 45–47
American youth cults, 119–125
Applied anthropology, 93
Autarky complex, 66

Behavioral analysis, 92–96, 160; criticism
    of, 94
Benabarre (Spain), 69–71
Bhagavad-gita, 123
Black Americans, culture characteristics,
    128–129; urban delinquents (Vice
    Lords), 129–131; urban families, 127–
    129
Blood Indians, 92; women, 107
Boundary-maintenance, 37–48; Gypsies
    (Spain), 39–42; Hutterites (North Amer-
    ica), 42–44; Jigalong Mob (Australia),
    47–48; Navajo, 45–47; Nilgiri tribes
    (India), 38–39; Tiwi (Australia), 38;
    Zuni, 45–47
Buddhism, and modernization, 59
Burgbach (Germany), 76–78; women's
    adaptation, 110

Caste system, 63
Chicanos (see Mexican-Americans)
City, the, 54–55, 157–158; emigration to,
    69–71; and the peasant, 56
Colonial mentality, 33
Community, reification of, 44

Conducive base, 108
Conscientizacion method, 96–97
Consumer consumption, ceiling on, 72
Contingent stimuli, 93
Coping strategies, and acculturation mini-model, 32–33; intelligent parasitism, 48; Maori (New Zealand), 26–27; Menominee Indians, 89–92; Skolt Lapps (Finland), 29–30; Tanala (Madagascar), 27; Tibetan nomads, 25–26; variation in, 61–72; Yungay (Peru), 28–29
Counterculture, 120, 162; Hippie cult as, 122
Cultural awareness, 96–97
Cultural borrowing, reciprocal, 22–23; *see also* Diffusion
Cultural compulsive, 3, 7; and innovation, 16
Cultural diffusion (*see* Diffusion)
Cultural focus, 13
Cultural level, of human life, 5
Cultural persistence, 4; *See also* Persistence
Cultural pluralism, 140, 162–163
Cultural sensitization, 97, 160
Cultural therapy, 96–97
Culture, definition of, 4
Culture Area model, 18
Culture Circle model (Germany), 17
Cults (*see* Youth cults)

Decision-making model, 97–102; Fur of Darfur (Sudan), 99–100; Manus (Admiralty Islands), 98–99; Schönhausen (Germany), 100–102
Delocalization, 29–30
Developing societies, 58–59
Diffusion, compared to acculturation, 7–8, 17; mini-model, 17–23; and modern man, 18–19; older models of, 17–18
Disaster identity, 28

Eclecticism, in research methods, 163
Ecological mini-model, 25–30
Emic vs. etic approaches, 161
Emigration, to cities, 69–71; Black Americans, 128
Emulation, 33–37; Kaktovik Eskimos, 36–37; "lagging," 63–64; Manus (Admiralty Islands), 35–36; Palau, 34–35
Emulative model, 34
Entrepreneurs, 98–99; Paliau of the Manus, 98–99
Environment, and sociocultural system, 8, 25–30
Equilibrium, of system, 8; and modernization, 62–63
Ethnocentrism, as boundary maintenance, 38; Tiwi, 38
Event-analysis, 161
Exploitation, mutual, 47–48

Familistic individualism, 46
First-order contacts, 60
Folk city, 56
Forced acculturation, Tiwi (Australia), 49; Umotina Indians (Brazil), 48–49
Friend-of-a-friend syndrome, 70–71
Functionalism, 8
Fur of Darfur (Sudan), 99–100
Fusion, 157

Ghost Dance, 15–16, 48, 87
Ghost sickness, 138–139
Gopalpur (India), 61–63
Grand model, 4–9; overview, 143
Grossenhäuser, 76–77
Gypsies (Spain), 39–42; image of, 41–42

Hippie ghetto, 122
Hutterites (North America), 42–44; persecution of, 43; socialization, 43–44

Indian Protection Service (Brazil), 48–49
Individual level, of human life, 7, 85
Industrialization, Hal-Farrug (Malta), 82–83; and urbanization, 148
Inferiority feelings, and emulation, 34; and modernization, 63
Innovation, 159–160; concept of, 13; examples of, 14–16; mini-model, 13–16; preconditions for acceptance, 16; as psychocultural process, 86; technological, 29–30; as two-step process, 16
Instant communication concept, 147, 149
Instrumental Activities Inventory, 97, 100–101, 160
Intelligent parasitism, 48
Internal control, 95
International Society for Krsna Consciousness (ISKCON), 123–125

Japan, and modernization, 78–81
Jigalong Mob (Australia), 47–48

Kafir Wars, 87
Kaktovik Eskimos, 36–37; women's adaptation, 111
Kinship, and urban Black Americans, 127–129; and urbanization, 73
Kippel (Switzerland), 65–67

Life styles, in city, 55
Limited good, concept of, 56–57
Loneliness, and youth cults, 120
Love and sex, Black Americans, 128; Mexican-Americans, 134
Lugbara (Africa), 50–51

Machismo, 133–134
Male role, German peasant, 110; machismo, 133–134; urban Black American, 127–128; Yir-Yiront, 21–22

Malta, and industrialization, 82–83
Manly-hearted women, 107
Manus (Admiralty Islands), 35–36; leadership in, 98–99
Maori (New Zealand), 26–27
Marginal man, 86; as innovator, 15
Marriage, in ISKCON cult, 124–125
Mass media, and innovation, 16
Mazeway reformulation, 86–87, 160
Mental configuration, 86
Mexican-Americans, 131–134; acculturative groups, 132–133; Baby Mafia (Family), 134–136; Chicano prisoners, 134–136; class distinctions, 132; fatalism, 133; La Raza, 132; machismo, 133–134
Mini-model, 9; acculturation, 31–51, 144, 154, 157; decision-making, 160–161; diffusion, 17–23, 153, 156; ecological, 25–30, 144, 153, 156–157; innovation, 13–16, 153, 156; modernization-urbanization, 53–84, 154, 157–159; overview, 143–145; psychocultural, 85–102, 154, 159–160
Minority groups (United States), 126–140, 162–163; American Indians (see American Indians); Chicano prisoners, 134–136; Mexican-Americans (Chicanos), 131–134; urban Black delinquents (Vice Lords), 129–131; urban Black families, 127–129; values of, 117–118
Mission, sense of, 113
Missionaries, and mutual stereotypes, 47–48; and syncretism, 20
Modern man, and diffusion, 18–19
Modernization, and assumptions about, 66–67; Benabarre and Almonaster la Real (Spain), 69–72; Burgbach (Germany), 76–78; Gopalpur (India), 61–63; Japan, 78–81; Kippel (Switzerland), 65–67; K'un Shen (Taiwan), 81–82; meaning of, 158; models for, 59; nonrevolutionary, 78–83; Orašác (Yugoslavia), 67–69; and Polynesian personality, 95; resistance to, Qemant (Ethiopia), 74–75; Vasilika (Greece), 63–64; Zinacantecos (Mexico), 75
Modernization-urbanization mini-model, 53–84; introduction, 53–54; and network analysis, 60–61; resistance and persistence, 73–78; variations in coping, 61–72
Moral order, rebuilding of, 83–84
Mother-child relationship, urban Black American, 127; and urbanization, 95–96

Native Americans (see American Indians)
Native American Church, 88–89
Network analysis, 60–61, 70–71, 158–159
"New people" of Lugbara (Africa), 50–51
Nilgiri tribes (India), 38–39

Orašác (Yugoslavia), 67–69

Palau, 34–35
Pan-Egyptian Diffusion Model (England), 17
Parental Mediation Model, 95–96
Peasant stage, 53–54, 56
Peasantry, 56–58; definition, 57; in developing Socialist state, 67–69; German Bauern, 76–78
Persistence, of American values, 113–118; Toba Batak (Sumatra), 73–74
Personality, and modernization, 95
Peyotism, 89–90; Cheyenne, 20; Menominee, 88–89
Postpeasant stabilization, 60
Primitive stage, 56
Protestant ethic, 113; and Navajo values, 136
Psychocultural mini-model, 85–102

Qemant (Ethiopia), 74–75

Rationality, of the city, 55; economic, 78
Reactive movements, Melanesia, 88; Xhosa (Africa), 87; see also Revialization movements
Reality, scientific vs. sociocultural, 157
Reciprocal borrowing, 22–23
Red Power groups, 140
Reinterpretation, failure of, 21–22; and syncretism, 19–22
Religion, as boundary maintenance, 42–44, 74, 75; from innovation, 15–16; and syncretism, 20; and youth cults, 121
Replacement, 157
Revitalization movements, 87–89; ISKCON cult as, 123; see also Reactive movements
Revolution, and forced acculturation, 48; nonviolent, 119; and the peasantry, 58
Role-playing, and acculturation model, 32; single and many-stranded, 60–61

Schönhausen (Germany), 100–102
Science, and traditional values, 82
Second order contacts, 60
Secular-urban stage, 56
Self-consciousness, and moral order, 83–84
Self-sufficiency complex, 66
Skolt Lapps (Finland), 29–30
Snowmobile revolution, 29–30
Social class, and disaster identity, 28; new middle class, 71, 80–81
Social control, as boundary maintenance, 46
Social interaction, nature of, 39
Social interaction level, of human life, 5–7
Socialism, peasants in, 67–69
Socialization (Hutterites), 43–44
Sociocultural change, acceptance of, 33–37; definition, 4; and the future, 146–149;

grand model for, 4–9; introducing, 48–51; introduction, 3–4; mini-model for, 9; *see also* Mini-model; and persistence, 103–140; and psychological adaptation, 89–92; resistance to, 37–48; substitutive vs. transformative, 77–78
Sociocultural system, 5
"Soul," 128, 131
Spontaneous behavior, 7
Syncretism, 157; by individuals, 21; and reinterpretation, 19–22
Syncretization, 17; *see also* Syncretism
Swazi (Africa), 21, 50

Taiwan, and modernization, 81–82
Tanala (Madagascar), 27
Technoeconomic differentiation, 29, 30
Tibetan nomads, 25–26
Tiwi (Australia), 38, 49
Trait tracing, 18, 31
Tri-Ethnic Research Project, 94–96
Two-step process, 16

Umotina Indians (Brazil), 48–49
Urbanization, 54–55, 147–148; and mother-child relationship, 95–96; Toba Batak (Sumatra), 73–74

Vailala madness, 88
Values, changing, 116–117; constant (core), 116; minority group, 117–118; traditional to emergent, 114–117
Values Projective Technique, 114–117
Vasilika (Greece), 63–64

Vice Lords (Chicago), 129–131; gangbanging, 130; ideological sets, 131; wolfpacking, 130
Vicos Project, 93–94
Voluntary acculturation, "new people" of Lugbara (Africa), 50–51; Swazi (Africa), 50

Warriors Society, 108
Women's role, 49, 161; adaptation to change, 105–112; Blood Indians, 107; German peasant, 110; in ISKCON cult, 125; Kaktovik Eskimos, 111; Menominee Indians, 107–110; Japan, 80; urban Black Americans, 127; Zapotec (Mexico), 105–106
Worker-peasant, 65–67, 67–69
World view, 85; and innovation, 16
World War II, and American Indians, 45–47
Wovoka, 15–16, 48, 87

Xhosa (Africa), 87

Yir-Yiront (Australia), 21–22
Youth cults, American, 119–125, 161–162; and drugs, 120–121; Hippies, 122; International Society for Krsna Consciousness (ISKCON), 123–125; problems of, 120; proliferation of, 120–121
Yungay (Peru), 28–29

Zinacantecos (Mexico), 75